Other titles by the same author:

Goodnight AH 2020
Religions and the European Union AH 2020

A
DIPLOMAT'S
LIFE

MEMOIRS
OF A BELGIAN
DIPLOMAT

BARON PHILIPPE GUILLAUME

authorHOUSE®

AuthorHouse™ UK
1663 Liberty Drive
Bloomington, IN 47403 USA
www.authorhouse.co.uk
Phone: UK TFN: 0800 0148641 (Toll Free inside the UK)
       UK Local: 02036 956322 (+44 20 3695 6322 from outside the UK)

Published by AuthorHouse 09/23/2020

ISBN: 978-1-7283-5541-2 (sc)
ISBN: 978-1-7283-5542-9 (hc)
ISBN: 978-1-7283-5540-5 (e)

Print information available on the last page.

This book is printed on acid-free paper.

Originally published as Ma Vie de Diplomate. Translation into English by Luciana Ruas.

Front cover by Dominique Guillaume.
Back cover by Emmanuel Guillaume.

Treat your friend as if they might become an enemy,
Treat your enemy as if they might become a friend.
                                        (Chinese proverb)

Fortiter in re, suaviter in modo.

FOREWORD

At first glance, it may seem that my scribblings fall into a trap that has ensnared many diplomats before me who have published their memoirs but shared few memories.

What I'm trying to do, which is quite the opposite, is use my experience to demonstrate that a country like Belgium has an effective diplomatic network, which has its role to play in building and maintaining relations between nations. Transported into the heart of this network, readers will readily agree on the modest nature of the position I held. However, this position was made substantially more notable by the efficient work done by both my predecessors and younger colleagues.

I write in the hope that the young people who venture to read my words conclude that this fascinating profession deserves to be delved into headfirst. As for older readers, these pages will provide explanations as to the policies followed within the timeframe covered.

I write from memory alone, not having accessed the Ministry of Foreign Affairs Archives.

PG.

Author's note: the passages in italics (historical anecdotes, political details, etc.) have been written to portray situations from a different angle, therefore shedding a different light upon them.

You may note that my analyses of the different countries where I was posted seem outdated. These texts are the fruit of a good translation of my French book published in 2007. Updating it would not have reflected the circumstances I experienced.

I

MY YOUTH

(1934–1960)

I was born in Peking in 1934 while my father was serving as the representative of Belgium in China. At the time, the Belgian mission was called the legation, and my father held the title of Belgian Minister.

My father comes from a long line of civil servants. My great-grandfather, Henri Guillaume, general-major, personal aide-de-camp to the King, member of the Royal Academy of Belgium, was Minister of War from the second July 1870 to 10 December 1872. On 15 July 1870, he mobilised the army to prevent an invasion from one of the belligerents of the Franco-Prussian war. Ever concerned with the wellbeing of both officers and soldiers, he implemented several reform bills that left their mark on the Belgian army. He advocated, among other things, for military service and the re-structuring of army schools (war, military, cavalry and NCO schools). In recognition, King Leopold II granted him the title of baron, a title subsequently passed down through his entire lineage.

My grandfather, Paul Guillaume, was a diplomat. While stationed in The Hague, he became well-acquainted with the Belgian-Dutch problems concerning the Scheldt, and his book is—to this day—the most complete work on the subject, even in The Hague. He married Euphrosine Gradisteanu, a young Romanian woman who was lady-in-waiting to Queen Sylvia of Romania. Both of them died in 1917. They had four sons. The eldest, Gustave, was an excellent diplomat who produced notable writings on the Balkans. He died in 1938. Their second son, Emmanuel, forged a distinguished career path in the railroad industry. A lover of philosophy, he corresponded with the great minds of his time. Their third son, Baudouin, pursued a career in the military, and then went to Shanghai, where he would manage *Crédit foncier d'Extrême-Orient*, a prosperous subsidiary of *the Société Générale de Belgique*.

My father, Jules, was the youngest of these siblings. He was destined for the bar, but the circumstances brought about by the 1914–1918 war led to his law studies being cut short. He became secretary to the Belgian delegation at the peace conference held in Versailles. Highly valued by the delegation, the department invited him to become a diplomat, a position he accepted. He was appointed chief of staff to the Belgian representative on the High Allied Commission for the Rhineland. He would go on to be posted in Bucharest, London, Peking, Mexico, and Paris.

Following his position as deputy to the Belgian Military High Command in Cologne, he was appointed first secretary to our Peking legation. China, which was very unstable and nationalistic, was infested with warlords. The Belgians were building a railway in central China (Longhai railway). Learning of the abuse suffered by his people in July 1927, the Belgian Minister was concerned. Unable to gain reliable information on the matter from the Chinese, he decided to send my father, who was unmarried, so that he may examine the veracity of these rumours, first-hand. He himself lived in Peking with his family.

The political instability faced in the country led to the Chinese barring the entry of foreigners to the region, which was imposed through the requirement of a visa. My father's application was rejected. Undeterred, and having got word that a train would be running on the Belgian-built track, he made the firm decision that when it did, he would be on it. His visa application was swiftly approved; the Chinese did not like to lose face.

The Time correspondent went with him at his own risk. The train set off. My father, who had his suspicions, worried that his carriage would be unhooked from the rest of the train en route, to ensure that he did not reach his destination. He travelled in the engine. Arriving safely, my father and the American went about their own business. Boarding the train to return, my father enquired as to the journalist's whereabouts. The Chinese announced that he had been buried alive, pointedly adding: "you could have faced a similar fate. We told you not to come here".

In 1933, he married my mother and went to China for the second time, now as Minister of Belgium, stationed in Peking. In 1937, the Belgian and Chinese governments agreed to elevate their respective missions to the rank of embassies, a step that was instigated by my father. It is worth noting that in the 19th century, only the major world powers exchanged ambassadors, which gave them precedence over the ministers. Following the 1914—1918 war, these major powers allowed Belgium to exchange ambassadors with them. A privilege granted purely as protocol, the gesture served to reward Belgium for the heroic actions of its soldiers. This elevation of Belgian-Chinese relations led to a need arising for a new leader to be appointed. We left China and headed for Brussels. My father was to be posted to Moscow next. He was appointed ambassador to China in 1937, then to Paris in 1944.

My mother, Élisabeth Wittouck, came from a family of industrialists. Her father's family can be traced back to Sint Niklaas Waes. My grandmother, Albertine Brandeis, was a young Austrian girl of Jewish descent, who was bright and very well brought up. They had three children. The eldest, Jean, would go on to take over the family's industrial affairs. My mother came next. Marie Thérèse was the youngest. She married Jean Ullens de Schooten, a skilled diplomat. Widowed at an early age, she made her way to Iran, publishing books on the local tribes with whom she lived for some time, sharing in their lifestyle and traditions before moving on.

In Peking, my parents led a very active life, mostly in circles made up of the city's foreign population. At the time, diplomatic relations with the Chinese were carefully conducted, most formally.

But how can I begin to describe this China, the place where I took my first breath?

China was unstable in 1934. The powerful Shanghai "green gang"—considered to be one of the most powerful secret mafia organisations in China—dealt in arms and the drug trade, among other things. They supported General Chiang Kai-shek.

In Peking (Beijing), however, far away from Mao Zedong's battles against the powers-that-be and the war with Japan, the tempo of the lifestyle lived by the diplomatic corps, made up of my parents, among others, was set to the pace established by the peace treaties entered into after the Boxer Rebellion of 1900. These included important jurisdiction privileges, which resembled the capitulation treaties imposed on the Middle East by European powers. It became my father's responsibility to judge the Belgians in China.

The Belgian legation was located in the legation district, bordering on the Peking Wall, which has since been destroyed and replaced with a boulevard. This district, which had been granted to "foreign barbarians" after the defeat of the Boxers, housed all the major European missions. A brave Catholic priest held services there, in a small chapel, on Sundays. This land was claimed by the legation and a wall was built around it, encompassing the houses inhabited by Belgian diplomats as well as the offices of the legation itself. Barracks were built further back, big enough to house around twenty soldiers who were stationed to embarrass the Chinese. When he took up his post in 1933, my father asked that they be sent home. What could such a small unit do if we were ever in real danger?

On the day I was born in Peking, Hitler had Chancellor Dollfuß of Austria assassinated. The latter, a right-wing chancellor, established a corporate, nationalist state on 1 May 1934. He arrested the socialists and especially the Nazis who supported the country's unification with Germany. Chancellor Hitler thus committed his first crime outside Germany. Nazism began to spread across German borders, and the Anschluß movement was underway.

This international drama did not affect my early childhood, so I will limit myself to attempting to describe the environment within which I was living. Cartier de Marchienne, one of my father's predecessors, built the house we lived in, in a pure Bruges style. Described by Marguerite de

Yourcenar in her memoirs, it stands out in the Chinese landscape, just as a Chinese-style house would do in Bruges.

Still only a child, and never having set foot in my homeland, a certain feeling of pride struck me every time I read the words "made in Belgium" inscribed on our taps. Halfway down the stairs, a stained-glass window depicting the Belgian coat of arms let in shimmering light. The central lawn, which was protected by stone lions that my sister and I would climb on, was lined with several houses that had also been built in the Bruges style: the councillor's house, the chancellor's house and the offices.

> *"It is not a bone, Madam," was the sentence proclaimed by the gynaecologist, acknowledging the impossible nature of satisfying my mother's curiosity about my gender using radiography. However, as she travelled through Canton (Guangdong), she drank the measure of snake venom required by the Cantonese pharmacopoeia to provide her with a son.*

[Unwilling to meditate in front of the Temple of Heaven in Peking and indifferent to being in the location where the Son of Heaven was praying to Heaven.]

> *In China, every parent wants a son—when asked how many children he has, a father will only answer with the number of male children. The Chinese believe that a male firstborn is a sign of good fortune. Our Chinese translator, a former member of the imperial court, gave me the gift of a stylised silver padlock – the key to happiness. When my sister was born, they consoled my mother with the kind words that, alas, they had faced similar circumstances. My brother was born in Brussels. When my youngest sister was born, they congratulated my mother for having given birth to the fourth leg of the table of happiness.*
>
> *A few weeks after I was born, my parents went travelling around China. The Belgian diplomatic installations in the country were not limited to Peking, rather, were distributed among three cities: Tientsin (Tianjin), Shanghai, and Nanjing.*

Upon their departure, my mother left me with an American. A very modest Christian Scientist, she even extended her modesty to me, a mere baby at the time. When she got back to Peking, my mother heard from the horrified American about how every time she changed me, all the Chinese people in the house would peer through the keyhole. My mother understood immediately. The American woman's modesty had led them to believe that my mother had given birth to a daughter. And wanted to hide the fact. My mother displayed my naked body to them, thus satisfying their Chinese curiosity.

Our early childhood went by peacefully and unremarkably. Mercenaries, and particularly our am-ah (nanny), took care of us. I spoke Mandarin to her, and English to the Westerners. I was taught French by one teacher, Dutch by another, and a third taught me German (although she was let go in May of 1940).

We spent sweltering summers in Pei-ta Ho (Beidahe), a seaside resort on the coast of the South China Sea, which is still popular today. My parents owned a house there. In Peking, spring or autumn weekends would mean a trip down a dusty dirt track to the Summer Palace. My parents rented a pavilion next to the marble boat (a wonderful life-size marble reproduction of a junk, moored by the lake). Lotus flowers littered the ponds, and a boat trip caused quite a stir, as we had to weave a path through the wonderful flowers. In winter, the cold and wind would set in. Sometimes a westerly wind would bring sand from the Gobi Desert.

We had barely made it back to Brussels when the Japanese—Chinese war broke out openly. Until then, the countries had contented themselves with intermittent clashes. Immediately concerned, Belgian investors (Société Générale, Empain, etc.) asked the government to send my father back to China to keep an eye on Belgian interests, a task he was very well-acquainted with, having already dealt with such matters in previous missions.

In China, Belgian companies were building trams, railways, and telephone exchange offices and played a significant role in banking. These companies had also established a network of businessmen across the country. Let us not forget that our sovereign, Leopold II, wanted to colonise China at the end of the 19th century and was already sending representatives of the Belgian state's foreign trade to the country in order to do so.

The Japanese soon occupied Beijing. The Chinese government left for Chungking (Chongqing), a city on the Yangtze River in the centre of the country. They requested, however, that the diplomatic corps remain in Peking so that they would not have to admit to the world that China was losing its capital. I remember the Japanese troops marching into Peking and the turmoil that ensued.

Towards the end of 1941, my parents left for an inspection tour of our Embassy's various offices, planning a route that took them through Chungking so that they could make contact with the Chinese government. Having arrived in Canton (Guangdong), they decided to stop off in Hong Kong on their way back to Beijing. Just then, the Japanese-American war (1941—1945) broke out in Pearl Harbour (on 7 December 1941). Roosevelt immediately declared war on Germany, Japan's ally, therefore leading the British, the Belgians, and other European nations to declare war on Japan in solidarity.

The Japanese, who had already made it to Canton, invaded Hong Kong by land. My parents were imprisoned and forced to stay in their hotel. Japanese officers then invaded the hotel, looking for white women to rape. Hiding in their bedroom, my parents could be heard mimicking the sounds a Japanese man would make with his white captive. Their ploy was successful; my mother spared from the traumatic ordeal. The next day, the Japanese led them before the firing squad. My mother threw herself before my father, declaring that if they were to be executed, at least they would die together. Back in Beijing, the Japanese coldly announced the death of our parents. We broke down. Tokyo had banned executions, but this information had not yet made it to Beijing. The Japanese then sent my parents back to Beijing in the bottom of a boat, crammed in amongst a dense, suffocating crowd. Their return to us in Beijing brought unspeakable joy.

> *Half a century later, I made my way to the exact spot*
> *upon which this tragic episode had taken place in southern*
> *Hong Kong. The beauty of the place cancelled out any trace*
> *of the violence that had once taken place there.*

On 1 April 1942, (April Fool's Day itself (!) brought an unexpected development) Japan announced a reciprocal repatriation agreement for diplomatic missions between Japan and the countries it was at war with. As agreeable as ever, the Japanese allowed us to take as many moving boxes as we wanted. This meant my parents could take several Chinese pieces of furniture back with us, which we kept, and which my brother and two sisters still have to this day.

Leaving China, we headed for Lourenço Marques (Maputo) in Mozambique on a Japanese ship, the Kamakura Maru. The Portuguese colony felt like a peaceful haven to us. The German consul was staying in the same hotel as us. Regardless of our respective parents banning us from seeing each other, we still managed to play with the consul's son.

As soon as he was on dry land, my father made his way back to free China, back to his position. He settled near the Chinese government in Chung King (Chongqing). We stayed in Africa but left Lourenço Marques for Johannesburg, where both the economy and education systems were more developed. My mother found herself alone with four children, including my youngest sister who was only two, and my brother who suffered from kala-azar (a severe form of visceral leishmaniasis), a disease prevalent in eastern Asia but which the South Africans were not familiar with.

In 1942, apartheid had not yet been introduced in South Africa, but relations between the black, indigenous and white communities were strained. We settled into life in Johannesburg. I took the bus to the Marist brothers' school every morning. A strict, formal method of teaching was employed, and the South Africans took part in daily military exercises: my Belgian nationality meant I was excused. I did not, however, escape a leather strap to the hands.

Our gardener was a man from the powerful Zulu tribe. The same Zulus who were ruled by King Chaka and who defeated the British at Isandlwana in 1879. This was of no matter until one day when I was playing in our garden. Having probably drunk or smoked, he developed a deep rage, and swinging his machete to slice off a section of thorny reed, he began his pursuit, whipping me from head to toe. All I was wearing was my swimsuit. My mother ran out, picked me up and took my bleeding body to the police station. The commissioner advised her not to take any action. If she did, the tribe could vow revenge. We went home. Escorted, this time, by his father, the gardener apologised. My mother kept him on.

Arguments between the Zulus would often break out. The most impressive, from our perspective as children, took place one evening in the family kitchen. Insults and knives flew through the air between the two protagonists. My sister, who found herself below the flight path of these knives, was amused by the episode. My horrified mother forbade me from joining her and ordered her out of the room.

My father left China and joined the Belgian government in London. Once the war was over, he was appointed to Washington as Ambassador. Before taking up the position, he went on a tour of the Belgian companies in the Belgian Congo. The Congo had, in fact, played an important role, having helped the United States by supplying it with rubber, quinine and uranium during the war. We met him in Elisabethville (Lubumbashi), the mining capital of the country. He decided to send us to Washington early. Commercial airlines had been banned, which meant we had to travel in military planes. Our first stop was Lagos, a simple city in Nigeria at the time, but an important stop for American aviation, nonetheless. It was here that the seriously injured pilots were brought, before being taken to a large hospital in Natal (Brazil).

A week spent at the English club in Lagos flew by, during which we learned to dive from a high springboard. Soon enough, we boarded a military plane transporting American airmen coming from Europe. I was very impressed by their bandages, wound around wounds on their arms, heads and elsewhere.

We stopped at Ascension Island, a British rock in the middle of the Atlantic, which had been rented by the United States as a military base. Nothing grew on the island, so the army had to import all their food. We went on to land in Natal, the Brazilian city positioned closest to Europe. A high fever due to an ear infection caused by a poorly executed dive in Lagos earned me a week's stay in the military hospital. The only child, I found myself inserted into the lives of the wounded soldiers. As soon as my temperature was back to normal, I was running around and playing with them.

A military plane finally took us on to Washington. What I found upon landing was a country at war. A feeling of generosity for prisoners of war could be felt strongly among the general population. However, I also saw posters urging Americans to think about 'their boys' and not throw whole loaves of bread away. This level of consumerism shocked me, especially under those circumstances.

My mother moved us to Manchester-by-the-sea in Massachusetts, where a Belgian friend would keep an eye on us while she joined my father in London, on the flagship of a convoy in which warships surrounded and protected commercial ships. In the middle of the night, one night, the admiral called her on-deck to observe an attack on a German submarine.

After the liberation of Brussels on 4 September 1944 (and the London Convention entered into with the Netherlands and Luxembourg on 5 September 1944, which would later lead to the establishment of Benelux), the government returned to Belgium, and the Ministry of Foreign Affairs found itself in the premises located at number 8, Rue de la Loi. My father, who was supposed to join us in Washington, was posted to Paris at the last minute by Mr Spaak, Minister of Foreign Affairs.

My mother came back to pick us up from Manchester-by-the-sea, and we boarded a military plane filled with nervous airmen on their way to the front. Our innocent little faces set them at ease during the journey. We waged paper plane wars against them. Landing in Great Britain, we discovered that we would not be leaving for Paris the next day because it had just been bombed. We spent Christmas at the mess with the soldiers. The room buzzed with a combination of over-excitement and nostalgia. The dense cloud of cigarette smoke clouded our vision. At the end of the meal, we each got our ration of plum pudding.

Our arrival in Paris ("The City of Lights, where a thousand lights sparkle") could not have been more dismal. It was dark, and the curfew was ominous. It was cold.

Our relations with France were still strained: on 5 September 1940, at the request of the Germans, the French had broken off diplomatic relations with Belgium. During the war, one consulate survived in Paris.

Relations were resumed when Charles de Gaulle was elected to the French government.

The situation France found itself in was concerning. The country was in mourning. Six hundred thousand were dead. Industrial production had halved, the country's financial reserves were non-existent, and inflation had set in.

The supply of foodstuffs, which could still only be obtained with stamps, even several years after hostilities had come to an end, improved only slowly and was incomparable to the situation in Belgium. In France, bread was made using corn. In Belgium, we used wheat. In France, there was no access to sugar, cream or chocolate. We bought all of that in Belgium. The journey from Paris to Brussels took a day, and we would go through five or six spare tyres. If the same trip were to be made by rail, the French train would stop at the border. Passengers had to get off the train to go through French customs and security. They would then walk across the border to the Belgian customs and security and get on a Belgian train.

It was in these precarious conditions that the new directions French policy would take were being decided.

Returning to Paris in 1944, de Gaulle wanted to create a semblance of continuity between the current and pre-war governments: he moved into his former office as Secretary of State for National Defence. My father presented him his credentials in this office.

Returning to his old offices appeared not to have been a decision de Gaulle made on a whim, rather, it was an action that would seize the period during which Marshal Pétain was head of state and throw it into the dustbins of history. Retroactively, France then became an ally to the powers who were at war with Germany, which allowed the country to avoid occupation by the Allies and gave it the right to an occupation zone in Germany and Austria. Successive French governments would follow de Gaulle's lead, up until Jacques Chirac recognised the "imprescriptible debt" the State owed to the victims of the Vichy regime, on 16 July 1995.

Under de Gaulle's first government (3 June 1944 — 20 January 1946), France caught its breath and let a deep desire for change take root. The return of those who had been displaced and the various Resistance movements left their mark on the political landscape. My mother would spend hours with the Belgian Red Cross, waiting for the returned Belgian prisoners and deportees to arrive.

Wanting to create a new Christian path that opposed Nazism as much as it did Communism, the Holy See put forward a proposal for a Christian democracy. In France, a party was founded according to this new theory; the Popular Republican Movement, MRP. Among its ranks was Robert Schumann, who would go on to be one of the founders of the European Union.

France's left was divided. On the one hand, there was the French Section of the Workers' International (SFIO), which was founded in 1905. On the other, there was the Communist Party, formed by a split in the SFIO in 1920 and with the collaboration of the CGT union (General Confederation of Labour). The Communist Party became the most powerful post-war party, winning 114 of the seats despite its pro-German position, until the 1941 invasion of Russia and thanks to the role it had played in the Resistance. My parents invited Maurice Thorez, the leader of the party, to a dinner party held at the embassy. The members of the French aristocracy who also attended were visibly concerned about having to share a meal with a communist.

The traditional right went back into its shell for a while.

Little by little, the Communists lost enough ground to loosen their grip on national power.

If I step back and take a look at Franco-Belgian relations, it becomes clear that beyond a certain linguistic affinity with one part of Belgium, and a relationship that dates back to feudalism with the other, relations between France and Belgium are made up of both very happy times, in which the countries are allied, and times scarred by occupations and misunderstandings.

In 1944, Belgian-French relations had not yet healed from the damage done in May 1940. Unwilling to admit to the defeat of the French army, Paul Reynaud, the Prime Minister of France in May 1940, criticised King Leopold III and removed him from the Legion of Honour after the Belgian army surrendering. Rising to power soon afterwards, Marshal Pétain, a soldier who was well aware of Belgium's military circumstances, reinstated him in the Legion of Honour, stressing his admiration for the courage the King had displayed during the Belgian campaign, to our ambassador.

Belgian opinion was also divided. The million Belgians who were still in France after the war did not make my father's task any easier. He would never get Paul Reynaud to admit to how wrong the position he had taken in 1940 had been. Trust was, however, gradually re-established between the two governments and between the two peoples, eventually leading to the beginnings of regional European agreements that were supported by the United States. I was picked on with a nickname that followed me from school in Paris, to Cours Saint-Louis, and even to boarding school with the Oratorians of Pontoise. They called me *"petit Belge"*.

It was in this variable climate, one that oscillated between love and hatred, that the two countries, along with others, succeed in creating a new Europe via the Treaty of Rome. My father was very active in negotiations.

But the wrinkles of the past don't disappear just because you're smiling on the outside. Gallican, rebellious France, driven by a self-image, shaped by an illustrious military and political past in which it rejected external authority, accepted this cooperation between Europeans in spite of itself. It stood in stark contrast to Belgium, a country that had definitively abandoned the neutralist policy drawn up by its government at the end of the thirties and, taking a gamble, demonstrated the advantages of opening its borders. To its partners in the venture, this Belgium became the new European conscience.

One day, my father received instructions from the Ministry to swap the Embassy's coal boiler for oil heating. The embassy was at rue de Surène, only a stone's throw from the Élysée. In digging a hole to bury the tank, we came across a mass grave. Intrigued, my curious nature led me down into it. The bones had been placed there: this building had belonged to Lafayette among others. Who had buried these bones? Would we find more in the basement? The thought that a mass grave lay under me as I slept intrigued me. It felt like part of the mystery of history and of life.

I had now left school and had to choose a career. The variety and periodic changes in lifestyle that life as a diplomat could give me steered my choice. This path led me to enrol in the Faculty of Law of the University of Paris, rue d'Assas. I also took courses at the Institute of Political Studies "Sciences Po.", at Rue Saint-Guillaume.

While I was at university, the minds of the population were taken up with the Algerian war (1954—1962). My fellow students were no exception. Some did not return. On one side of the conflict were the French soldiers, who had a very pleasant lifestyle, along with settlers who had become rich thanks to cheap labour. On the other, the Algerian side, was the F.L.N. (National Liberation Front), the instigators of the war.

The Front, who purchased their weapons in Belgium, became a source of great shame for me during a field trip to Belgium one day. The other members of my seminar on economic geography and I had been taken to visit our arms company, where we would find weapons engraved in Arabic. The weapons had very clearly been manufactured for the F.L.N. Later, when I came to manage Foreign Affairs with Algeria, I would meet several officials who would explain that they had found refuge in Belgium, as a means to escape the French.

In addition to going to class, my parents would insist that I periodically attend dinners they would host. I did, although reluctantly. Fleeting memories still crowd my mind when I think of writers like the brilliant but sinister Mauriac, the lighter and more cheerful Maurois, and Cocteau who, when dining with Queen Elisabeth one day, did not let her get a word in edgeways. On another occasion, during a luncheon held at the Embassy, Maurice Chevalier would sing his song, "Manneken Pis", while clutching my hand.

Queen Elisabeth of Belgium would often stay with my parents. She was always joined by one of her ladies-in-waiting, either Baroness Grenier, a major player in Italian football betting, or the Princesse de Caraman-Chimay, the Countess of Greffulhe's sister. Brilliantly intelligent and mischievous in nature, mid cold war, Queen Elisabeth would decide to go to Beijing to meet Mao Zedong, to taunt the Belgian government, despite its unfavourable opinion. Ever daring, she sent my father a postcard from Beijing. On it, was a picture of the Chinese imperial crown.

The Countess of Greffulhe once attended a cocktail party at the Embassy, beautifully dressed in a purple haute couture ensemble with purple boots. Striking despite her advancing

14

years, her personality made her radiant. She was a friend to the entire city of Paris, hosting the most famous writers and philosophers in her living room, even serving as inspiration for Proust's character, the Duchesse de Guermantes. My parents knew her well. My father asked her, as he did of many others, to intercede, with the aim of getting Paul Reynaud to retract his unjust incrimination of King Leopold III in 1940. When she took her last breath at the age of 92, whilst in a hotel in Geneva where she had gone to support a young writer, my father predicted that his own death would also take place in a hotel. He would pass away in his hotel room in Stockholm a decade later.

Apart from these social events, I also attended several meals hosted by my parents with the aim of increasing the likelihood of the French accepting the treaty that would establish the European Defence Community (EDC). It was eventually signed on 27 May 1952. My father became particularly active in the matter, and a rumour even went around about him being appointed head of the military organisation. His friends had already nicknamed him the "General Baron". Signing a treaty is one thing, ratifying it is quite another. Five of the countries ratified it: Belgium, Luxembourg, Germany, Italy and the Netherlands. The sixth, France, was hesitant despite the treaty's deadline for ratification. Quickly becoming impatient, Spaak begged my father to intervene. The latter asked in vain that Spaak be patient, as the French government, led by Mendès-France, wanted to end the First Indochina War (1946—1954). He had just signed the peace of Geneva, on 21 July 1954, after the French defeat at Dien Ben Phu (3 February 1954).

Just as in 1940, defeated, the French army surrendered once again. The French government, ever wary of the German military, could not face giving up control of its army under these delicate circumstances. Visiting my father's house one day, I would overhear Marshal Juin, who served under Pétain and only surrendered to the allies in Tunisia in June 1943, saying that the idea of German sergeants commanding French soldiers was unthinkable. One Saturday in August 1954, Mendès-France, his wife and children paid my parents a visit. Only milk was served, in honour of the campaign he had launched encouraging the French to drink more milk. After lunch, he began talks with my father. Agreeing to present the treaty to Parliament, Mendès-France would refuse, however, to stand in support of it. The Assembly rejected the treaty on 29 August 1954. The Six would then fall back on the WEU, an organisation created at the London conference, held from 28 September to 3 October 1954.

> *While I was posted in Paris, Ambassador Rothschild – who had been Spaak's Chef de Cabinet when the CED had failed - criticised my father for his lack of firmness with Mendès-France. I replied that, quite the contrary, it had been Spaak's intransigence that led to the failure of the treaty.*

This demonstrates the curious theorem that was developing within the European Union. Benelux was the thread that guided its development, the guinea pig on which integrations were tested. While the Franco-German agreement drove the Union, major failures came as a result of a Belgian-French disagreement: the CED in 1954, and the Fouchet plans (1961—1962), the details of which shall be provided later, in the chapter devoted to my time posted in Paris.

The first agreements establishing the Benelux Economic Union were signed in 1958, leading to the gradual integration of the Netherlands, Luxembourg and Belgium. The degree of integration was steadily increased, serving as a testing ground for the remaining members of the European Union. Working in the shadows, unbeknown to all but specialists and politicians, Benelux played a key role in the conception of the European Union.

The Franco-German agreement, which had the support of both de Gaulle and Adenauer, seemed, a priori, to uphold ideas that opposed the spirit of the Treaty of Rome. By creating the European Union, members would establish a rule of equality amongst themselves. What, then, were the others to think when the two most populous and richest states made separate deals? Experience has shown that it was precisely this tandem that became the driving force of the Union. How? These two states, which had few naturally common interests, did not compete with one another. State reason guided the agreement. In addition, thanks to the incessant meetings taking place among officials at varying levels of power, the two administrations and their politicians got to know each other, therefore gaining empathy and understanding for each other's problems. As a result, reaching a common standing despite the difficulties they faced became an easier task for them to manage.

I left Paris for Belgium. 18-months of military service in the navy followed, during which I rose to the rank of deck officer at the Sint Kruis barracks, near Bruges. A few weeks later, I passed several exams that, when combined with the degree I'd finished in France, gained me a PhD in Law from the University of Louvain. Soon after, I boarded the "Kamina" troopship.

Two months in a dry dock in the port of Antwerp had me taking part in nightlife populated by sailors from all over the world, all of whom were both drunk and exhausted.

The young tradition of the Belgian Naval Force dates back to the Second World War. The general officers I met had served as young officers in the British Royal Navy (Belgian Section). In 1946, it became the Belgian Navy. They were not haunted by their duties come nightfall, which meant that the atmosphere was more relaxed. The young generation of officers, however, was infinitely more disciplined. Initially due to the influence of the British, then that of the Dutch, one lunchtime a week while at sea we would dine on an entire Indonesian 'rijsttafel'.

In the following months, we twice transported the para commandos to their base in Kamina, in the province of Katanga in the Congo.

The other officers of my rank served on minesweepers, a weapon for which the Belgian Naval Forces ranked first among the allies. The Allied Mine Warfare school was in Ostend. My last call to arms was on a minesweeper.

When my military service came to an end, I married Monique d'Aboville, a French woman with a diverse background (with roots from both Sarre and Savoie), but who was originally from Normandy. Our marriage was not a happy one. We had four children, Emmanuel, François, Agnès and Dominique. They are now in their fifties and over. Emmanuel has a daughter, Élise, with Sophie Stinglhamber, François has three daughters, Catherine, Hélène and Amélia with Ania Pabis, Agnès has three daughters, Thérèse, Bettina and Mélusine with Bernard Boon-Falleur and

Dominique has two daughters, Sarah and Myriam, and a son, Séraphin with Chantal Umulisa Gayawira. Catherine married Charles Duval-Leroy and had two daughters, Olympe and Celeste.

It was then that I set my sights clearly on being a diplomat. All I had to do was pass the diplomatic entrance exam.

The Department, however, did not hold an entrance exam in early 1958. While I waited, having finished my military service, I became secretary to Baron Moens de Fernig, general commissioner of the Brussels World Fair. The general theme of the Exhibition was "For a more human world", that is to say, "take stock of the world so that together, the men of our time can prepare to build a more human world".

The Exhibition therefore excellently reflected the political and humanitarian concerns of the time, as well as the technological hopes and fears. Forty-two million visitors would pass through the pavilions hosted by 43 countries. I met several heads of state and other important figures.

> *By chance, we happened to host representatives from both from the Vatican and Moscow, as little as two days apart. I remember the glorious nature of the Vatican prelates, led by Cardinal Siri of Genoa, coming hand in hand with a clear arrogance.*
>
> *The Russians, who came with their president, accompanied by Mikoïan and Mrs Federovna, gave our sovereign, King Baudouin, the gift of a performance by the Bolshoi theatre. The Soviet president's secret services demanded that around fifty members of the KGB also be allowed into the royal box: I closed the door in their faces and stood in front of it, barring their entrance.*
>
> *At Baron Moens' residence, the two delegations were served the same tomato sauce. It was, however, presented in a different manner for each, named cardinal sauce for some, red sauce for others.*

The architectural marvels at the Exhibition fascinated me. Now was the time for architects to put their daring theoretical assumptions into practice, the most impressive of which I have to share. One was the

Atomium by engineer André Waterkeyn, which represented an iron crystal magnified 165 billion times. Another was the Civil Engineering Arrow, which I walked almost all the way along before it was closed to the public. Yet more included the dome of the UN pavilion, which had walls thinner than an eggshell, if an egg had the same diameter as the construction. The Philips Pavilion, built by Le Corbusier, with its one hundred loudspeakers scattered around a membrane structure and supported by masts, became the birthplace of new Musique Concrète and electronic music. The Exhibition marked the end of post-war reconstruction with these new exploits. The pavilions of the Belgian Village from 1900, nicknamed "Joyful Belgium" depicted the "Belgian way of life".

To counter the morbid, deadly unleashing of science that took place in Hiroshima and Nagasaki, the Brussels Expo 58 stood against the new adventures science was embarking on outside its military uses, in the International Science Hall, where it took an enthusiastic look into the future.

The exhibition set the stage for a new era, which was all the more euphoric since the Treaty of Rome had been signed the previous year, on 25 March 1957. The European Community began to settle into Brussels. The city underwent a structural reform, in which peaceful boulevards designed in the days of King Leopold II were transformed into rapid intra-urban roads. King Baudouin's reign has come to be defined by the latter. Suddenly, Brussels shed its lowly image of simply the Belgian capital, becoming, instead, one of the most important decision-making centres of the world.

The Belgians seemed happy, and to have reconciled with each other. The royal question became a thing of the past, making way instead for the first skirmishes of linguistic disputes to come to a head.

Belgium reigned confidently in the Congo. At the 1958 Exhibition, the Congo and Rwanda-Burundi section was imposing and colonialist in appearance. It exhibited the successes of colonisation, and the Belgians could clearly see themselves remaining in the Congo, Rwanda and Burundi for many happy years.

However, many Congolese people came to see the Exhibition. They noticed that white people worked a lot and were the ones with all the jobs. They were able to see the lives led by white men other than those of the colonisers in the Congo. Belgians waited on them in restaurants. This Belgian way of life made the 300 ethnicities of Congolese visitors, who, for six months, were living together for the first time, stop and think. They came together, talking of self-determination and claiming back their rights to participate in running their country and their affairs. They wanted a say in the decisions that had been made for them. Two years later, Belgium would grant them their independence.

> *I witnessed a curious matter of protocol. King Leopold III was to host the Mwami (Tutsi King) of Rwanda, who had come to inaugurate the Rwandan pavilion. But who should be the first to enter the room? The Mwami believed that, as he was the ruler of Rwanda and King Leopold III had abdicated, it would be up to King Leopold III to allow him to go first. King Leopold III, however, believed that he was entitled to go first, as the Belgian administration considered the Mwami to be a local chief under the Vice-Governor of Rwanda-Burundi. The result was that they made their entrance together, stretching their hands out in greeting at the same time.*

Despite the moves made towards peace in the exhibition, the Cold War loomed with the first popular manifestation of the new Soviet power. The Soviet pavilion housed a sputnik replica, the first satellite sent around the Earth, on 4 October 1957, seven months before the exhibition opened and six months after the signature of the Treaty of Rome. This satellite beeped at a wavelength the Soviets communicated at. I picked up the signal on my little crystal radio. In comparison, the American pavilion, the most important circular building in the world, looked rather dull.

Two very important cultural events were held simultaneously in the International Arts Hall. They showed the important cultural role Belgium played. One, the exhibition devoted to Fifty Years of Modern Art, showed Magritte, Delvaux and the prestigious school of Laethem. The other was devoted to Man and Art.

An American company, Pan Am, invited me to an inaugural flight of a Boeing with jet engines. The technological revolution between the propeller engine and the reactor impressed me deeply. We left Brussels, flew over Paris half an hour later and were soon back in Brussels. The silence of the plane appealed to us, as well as its speed. We were each given a glass of champagne, and the crew suggested we place the glass on our tray tables: the glass stood firm, as the plane did not vibrate. It was fascinating.

It was in this atmosphere charged with a new energy, in this Europe that was so battered and bruised from the Second World War, that I found myself making my way into a career as a diplomat, at the age of 25. What had I acquired along the way? Being able to speak several languages: Dutch, French, English, later adding Spanish and German, which I have relearned since 1940. I no longer spoke Mandarin. A law degree from the University of Paris, studies from the Paris Institute of Political Sciences and a PhD in Law from the University of Louvain.

II

INTERNSHIP AT THE MINISTRY OF FOREIGN AFFAIRS

(1960—1963) BRUSSELS

Finding myself going into Foreign Affairs on Good Friday 1960, I was flooded with excitement. I finally had a stable job, making me financially independent. I was earning a monthly salary of 9,000 Belgian francs, or 225 euros. I was participating, if minimally, in the public life of my country, and stood before a gateway to the wider world. The next day, on my way to work, I encountered a pigeon trying to find its way into those very same buildings, its indelicate manners displaying its lack of awareness of the hushed politeness expected of diplomats. Relieving itself on my head, it filled me with humility. It was this feeling what would guide me on my journey through the fascinating profession.

What did my future hold? Belgian representation abroad is divided into two branches: diplomatic relations, meaning relations between two states through embassies held by each state in the capital of the other. An ambassador may be assisted, depending on the importance of this relationship, by a counsellor, a first secretary, a secretary or an attaché.

As for the second branch, consular relations, these deal with matters concerning individuals or companies: visas, civil registrations and defending the interests of companies abroad. As a general rule, our ambassadors also carry out the duties of a consul. In countries where Belgium has several interests or a large Belgian colony, however, the government establishes a consulate or consulate general in an important provincial city (for example Rotterdam, Lille, Munich, New York, etc.)

This same division can also be seen in the Ministry of Foreign Affairs. Alongside a general directorate, which manages personnel, protocol and a variety of small services, the Directorate-General for Political Affairs deals with political relations; Foreign trade and economic relations (commercial relations are dealt with by the European Union, as established by Article 133 of the Treaty of Rome), and, finally, the Directorate-General for Consular Affairs deals with the problems faced by individuals.

When I started at the Ministry of Foreign Affairs, it felt like a club. Everyone had the same opinions and followed the same policies. Belgian consensus was resolutely UN, Atlanticist, European and pro-colonialist and the few politicians who strayed too far from this school of thought were immediately weeded out. This consensus, which was a major asset to the Department, made detailed directives unnecessary.

Belgian foreign policy didn't go much further than that. Our pioneering businessmen, creators of economic and financial empires in China, Egypt, Iran, Russia, the Ukraine and Latin America, did not pass their entrepreneurial spirit down to their heirs. The result was severe restrictions being placed on our commercial and industrial network, as well as on our diplomatic horizons.

Suffice to say that the events in the Congo in 1960 and the gradual broadening of our diplomatic horizons, thanks to cooperation between European nations, significantly changed the Department's approach to international issues. These circumstances, combined with a healthy diversification in the personnel recruited and the flaws that would eventually come to light in the Belgian consensus, had brought an end to that jovial team spirit by the end of the century. The intrinsic quality that could be expected of each diplomat, however, never faltered.

Going into the ministry, I entered the NATO service. That being the case, I swiftly set about making a methodical inventory of the problems in the organisation.

The Cold War was in full swing. Tensions between the West and the Soviet Union ran extremely high. The Communists, who had acquired a large military arsenal, had clear military supremacy over a still-weak

NATO; the Soviets' populist approach appealed to the new states born out of former European colonies, and economic success placed the Soviet Union second only to the United States in the Global Business & Economics Anthology. In Western Europe, the traditional political parties succeeded in removing the Communists from their governments. Still, in certain countries (France, Italy and Spain) these parties managed to retain a high level of power. The economic situation in Belgium was starting to become a problem. Belgo-Congolese Round Table negotiations aimed to lay out the terms of the Congo's independence but came to an end with a strange sense of indifference.

NATO (The North Atlantic Treaty Organisation) continued to act as a military shield, preventing a new war from breaking out in Europe. How? The first pillar: the Washington Treaty of 4 April 1949, which created the North Atlantic Treaty. This treaty stipulated that in the event of an armed attack against a member state of the treaty, each member would decide on the action it deemed necessary, which could include deploying armed forces, to restore and ensure security in the North Atlantic region.

But why was it formulated so vaguely? Because the leading state in the treaty, the United States, demanded that the US Senate retain its privilege to declare war.

The second pillar, the North Atlantic Treaty Organisation, handed command of the allied armies over to an American general. If an attack were to be launched on any member of the Alliance, the general would respond immediately, without waiting on a vote taken by the American Senate.

It was set up following the Korean War (1950—1953), which had demonstrated the fragility of the West.

The official aim of the Washington Treaty and of establishing NATO appeared to be defending Western Europe against the USSR. The treaty was also, although less visibly, a powerful means with which to force member states to get along. This was the case for France and Germany, but also eased the often-strained relations between Greece and Turkey.

The United States added an economic proposal to this military approach, the Marshall Plan: a generous aid within an organisation were ex-countries at war would meet and coordinate their economic policies in order to build a rich and peaceful Europe.

What were the Americans aiming to do? They wanted to keep their troops in Europe, something they could afford to do thanks to economic aid provided by American taxpayers. They soon found that building a strong, peaceful Europe that would be capable of resisting the Soviet allure would give them a strong competitive advantage. Without this America could lose a very important trading partner. This was especially true as, except for Egypt, Sudan and Ethiopia, the rest of the African states were still part of European empires. In an attempt to prevent the American economy from crashing, the US had to pull out all the stops to ensure that these riches did not fall into Soviet hands.

By turning Europe into a sanctuary, safely nestled under its protective nuclear cover, the United States thus moved the fight against the Soviet Union over to the other continents; a fight that was not only military but also political and economic. It was, in short, the Cold War.

The delicate balance of military relations between the East and West can be determined through an analysis of the following data.

The USSR had notable territorial superiority thanks to its Siberian hinterland, and despite disputes with its neighbours over almost all the land borders it had established by force. Economically, the USSR developed at an impressive rate and, in 1959, Khrushchev did not hesitate in saying "We shall bury you" to Vice-President Nixon. A closer analysis of the quote reveals that it could, in actual fact, have contained a shred of realism. Only, however, if the Soviets continued to work as hard as they had been working and managed to keep their place at the forefront of technological development on the one hand, and if the West didn't wake up on the other.

The West sought refuge in countries that did not share a border. The Atlantic stood between the United States and Canada, and Europe. In Europe, if we work our way from North to South we find a very lonely Norway bordering on the USSR; next is the fragility of Hamburg, which, only a few miles from the Iron Curtain, risked being separated from the rest of Germany in as little as a few hours; Great Britain followed, which, thanks to its insularity, became a possible place to which to withdraw; and finally the Rhine, which stood two hours from Brussels and the Iron Curtain. Spain was not a member of the Alliance and stood between Portugal, a member of the Alliance, and the other States. Greece, and especially Turkey, which bordered on the USSR, joined the Alliance despite sharing no land borders with the other States. Turkey, however, was able to block the Soviet fleet stationed in Sevastopol from sailing out via the Black Sea.

The West's territorial vulnerability was exacerbated by its conventional army, which was infinitely smaller than the multiple Soviet divisions. In addition, President Eisenhower slowed the development of the "military-industrial complex" — one he considered to be of a considerable size, absorbing more than the net income of the entirety of American businesses. Nevertheless, he monitored the USSR closely using U2 spy planes. A pilot of one of these planes, who was captured by the Soviets on 1 May 1960, created major turmoil in Russia–United States relations. This was the first major crisis I got to experience in the world of Foreign Affairs.

Eisenhower managed to maintain a balance of forces thanks to the large nuclear arsenal under his control. This nuclear force was not part of the NATO forces. The doctrine of American military deterrence, which had been approved by the Atlantic Treaty member states, is based on an overwhelming nuclear response. This policy encouraged the Soviets to produce nuclear weapons that were comparable in size to those in the US. They also mastered building nuclear rockets. Sputnik, launched in 1957, proved as much.

Faced with these new circumstances in December 1957, the USA transferred part of its nuclear weapons to NATO. The UK would follow suit. The Supreme Headquarters Allied Powers Europe was therefore granted a wider range of defences.

Next, the United States would suggest they alter their response to any aggression to a "graduated response". To us, this new military theory seemed reasonable, although it was a bit of a leap into the unknown. If the Soviets invaded Western Europe using only conventional means, they would have a clear advantage thanks to their geographical position, the size of their troops and their conventional arms. The United States was renewing its promise to intervene, but the commitment it was making was becoming blurrier. What would a US President do if the Soviets threatened the United States with their nuclear bombs should they intervene in a conventional soviet invasion of Western Europe?

On 4 May 1962, the ministers of member countries adopted the "Athens Guidelines", the aim of which were to keep the USSR within its borders. They also laid out the techniques to be used in a graduated military response and the line that would need to be crossed to require a nuclear response. The US committed to consulting with its allies before proceeding with the use of nuclear weapons. Overwhelming nuclear deterrence was thus followed by a graduated response, that is, a response that would always be more forceful than the attack had been. This new theory meant that the use of nuclear weapons could be avoided.

> *As part of the deployment of American nuclear weapons in Europe under the command of the SHAPE, I was tasked with translating a very secret Belgian-American agreement from English into French. This agreement would allow the United States to store nuclear weapons in Belgium. The officials responsible for this agreement had it signed by Pierre Wigny, the Belgian Minister for Foreign Affairs, in the midst of the Congolese crisis as he rushed between two meetings. Later, when he took over the ministry, Mr Spaak was questioned about this agreement in Parliament. He hadn't known it existed. The administration exhumed it from the safe it had been kept in, displaying the undeniable evidence. Mr Spaak thought the process under which an agreement of this importance had been signed was very cavalier, explaining as much to the House of Representatives. And rightly so.*

The new American president, Mr Kennedy, rose to power in January 1961. He criticised the Eisenhower administration and blamed the president for the US falling behind, technologically speaking. Industries within the country were called upon to restore the US armed forces to the technological superiority they had once held. The United States overtook the Soviet Union, taking back its position as the leading military power once again.

The erection of the Berlin Wall by the Soviets and the East Germans on 13 August 1961 would be the first test faced by the new US policy. The West made it known that as long as West-Berlin maintained its standing, a military response would not be triggered. For Westerners, this meant free passage of military convoys to the western areas of Berlin by air, road or rail, as well as the free movement of the four Allied Powers' soldiers throughout Berlin.

Although the solution to the crisis was not in the best of Western interests, it didn't fundamentally harm them either. Berlin was supplied efficiently, strengthening the understanding reached by the Germans and the Allies. President Kennedy made his way to Berlin to reinforce his desire to keep West Berlin in the Western fold. Whilst there, he made his famous speech, "Ich bin ein Berliner", reassuring the inhabitants of the city.

From then on, each time Germany tried to stray a little too far from the West, a reference would be made to the precarious position the city of Berlin found itself in, and the country would fall straight back in line.

A closer look would reveal that the balance of powers was changing. The Soviets had scored an important point. Three years earlier, the USSR would have yielded to the threat of a nuclear response from the US.

Later, we would learn that Khrushchev, First Secretary of the Communist Party and President of the Council of Ministers of the Union of Soviet Socialist Republics, had urged his allies to use drugs as a weapon with which to destabilise the West, in 1962. This would be done using specially equipped Kintex trucks that would ferry opiates through Bulgaria. This supply of drugs to the West is also what raised the funds needed to finance terrorist groups.

The Cuban Missile Crisis on 22 October 1962 would be the second test. The United States did not ask NATO to intervene. Regardless, Charles de Gaulle expressed his solidarity immediately.

The final agreement, made on 20 November 1962 (drawn up without consulting with either NATO or Fidel Castro, Chairman of the Cuban State Committee), it stipulated that the Soviets were required to dismantle their bases in Cuba and withdraw their missiles. The United States openly accepted that the Soviets were the guardians of Cuban sovereignty.

By admitting the Soviet hold over Cuba, however, Kennedy renounced one of the fundamental principles of the 1823 Monroe Doctrine, which stated that no European power may interfere in the relations of any country in the Americas. This policy of abandonment left a bitter taste in my mouth. History has proved that this would mark the beginning of a new era in which the United States, while still extremely powerful, no longer had access to a weapon that worked as an absolute deterrent, except for on the European playing field.

Although this was presented as a victory for the US, it allowed American leaders to see the levity with which their president made his decisions. In fact, at no point did he envisage Cuba being invaded, believing, incorrectly, that such an action would provoke Soviet retaliation. The CIA misunderstood the message, believing that they no longer had the president's support. Moscow was well-aware that the United States no longer had a deterrent. The USSR would intervene in Nicaragua a few years later with almost complete impunity.

During the same period, I also acted as secretary to the joint National Defence/Foreign Affairs administrative committee, which allowed me to gain insight into our policy in this area.

Although they were under pressure from a war in full swing, the US Food and Drug Administration authorised the first contraceptive pill ever to be marketed. A catalyst, the pill transformed the way of life of the entire population. From then on, it would be women who would decide whether or not to have children. They could take charge of their own lives and destinies, no longer being confined to their homes.

The pill also marked the beginning of sexual liberation and the right to pleasure. The tension of the Cold War and all the restrictions imposed as a result became less bearable. The pill put an end to a certain delicate eroticism where, as the Chinese say, intrigue was created between the jade sceptre and the coral cave.

It would, however, take another generation for women to be granted roles in management, in both the private and public sectors.

Having barely settled into the role, the Chef de Cabinet appointed me secretary of an ad hoc working group created to manage the Congolese crisis in early July 1960.

Once Asia had been decolonised, the African colonies began to shake off the colonial yoke. The first revolts began in the 1950s. In 1958, Charles de Gaulle granted the French African colonies their independence. Belgium was given no prior warning. French West Africa, French Equatorial Africa and Madagascar thus became independent. Only the Belgian, Portuguese and Spanish colonies now retained their colonial ties.

The end of colonial reign was drawing near, causing the January 1959 riots in Léopoldville (Kinshasa). With the two colonial wars that had recently been lost by Europeans in Africa (Kenya and Algeria) fresh in their minds, the Belgian authorities were quick to grant them their independence. A round table was held between the Belgians and the Congolese in Brussels, to determine the terms of independence and the ways in which future Congolese institutions would operate.

On Independence Day, Prime Minister Lumumba was harshly critical of Belgium. A few days later, the Force Publique mutiny broke out in the Congo, Congolese soldiers rebelling against their Belgian officers. General Janssens, the Belgian commander of the Force Publique, was forced to resign on 7 July 1960.

We were dismayed. Only a few weeks earlier, the whole of Belgium had laughed at the mere idea of decolonisation. The word "independence" didn't even exist in Swahili! We didn't believe the Congolese would choose to give up the material advantages they had been granted by the Union Minière (copper) and Forminière (diamond) social policies. Life expectancy had doubled for workers of these unions thanks to a policy that was far more generous than any the French or the British had granted their colonies. True independence was unimaginable. The uprising of the Force Publique, which had been created in 1885 to defend the country and was responsible for ensuring the economic development of the colony, was incomprehensible.

And yet, in the words of Jaques Brel, "chez ces gens-là, on ne rit pas", (those people do not laugh). The Congolese wanted "independence, true independence".

The officials at the working group created for African affairs made sure everything went smoothly with the independence celebrations in Léopoldville and the founding of the new Congolese government. The four diplomats in the working group I coordinated left their posts temporarily, to manage the Congo crisis.

The group moved into the Minister's quarters at 8 Rue de la Loi, pulling together makeshift offices that didn't contain a single file. Events unfolded quickly, one following on swiftly from the other: on 11 July 1960, the province of Katanga broke away and proclaimed its independence. Two days later, the Belgian para-commandos entered Léopoldville and restored order. On 14 July, with Belgium's consent, the UN Security Council decided to deploy peacekeepers to the Congo.

On the very same day, Congolese Prime Minister Patrice Lumumba broke diplomatic relations with Belgium. Mr Hammarskjöld, Secretary-General of the United Nations, berated us, as well as the Union Minière du Haut Katanga which produced copper and other metals. A message from our embassy in Stockholm informed us that Mr Hammarskjöld's brother ran the copper industry in Sweden. Did his harshness mask a hidden Swedish agenda? Was Sweden trying to get hold of the Union Minière's copper? The task force hesitated, before deciding not to make this information public.

> *Messages were sent by telex. The ministry only had one device. One day, mid-crisis, the New China News Agency (the official Communist China press agency) hacked into it for 48 hours. The system meant that the receiver could not cut off communications, which meant our telex was rendered useless, both for sending and receiving messages. The RTT (now Belgacom) installed new lines the next day. We also bought a few new devices.*

On 21 and 22 July, the Congo affair was taken to the UN Security Council. We managed to keep up with the debates thanks to the INR (public television). We listened to the Soviet speech, not expecting anything good to come of it, and rightly so. Henry Cabot Lodge, the US representative, however, would prove to be the most vindictive against Belgium. Schurmans, one of the advisers of the small working group, Papeians de Morchoven, the direct assistant to Mr de Staercke (permanent representative to the Atlantic Council), and I were aghast. In an international context, where the West is eternally on the defensive, it seemed irresponsible to stab Belgium, a faithful ally, in the back.

It was 3 am in Brussels when the Chef de Cabinet decided to consult with Gaston Eyskens, the Belgian Prime Minister. We woke him up with our concerns, quickly going on to discuss what the appropriate reaction would be. The idea of severing diplomatic relations and recalling our Ambassador in Washington for consultation was quickly dismissed.

Eyskens, however, was in favour of recalling André de Staercke. He wanted to make a strong point to the Americans. Papeians de Morchoven was put in charge of phoning him. The phone barely rang: de Staercke was reading "Lives of Illustrious Men" by Plutarch. He refused to follow orders:

"You can't do this to the Americans." And that was that. No one went against him.

> *While Belgium was indebted to the United States for having freed it from its German occupiers, not once, but twice, the American government owes Belgium for its victory in the war against Japan, at least in part. Thanks to the latter's management of the Congo, American soldiers at war in the Pacific had access to quinine and rubber (important for vehicles), and the army used Congolese uranium in the two atomic bombs launched on Japan — in Hiroshima and Nagasaki.*

After the legislative elections in Belgium, Paul-Henri Spaak left his position as Secretary-General of NATO, replacing Pierre Wigny as the Belgian Foreign Minister. The working group was dissolved, and I went back to the office. A bit of calm would do me no harm.

I spent a few months working on political relations with Eastern Europe. Tensions were still running high in the communist countries, and everyone was on high alert in case we needed to spring into action due to another coup. The West was clutching at its defences. Khrushchev, head of the Soviet Union, made threats against the West.

In this turbulent, unpredictable atmosphere, a double negotiation about diplomatic and consular relations started up in Vienna, between all the world states. I participated in these negotiations actively, from Brussels.

Eastern European practice considered that asking how much tomatoes cost at the market could be construed as economic espionage. We therefore had to protect our diplomats and our consuls from any drastic beliefs a host country may have. A difficult balance was struck regarding the privileges and immunities granted to both missions and individuals. The meeting quickly turned to a confrontation between East and West.

Following the assassination of Lumumba, the Soviets, working behind the scenes, provoked demonstrations in front of Belgian embassies around the world. In some countries, these protests took a very aggressive turn. Our embassy in Cairo was burned down, the flames burning so fiercely they melted the silverware in the vaults.

Shortly before I left Brussels for my next post, I went on a very short trip to Rwanda. My father had to go there as the King's representative at the independence ceremonies held on 1 July 1962. My father's heart problem was reason enough for the Ministry to grant me permission to accompany him, at the request of my mother.

The Rwandan population is made up of several ethnic groups: Tutsis, Hutus and some Twas. It's the Tutsis who traditionally exercise both political and military power. The Hutus, who make up the majority of the population, are farmers. In 1952, Belgium began to favour the Hutus over the Tutsis.

After the late 1959 riots, the Hutus began taking over positions of power from the Tutsis. The Belgian government, supported by the clergy led by the Archdiocese of Mechelen, which was omnipresent in Rwanda, did not prevent the massacres and the expulsions of Tutsis by Hutus. Consequently, the Hutus did not express animosity towards these Belgians and, quite naturally, were the ones to make up the first Rwandan authorities after independence.

Arriving in Kigali on the eve of the celebrations, I attended the last day of the Belgian mandate of the country by accompanying my father as he went on visits to the newly formed future authorities. They had set up in the office area of a school. The Belgians were concerned the future president, Greg wa Kayabanda, would take a leaf out of Lumumba's book at the Congolese independence ceremonies. This worry dissipated, however, with Kayabanda's reassurance that he would do nothing of the sort, and would, instead, deliver a very moderate speech.

The next day, Rwandans, led by President Kayabanda, took over from the Belgians who had previously been in power. After the official ceremonies, we watched as Tutsi dances were put on, performed by Hutus.

Back in Brussels, the Department asked me for a report. I settled the matter by proposing that the Belgian Ambassador be changed, as until the day before he had held the position of vice-governor of Rwanda. The lack of clarity caused by this situation could be very dangerous for Belgian-Rwandan relations, as it could become hard to distinguish between what he could do in his previous position, as vice-governor, and what he could do in his new one, as Ambassador. The Department followed my suggestion to the great relief of the Rwandans, and the Ambassador left Kigali.

Years later, the former governor of Rwanda-Burundi, Jean-Paul Harroy, told me that after the 1960 events in the Congo and thanks to the tense relations between Belgium and the UN, he asked Spaak for instructions on which policy to follow. He replied, "let go of one of the two countries (Burundi) to satisfy the UN and keep the other (Rwanda) close". Thus, over the years, Burundi has been tossed around from the Russians to the Chinese and French while the Hutu's Rwanda has been kept close to Belgium, in the lap of the "Mechelen", that is, the city where the archbishop, leader of the other Belgian bishops and their bishoprics, had his seat.

The first regular America-Europe television link via American satellite, Telstar, came about around then. The links between the two continents were becoming tighter via a new channel: the televised image.

Sometime after this trip, I took the language exam that would signal the end of my internship. The personnel department announced that I would be appointed to Kingston, without specifying the country. There are, in fact, several Kingstons jostling around the world that could house a consulate. I, however, was posted to the capital of Jamaica.

We decided to make our way there by boat, to make the journey a bit easier on my three firstborns, one of which was my baby daughter, not yet one year old at the time. Our boat was docked at Le Havre. Once on board, we waited 24 hours to hear that the crew was on strike and that the trip had been cancelled. We flew from Paris, stopping over in New York where a snowstorm was raging. The plane took us directly to Kingston. Upon landing safely, the doors opened, letting the hot, very humid air come rushing into the plane.

We stayed in a tourist hotel for the first two weeks. Caribbean music played in the pool area. The first few days filled us with wonder. Nothing felt in the least bit familiar. Once the first week had gone by, I sought out a bit of peace as the children were sleeping badly in the dizzying atmosphere. We found a hotel outside the city made up of small satellite chalets. We quickly settled into one.

I started my search for a house.

III

THE ANTILLES

(1963—1965)

The jurisdiction of my first post as attaché included all the islands, states and territories of the Antilles, except for Cuba. Going into my first post in a so-called developing country, I conducted close examinations of the political and economic functioning of these countries through long conversations with prominent figures in each one. These Latin American, African or Asian countries managed to preserve the memory of humanity, a traditional way of life and the importance of family, managing also to maintain a strict morality and the unbreakable bonds of friendship. They also had a sense of innocence when faced with divine or obscure laws.

These traditions prevented them from being able to fully understand the West. They are also the guardians of an ecosystem that the Western world could not live without. It was therefore with a sense of both deep thrill and reverence that I attempted to break into this world – while also abandoning the sediments of Western history forged by revolutions and scientific progress.

In my following posts, I would meet other men, each of whom had their own problems, hopes and disappointments. I would attempt to measure the space and the tension of the dignity with which each of them lived their daily lives, whatever their social position. I would also note the refusal of certain castes to see man as a complete being and to accept that the sun shines for each and every one alike. However, as Claudel writes, *"even for the simple taking flight of a butterfly, all the sky is necessary"*.

The Ministry decided to divide the mission in the Antilles into two parts, as there was a lack of direct communication between Cuba and the other islands. Fidel Castro, who governed from Havana, eliminated widespread corruption and decadent lifestyles. He turned down American aid in order to get the economy going once again but on healthier foundations this time. He did, however, make an agreement with the Soviet Union. Moscow was taunting the country's northern neighbour. Washington took action, severing relations with Havana due to this agreement with the Russians. Cuba had its membership suspended from the Organisation of American States. European states maintained their relations with Cuba, whose political regime followed Latin American traditions.

As a consequence of this situation, any journey from Havana to a Caribbean island would take you through Mexico City; the only state in the region that had maintained relations with both the United States and Cuba. Taking this trip on a regular basis was clearly considered less efficient than asking Belgian diplomats to stay in Brussels and make their way from there.

Belgian interest in the region can mainly be measured economically and commercially. At the time, the extent of our trade relations with the islands under our jurisdiction exceeded that of our relations with Mexico. The politics of the time should not, however, be overlooked, as the Soviet presence in Cuba meant that the Caribbean became one of the frontiers of the Cold War between the West and the USSR. One of the islands switching sides would alter not only the political geography, but also the trade relations that went hand in hand with it.

The Department therefore decided to open a new mission and chose Kingston, the capital of Jamaica, as its location. Brussels, however, told us to move our embassy's headquarters to Santo Domingo, the capital of the Dominican Republic and the most important state in the jurisdiction.

I chartered an aircraft to carry the mission's furniture and files, each member of the mission's personal belongings and their cars. Everything was transported in a matter of hours. By boat, it would have taken several weeks as we would have had to go via Miami, which operated as a hub between the shipping lines serving the Caribbean islands. This exercise, of opening an Embassy, interested me, all the problems we faced were visible right from the very start.

Each island had its own, unique colonial heritage, but they all operated with a similar financial and economic rhythm, set to the pace of agriculture. Their system was based on the same financing methods as we applied to our agricultural businesses, in which banks would give them advances pledged on future crops. A large part of the crops harvested in independent states but financed by American or Canadian banks was being sold in the United States under long-term contracts.

The landowners, who were worried about the future of their country, poured their income into these same banks. This income would come to be equal to the amounts they were requesting as loans, which would mean that the option of self-financing was available to these farmers. The detour their money made, through American banks, however, allowed landowners to keep their income in a safe currency on the one hand, and permitted them to keep up their appearance as citizens of poor, third-world countries who needed to take out loans, on the other.

The islands that were part of the European Union (France — Guadeloupe, Martinique, Saint Barthélemy and Saint Martin and the Netherlands – the Windward Islands, including Sint Maarten, and the Leeward Islands, including Curaçao and Bonnaire) sold their crops within the European Union under the "ACP" (African, Caribbean and Pacific Group of States) agreements and were granted loans by European banks. Any surplus that was not absorbed by this variety of agreements was then sold on the global marketplace.

The only exception to this rule at the time was Cuban sugar, of which the USSR bought a large share at a fixed price.

An examination of these agreements led to an important question being asked: could these countries become financially independent? Their farming practices were certainly a testament to their wealth. In the Dominican Republic, for example, the soil was covered with a thick layer of humus. Japanese settlers took to harvesting rice three times per year. After a few years of this beautiful demonstration of work, the government drove them off the island, coming to the conclusion that they were getting rich at the expense of the Dominicans. I remember young Dominicans living calm, happy lives in the countryside, content with milk drawn from a wild cow and the fruits picked from three banana trees. Yet another day, as I walked through Dominican back lands, I heard that a woman had been stoned to death for not having waited her turn at a water well.

It was then that the Congolese expelled the Belgians. I suggested, in vain, that they come and settle in the Antilles.

In addition to agricultural wealth, some islands also benefitted from mineral wealth: bauxite, especially in Jamaica, and petroleum in Trinidad and Tobago. This type of wealth generated a more regulated financial flow throughout the year.

The small islands also lived off American tourism, and some islands had the added draw of being tax havens. Politically, the United States believed it had a direct interest in keeping these islands in its orbit, given that it was mid-Cold War. This was purely in the interest of maintaining their own safety. Christopher Columbus' point of entry to America, the Caribbean islands guard the way to the south of the United States and especially to the Panama Canal, the easiest way of travelling from the east coast of the United States to the West. The Soviets showcased their understanding of these connections by recruiting Castro after his revolution and by gaining a foothold in the isthmus that was Nicaragua.

The United States, their great unloved protector, therefore tolerated these tax havens. The significant revenue generated by the US for the governments of these islands encouraged them not to sway towards the communists, as Cuba had done. In addition, by allowing American exporters to invoice their exports at cost price and re-invoice them from their tax havens, raking in the profit, the American Treasury granted free assistance when it came to exporting.

Having just arrived from Europe, I settled in Jamaica. First, I found a house on a hill. It had a garden with several mango trees in it. We moved straight in. It did not look like one of these colonial houses with their old-fashioned charm but was pleasant to live in all the same, with its covered terrace and wooden walls. One of the house's permanent fixtures was a canopy over the bed, which we hung mosquito nets on. Later, once I had left, I would come to learn the small stream that trickled gently down the hill at the end of the garden had become a torrent and had washed away half of the garden.

Discovered by Christopher Columbus in 1494, Jamaica was first occupied by the Spanish and then by the English. The latter worked to develop agriculture on the island (cane sugar), quickly making it the richest English colony.

The Great Depression in 1929 generated major social conflicts in the cities, leading to unions being created and triggering the emigration of Jamaicans. A Jamaican diaspora of around 2.2 million people could therefore be found around the globe, compared to a population of 1.8 million who remained on the island, of which half a million were illiterate.

Bauxite began to be mined after the Second World War: Jamaica, the world's third-largest exporter, had reserves of 2 billion tonnes. It was sold to the United States and Canada.

Cultural life was almost non-existent, and booksellers only sold tourist books about the island's flora and fauna. During my short stay in Jamaica, I noted the public reaction to the premiere of the film "The Longest Day" with interest. While the Europeans and Americans felt in tune with the brave soldiers during the landing, the Jamaican audience applauded military successes on both sides, although their pleasure was pronounced when the British (who had colonised their island) and the Americans (their nosy neighbour) lost a battle.

In sports, Jamaica, a member of the Commonwealth, plays cricket on many grounds. Jamaicans also participate enthusiastically in the Commonwealth Games. Thanks to British influence, they also play football.

During my stay, Jamaica began to emerge from the colonial era. The island's varied population was made up of English and Canadian subjects loyal to the Crown (which explains why the main English and Canadian banks had branches there), black former slaves, Chinese and Indians (from India). All the ethnicities seemed to be present in this racial mix. Aesthetically, I found the Afro-Chinese to be most attractive. The island was also home to descendants of Ethiopians who considered the Emperor of Ethiopia (Ras Tafari) to be their sovereign.

The island's main agricultural produce included sugar, speciality coffee (Blue Mountain coffee), cocoa and bananas. The staple food was limited to breadfruit (or Artocarpus altilis), which was imported to Jamaica from the Pacific Islands to stem the 1780 famine. The fruit looks a bit like an elongated melon. Bland but abundant, it was baked, cut into chips, etc. The fruit was nowhere to be seen in the Dominican Republic where rice and peas could often be found served as the national dish. The country's national drink, punch, was made using light rum (one or two stars — with an alcohol content equivalent to that of beer).

> *Here is a recipe for Jamaican punch: one part of sour (fresh lime juice), two parts of sweet (sugar or syrup), three parts of strong (white rum with one or two stars) and four parts of weak (water) mix and serve over ice.*

While the south of the island, where the capital – Kingston — is located, has no beaches whatsoever, the north of the island, which is three hours from Kingston by car, is quite the opposite. Montego Bay and Ocho Rios' superb beaches bring in a steady stream of tourists. As I swam there, I marvelled at the diversity and beauty of the fish surrounding me. Somewhat surprisingly, many Americans who had been seduced by the beauty of the island had decided to settle there to see out their old age. They tended to stay for two to three years, then, getting bored of isolated island life, would make their way back to the continent.

After six months in Jamaica, the time had come to move the embassy to Santo Domingo, the capital of the Dominican Republic. This republic shares the island of Hispaniola with Haiti.

I found a building large enough to house both the Embassy offices and my family. Only one large road stood between us and the sea. It was unfortunate, however, that its waters were shark infested. If you wanted to swim, you would have to go a little further up the shore to one of the many coves, where a coral reef would stop sharks from reaching the shallows. The ambassador had his own house.

[50 km from Santo Domingo (Dominican Republic), at an evening organised at the beach for 80 guests, lit by a full moon. As an aperitif, each attendee was given a coconut, which had been picked on site, its top sliced off and its water mixed with rum. Meat was cooked in the embers of a huge wood fire. A French friend of mine with long blond hair played notes written by our most romantic composers on her harp.]

Since the Conquista, the Dominican Republic has considered itself to be the land Christopher Columbus loved most (*"la república la más amada de Colón"*).

> *The cathedral housed the bodies of the Columbus brothers, Christopher and Giacomo, for a long time. Once the Republic gained its independence, however, Spain claimed back the body of Christopher Columbus. The body of one of the Columbus brothers was therefore sent to them. But which one? To this day, no one knows who has Christopher's body, because both Seville, Spain, and the Dominican Republic claim to have it. As for Diego, no one has laid claim to his corpse.*

Like the other Spanish colonies, the Dominican Republic has had an eventful history. Just as the others, the republic became independent in 1821. Following internal disorder, Spain then recolonised it, at its own request, in 1861. After a revolution, it proclaimed itself independent again in 1865 (founding a Second Republic). In 1868/70, it sought, in vain, to be annexed by the United States. Sometimes I would read articles in the newspapers filled with regret that they were not a part of the United States and did not use the American dollar as their currency (although the peso was doing well). It was a curious state of mind to observe.

In 1930, Rafael Trujillo became president, thanks to the United States, going on to rule the country as prime minister some of the time, sheltering behind figurehead presidents at other times. He was assassinated on 30 May 1961, finally bringing an end to one of the worst tyrannies in 20th century Latin America.

When I arrived in Santo Domingo, political life groped for a more moderate form of power, exhausted by the years of terror faced during the Trujillo dictatorship. Each person I came across would tell me about Trujillo's assassination in their own way. About how it took place on the main road that ran alongside the sea, and about the two generals, who had since become democratic heroes (Opus Dei, a powerful force on the island, told me they would refuse to consider them assassins). It's worth adding that the press still condemned the deceased dictator on a daily basis.

> *Inspired by the dictator's murder, the most popular merengue tune is "Mataron al Chivo en la carretera", (they killed the goat on the motorway).*

But was the new regime more democratic? President Kennedy took the opportunity to set up a powerful Embassy to make this republic a case study of democracy in Latin America.

It was raining dollars, and the US Congress was monitoring the situation with huge interest. Part of the "Alliance for Progress" initiated by President Kennedy in March 1961 was discussed during the 1961 Punta del Este gathering of the members of the OAS (Organisation of American States).

The declaration concerned the Alliance for Progress, which was defined as a broad effort to provide all the peoples of the continent with a better life. The United States pledged to pay Latin America $20 billion over the following decade.

> *The Latinos played on the Spanish name of this policy "La Alianza para el progreso", as it can be read in two ways, either: "the alliance for progress" or "the alliance stops progress".*

This Alliance for Progress was not met with significant success, given the serious economic difficulties faced by the subcontinent.

> *A rumour went around in the Dominican Republic that two American Senators had come to inquire about the degree of democracy in the country. As they came down the steps from the plane, a lottery ticket seller rushed towards them. The chief of protocol, who came to greet them, took two tickets and gave them to the Senators. Two days later, their numbers were drawn. The Senators won the jackpot and made their way back to Washington, convinced that the Dominican Republic was perfectly democratic.*

In truth, the regime wasn't a far cry from a Latin American republic. Power was held exclusively by the closed circle of twelve families who were descended from the Spanish invaders, although it frequently changed hands as none showed the makings of a statesman.

In three words, economic and social life revolved around sugar, profit and pleasure.

> *The national drink, daiquiri, a mixture of lime juice, maraschino liqueur, sugar and white rum, is served over crushed ice.*

In summer, I would often see groups of friends in the protected bays, chatting in the water around a bottle of rum.

Living through a passing hurricane that raised the sea by several metres is one of the lasting memories I have of my time there. Despite the general ban on going out, I broke the rules to admire the magnificently raging waves. Water and power were cut. I've never felt anything quite like waiting for that hurricane. No one knew what was going to happen. The sky changed colour, from greens to the darkest reds. The radio broadcast the measures we should take over and over. If anything, only serving to increase the suspense. Meteorologists tracked the path the hurricane carved, predicting the area over which its eye would pass. The winds rose, the trees trying to resist, but in vain. The hurricane's hot breath shook everything in its path. Was it the devil's breath, or that of hell itself? The streets were empty. The first tiles shattered. Pylons fell. Corrugated iron roofs broke loose and flew away like freed razor blades. The hurricane blew hard, whirling in one direction. Later, once the eye of the hurricane had passed, the storm would blow in the other. The end came about slowly and revealed the wounds it had inflicted, both in nature and in mankind's creations. The next day, the city started to feel its way towards getting up and running again. No one cared about where the hurricane went next, going on to die in Florida once it had wreaked more havoc. Sadness and desolation followed the anguish caused by the announcement that the hurricane was coming. The eyes of those around me were no longer raised anxiously to the sky. Now they were lowered, filling with tears as they looked at the ground. Nature had testified to its power over humankind once again.

A Dominican friend of mine owned several dozen hectares of land covered in wild carnations. He told me that an American perfume company had made him an offer to buy the harvest, although he had not followed up on the proposal because he did not fancy doing the work it would involve. This Dominican, while intelligent, did not take into account the damage he was doing to his country's economy.

Literary life turned out to be almost non-existent, and the only books around came from Buenos Aires, the cultural capital of the Spanish-speaking states. The rare university-educated Dominicans all completed their further education in the US. Spain, which was still under Franco, was of no note, whether economically, intellectually or politically. The diet of most of the population revolved around a small number of basic items: rice, beans, a little meat, all cooked up together in fat. As the only fruits harvested were pineapples and bananas, on the first day of every year, each Dominican subject was given an apple, which would be imported from the United States.

In sport, the Dominican Republic, like the other northern Latin American countries, had a strong American influence, which is why the national sport is baseball.

Amid this intellectual desert, my British colleague invited me to lunch to meet writer Graham Greene. The man spoke little. He asked questions and listened. Prohibited from staying in Haiti because Duvalier had him down as a "communist", he came to the neighbouring republic of Santo Domingo, meeting exiled Haitians there instead. These exiles did an excellent job of describing the general atmosphere felt in Haiti, going on what I read in his book "The Comedians", which was published shortly after, in 1966.

I have tried to examine the Dominican Republic's characteristics by comparing them to the characteristics common to other Latin American states.

While North America was populated with people fleeing from the oppression of the Old Continent, the Spanish and the Portuguese came to Latin America and brought their traditions with them, believing themselves to be extending their motherlands rather than colonising new ones. Their social system was based on European feudalism – at the root of which was birth, blood ties and loyalty, geared more towards the individual than the constitution and its laws.

> *"If North America is that of Protestantism where the right to life, liberty and the pursuit of happiness is proclaimed" (Declaration of Independence, 1776), Latin America is the America of Catholicism where "the ruling classes consolidated themselves … as heirs of the old Spanish order. They broke with Spain but proved incapable of creating a modern society. … The newness of the new Spanish American nations is deceptive: in reality, they were decadent or static societies, fragments and survivals of a shattered whole." (Octavia Paz, El Laberinto de la Soledad, 1950).*

The Dominican population was made up of the descendants of the Spanish and of African slaves, who had been sent from Spain and Christianised (the ladinos), mixed with those imported directly from Africa (the bozales) and with those either from the French part of the island (present-day Haiti) or from the other Antilles.

As in the other Spanish-speaking Latin American republics, the president had concentrated political power. The president had to be male, as governing was a privilege granted exclusively to men, to a "macho". This power could be gained legally, in an election, or in a coup.

Other machismo traits included being tough at home, but unfaithful elsewhere. I saw proof of this school of thought many times.

A new president meant gaining recognition from foreign governments. Belgium never recognises a new government; only states. Countries in the Americas, however, recognise governments. They do so easily if the president is appointed legally; if he comes to power by force, they set conditions. Until a new government is recognised, bilateral relations are suspended, and any acts passed by the other state no longer recognised. This stops all trade, as the authorities no longer accept customs documents. Oddly enough, the US is one of the countries that practised this policy. During my stay, each time the government changed it would be business as usual for the Europeans as they dealt with the new leaders, while the governments of American states examined requests for the new government to be recognised.

I bore witness to this scenario several times. After Trujillo's death, the Dominican regime was hardly stable. Trujillo's first successor was Joaquin Balaguer, a man who had been very close to the former leader (June 1961/ 1st January 1962), followed by a Council of State, then a Civic-Military Junta, then a Council of State again, then Juan Bosh (February/September 1963), who was considered unreliable by the business community.

A triumvirate took power next (September 1963/April 1965). Its president, Donald Reid Cabral, imported British Austin motor vehicles. Legislation was changed immediately. Customs duties were rendered almost non-existent for Austin models and increased for other vehicles. Austins came flooding in. Failing to sell the cargo quickly, he parked unsold cars in a field. We called them "vacas" (cows). The IMF, which had arrived in the meantime, raised the Austin customs duties back to the normal rate, but it was too late; they had already been imported.

An inter-American agreement entered into in 1954 recognised that the president's opposition could seek refuge in any Latin American embassy. This opponent could then leave the Dominican Republic if they were going to the state whose embassy had given them asylum. This system generated a kind of diaspora of opponents spread across Latin America.

The Dominican Republic is located in a region of great imbalances: a high birth rate and an unexploited and unevenly spread potential – both of which weigh on the country's social life. This instability created a political stake that was monopolised by the country's two organised forces: the army and the Church.

The army controlled the population's instability as well as social instability as a whole; it forged a nationalism within the states. Since the 1960s, the struggle against communism has become an additional factor. Founded by the United States, it maintains close ties with the country. This exercise sometimes brought considerable material advantages, which became the stakes upon which the coup d'état would eventually be enacted.

One day, the Dominican army split in half: army against air force, troops and weaponry in the streets. The Netherlands did not have a permanent embassy in the country. The representative of the Royal Dutch oil company (Shell), asked to come and see me in the middle of the night. Both sides of the army were requesting his support. He didn't know which one to side with. We debated the pros and cons of each, together, and came to the conclusion that his choice came down to deciding between the plague and cholera. It would be best to simply stay out of it. He communicated our decision to both army clans. The next day everything was back to normal.

Customs duties rose by more than 100 percent for certain products, and the army invested in the particularly lucrative practice of importing these products without paying customs, declaring them unfit for military consumption and reselling them at the normal market price. The military thus pocketed both the commercial profit and the customs duties on the items. As these made up about half of the country's imports, I tried to contact the purchasing officers to offer them Belgian products. Impossible, I was told, as these would change as soon as they had made enough to have their villa built.

Heir to the Spanish Catholic Church (and a large-scale landowner), the Dominican Catholic Church was split between Opus Dei on the one hand, which was beginning to break into the Dominican Republic, and the cursillo on the other. The latter, which was a Catholic movement of renewal and evangelisation that put a strong emphasis on prayer, training and action, came to be present from 1962 onwards. Last but by no means least, the theology of Liberation was also beginning to make its way into the Republic.

A Belgian Scheutist priest made it his mission to look after the people in the slums. Matter-of-factly, he told me about the misfortunes faced by the population. Everything could be bought, and these people descended into debt worth several years of their annual wages in the process.

I put this to the test in my own home, where the launderer would pay the cook, who cooked his meal over the fire in my kitchen (a meal that I was, of course, funding). The cook, in turn, would pay the launderer to wash my dishcloths. It was

a vicious circle that put the brakes on any private initiative
that could arise.

This priest also told me about family life in the hovels: he wanted to carry out a census of the population by starting in one house and working his way along. When he went back to the first house, however, the residents would no longer be the same. The husband or wife would have left. The number of children would vary substantially. The only point that verged on positive was that the man of the house would take charge of whoever was part of the household at the time, although this did not mean that goods would suddenly come about in abundance.

Since 1959, relations between the United States and Latin America had been scarred by challenges and antagonisms on a global scale: East-West, North-South rivalries. From a commercial point of view, Latin America was still the United States' main partner. For the latter, this market, which the Americans saw as almost their own turf, was burdened by debts and showed no signs of opening up to the rest of the world. The events taking place in Latin America seemed to be matters of domestic politics rather than international relations. Their interest in the United States only went as far as the extent to which they affected bilateral relations. President Kennedy's assassination did not spark any spontaneous demonstrations – neither mourning his death nor celebrating it.

The Dominicans knew of the existence of European countries but thought of them a distant concept. Their only surviving relations with Europe were commercial. Antwerp, the location goods would be sent to, was a more familiar name to them than Belgium.

The relations between Latin American countries were quite different in nature. They seemed more like those of a family, with their quarrels and friendships. Its foreign policy made the Dominican Republic feel like it was a firm member of the Organisation of American States (OAS). The Dominican press reported news about the other Latin American countries in detail, further increasing the population's feelings of solidarity, especially with the other Spanish-speaking states.

It was through these reports that we followed the 1964 Chilean elections with great interest. Salvador Allende, who was too close to the Communists, was defeated, beaten by Eduardo Frei, a Christian Democrat.

The latter was elected with the support of the United States. He promised a "reformist", "transformist" and "developmentalist" government with his slogan "Revolution in Liberty", which gained popular support. This same population would vote Allende in, in 1970, having been deeply disappointed by their former leader's broken promises.

An Argentinian doctor and one of the leaders of the Cuban Revolution, Che Guevara had an aura that fascinated — or annoyed, depending on who you ask — the Dominicans.

In November 1964, my colleague Patrick Nothomb would be involved in a dramatic hostage situation in Stanleyville, alongside a number of Belgians. We asked the UN for permission to send our paracommandos in. At the request of the Department, I approached the Minister for Foreign Affairs to ask for his support before the United Nations, the story of which is worth telling.

The Minister of Foreign Affairs hosted me alongside other Dominican visitors, who were already seated around the ministerial round table. I asked for a moment alone with the Minister, believing that my approach may be unwelcome in a third-world country that seemed critical of Western politics. My request was denied, leading me to share the details of the situation in Stanleyville with the Minister and his visitors, as well as the support we sought. He assured me he would have no problem providing just that. The entire operation took no more than fifteen minutes. And indeed, when we took it before the UN, the Dominican delegate voted in our favour.

I did my bit alongside the other governments in our jurisdiction (Jamaica, Haiti and Trinidad & Tobago) by telex, without a hitch. We got a "yes" each time.

I would go to Port of Spain, the capital of Trinidad and Tobago, to deal with certain problems. This state, which was very different from the other Caribbean states, is certainly worth a visit. It is an archipelago made up of 23 islands, the two largest of which are Trinidad and Tobago.

From the beginning of the 19th century onwards, the British would populate these islands with Europeans (Germans and French), then Chinese, and finally Indian residents (from India). Governor-General Sir Solomon Hochoy was a Hindu. The Prime Minister, Sir Eric Williams, was African and a noted Caribbean historian: his book "Capitalism and

Slavery" left its mark on the history of slavery in the Caribbean. The rest of the government ministers were a mixture of ethnicities. A cocktail party held by the Governor-General resembled a UN meeting.

Belgian Benedictine monks from the monastery of Sint-Andries, near Bruges, set up a monastery on a hill where they would later found a school. It became the best school in the country, and the entirety of the bourgeoisie — regardless of their religious convictions — sent their children there. The Abbot seemed to glow from his openness. While we had dinner together, he told me about the long evening he spent with Fidel Castro once, when the latter was held up overnight due to his plane breaking down.

Among the country's main riches were petroleum, the petroleum industry, gas and sugar and, from 1907 onwards, the 50-hectare natural asphalt deposit at La Brea. The country's proximity to Venezuela made it sensitive to Latin American problems.

Sharing the island of Hispaniola with the Dominicans, the Haitians succeeded in creating the only state in the American hemisphere ruled by the descendants of slaves. Life in Haiti, a very poor country, was lived with a high cultural intensity. This country developed its own political life in the 19th century, one that was separate from the other Caribbean states. Rejected by the US and its slaving traditions, for whom a revolt led by the black population was inconceivable, they developed a sense of patriotism despite intrusions by both the French and the Americans.

A large number of engineers completed their education at the Agricultural Faculty of Gembloux. A minority of mixed-race citizens made up the bourgeoisie.

The population of Haiti lived in dire economic circumstances and developed at a very slow pace. A need for wood used to build fires on which their food would be cooked, led to them destroying their forests. These woodlands were not replaced by other crops – a missed opportunity to export food produce. The land did not provide them with any resources. Our consul informed us that his cement plant was only operational for half a day at a time: when he received an order for cement – which was payable in advance – he would give the order for the cement plant to start up for half a day.

Jean-Claude Duvalier was at the head of the country, having risen to power by chance. Unable to elect a president for their Republic, the

Haitians made Duvalier, a young doctor who had gained popularity for often treating his patients for free (and nicknamed "Papa Doc" as a result), interim president. The idea was that this would give the country's main parties time to agree on a candidate. The man took a liking to power, and when the Haitians asked him to give up his position, he went down to the port, hiring all the workers present as his personal bodyguards. To help him maintain his position, he gave them the right to control whether people lived or died. This group would become known as the terrifying Tonton Macoute ("Uncle Gunnysack") – known for ensnaring unruly children in their hemp sacks.

> *US President Kennedy aimed to clean up all Latin American policy. He wanted Duvalier out. As a wealthy man, his reasoning led him to believe that depriving the island of all commercial contact with the outside world, by issuing an embargo, would lead to the regime collapsing. The miserable conditions already faced by the Haitian population, however, rendered them unaware of any additional deprivation. Duvalier seemed helpless, but public rumour had it that he, a voodoo master, had cursed the American president. Kennedy was assassinated soon after, and that was how events were reported in the country.*

France would take a periodic interest in Haiti. At one point, it even sent Breton Roman Catholic priests to take charge of the country religiously, and therefore economically. As soon as they arrived, they confiscated all the material culture used in voodoo worship. The Haitians would quickly become aware that the priests were then selling the confiscated items to tourists. The government requested their departure and voodoo took hold once again. The religion flourished in Haiti, as many Haitians had emigrated from its epicentre: Benin. A mixture of Catholic and ancient rites, the gods held an important position in the religion. One of the most well-known gods, Baron-Samedi, possesses devotees when put in a trance. Voodoo practices are magico-religious and are nourished by curses and blood rituals (sometimes human blood).

Before I went to the Antilles, Maurice Garçon, a famous French lawyer, told me UNESCO had sent a scientist to Benin to find out about voodoo. Whilst there, he did not meet a single person who was willing to talk to him. One day, he happened to mention the fact to a boy who was cleaning his hotel room, who, unbeknownst to him, was the son of one of the country's greatest sorcerers. The boy took the scientist to see his father, allowing UNESCO to finally get to grips with the religion.

The day after I left Santo Domingo, headed for Brussels, the guerrillas descended from the mountain, overthrowing the triumvirate led by Donald Reid Cabral and taking over the city. And so, Kennedy's new policy of establishing democracy in Latin America came to an end, marking the start of a civil war between right and left-wing soldiers.

I went to the permanent Representation of Belgium to NATO, as a meeting had to be held by the Atlantic Council about the events that had taken place. I explained that what had happened in Cuba was repeating itself, but without Castro's input. The children of the bourgeoisie wanted to change the so-called democratic regime, which was, in fact, corrupt; they did not, however, request any aid from the Soviet Union.

The US, wanting to prevent what had happened in Cuba from happening again, stirred up the Latin American population and sent troops in to restore order. Our Ambassador had an acute attack of gout and had to be evacuated on an American ship, leaving the Embassy lacking a diplomat. The Department asked me if I thought I should go back. I answered that, in my opinion, the chancellor of the embassy should be able to manage the situation.

I stayed in Brussels for six months with my fellow graduates, preparing for the business review. As well as attending lessons on the various aspects of Belgian foreign trade, we would also go to establishments linked to foreign trade three to four times a week: export companies, the Port of Antwerp, the National Bank, the Office national du Ducroire for political insurance, etc. rounded off with a visit to the Netherlands and the Grand Duchy of Luxembourg. The final exam brought an end to our studies.

Next, I was posted to Bonn, the provisional capital of the Federal

Republic of Germany. Europe had undergone major changes in the time I'd been away: IBM had launched the memory typewriter: a revolution in the services sector. The Beatles were shining with the glory they had gained, and the Rolling Stones were beginning their rise to fame. The Beat Generation had begun in the United States, and its influence could be felt in Europe. Maria Callas ended her on-stage career in 1965.

During these visits, we would go to the province of Luxembourg. Senator Pierre Nothomb, my colleague, Patrick Nothomb's, grandfather, hosted us very elegantly in his castle in Habay-la-Neuve. Our families shared a similar history.

During the First World War, the Germans violated the neutrality imposed in the 1839 treaties by invading Belgium. As envoy extraordinary and minister plenipotentiary, my grandfather was the head of the Belgian legation in Paris in 1914. He believed that the end the Germans had brought to this neutrality was irreversible. Belgium should therefore be permitted to defend itself, by restoring its borders. As the population of Luxembourg did not support their young Grand Duchess Marie-Adelaide's pro-German position, he suggested that the country be annexed to Belgium.

President Wilson of the USA refused the annexation and 25-year-old Grand Duchess Marie-Adelaide abdicated in 1919, allowing her sister, Grand Duchess Charlotte, grandmother of the current Grand Duke Henri, to take her place.

He brought the initiative up with President Poincaré who agreed with him, arguing that France would be happy taking over Alsace and Lorraine. He considered the eastern part of the Dutch province of Limburg, of which Maastricht was a part, to be militarily cramped. He believed this made it indefensible by the Dutch, therefore making the Belgian city of Liège vulnerable. Maastricht must therefore be given back to Belgium. In order to allow Antwerp to become a port of war again, and for allied fleets to be allowed into the port should war be declared, the Lower Scheldt had to be returned to Belgium. These territorial modifications made to the Netherlands had to be made with the country's approval, and any losses had to be compensated for in Germany, on the left bank of the Rhine.

Senator Nothomb, who was a journalist at the time, supported this so-called imperialist Belgian policy. Beyens, a diplomat who became the Minister of Foreign Affairs, fought it. The latter would prevail, which led to my grandfather's departure.

While this was one of the reasons why he left his position, a second factor was also influential. My grandfather composed accurate descriptions of the various French political currents, particularly the party that was in favour of the war against Germany, in 1914. When they took Brussels, the Germans discovered the report and published it. Henri Poincaré, the President of the Republic at the time, showed no animosity towards him. The Belgian government, however – who was responsible for the secrecy of diplomatic missives — held it against him. A curious reaction, to say the least.

After the war, negotiations took place to revise the 1839 treaties. These concluded with the end of the neutrality regime imposed on Belgium — which thus recovered its full sovereignty — and the establishment of the Belgian-Luxembourg Economic Union and the Netherlands-Luxembourg agreement where The Hague represented the Grand Duchy in countries where it was unrepresented.

On the very same day, Senator Nothomb called me and my colleague Henry Beyens, the minister's grandson, and we smoked the peace pipe together.

IV

BONN

(1965—1969)

The German landscapes that surrounded me in my new post seemed lifeless after the luxuriance of the Antilles. Its inhabitants were forced to farm the land as a means of survival. This same problem was faced throughout Europe, particularly in the northernmost countries. Germany had become wealthy thanks to its work ethic and organisational spirit. During my time there, two governments came to power: Chancellor Erhard and the liberals (Kleine Koalition or small coalition), who were in power until December 1966, followed by the Kiesinger cabinet of socialists (Groâe Koalition or grand coalition).

> *After the generous, warm abrazo I had received from the Dominicans, I found myself being greeted with a restrained handshake and a slight nod.*

If I were to compare the lives led in so-called developing countries with those in the so-called developed countries, I would conclude that in the developed world, we were pushing further and further away from each other. The so-called developed population of the world was facing a breakdown of family relationships and friendships and losing its sense of family. Life was becoming dry, flavourless. It was losing its soul in search of the golden calf. Yes, we've found cures to countless diseases. We've increased life expectancy. We're richer in terms of our material belongings. We've been to the moon. But who's got it right, when it really comes down to it?

We settled in Bonn, on the left bank of the Rhine, while most of my colleagues live in Bad Godesberg, a closed universe excellently described by Le Carré in "A small town in Germany". The house had been occupied by my predecessor, and it met our basic needs but provided no additional luxury.

Our offices were located in an old bourgeois house, on the left bank of the Rhine. They neighboured the Presidential offices. From my own office, I found I had a superb view of the Rhine and the Siebengebirge, a hill range perched on the other bank of the river. To get to the Auswärtiges Amt (Ministry of Foreign Affairs), I would take a staircase down to the quays and then make my way up towards the Ministry. Some days I would make this trip several times. I never took notes, always trusting my memory.

The Ambassador's house was located in the prestigious Kommende. Built in 1254, it housed one of the centres of the German Teutonic Order.

Although I spent part of the Second World War in China, under Japanese yoke, my arrival in Bonn was marked by strong emotions brought up by the last world conflict. For many, 1965 Germany, 20 years after Chancellor Hitler's decade of power, was still haunted by its past and was struggling. When I left the Foreign Ministry in Brussels, my colleagues gave their condolences.

One day, while I was visiting Liège with my German-plated car, I stopped to ask for directions. I got a straight answer: no one helps the Boche here!

In contrast, a colleague who was posted to Bonn and still had a Belgian-registered car had a hateful phrase recalling the Belgian-French occupation of the left bank of the Rhine in 1920 scratched into the hood of it.

On the way to my post in Bonn, I saw a Belgian army Jeep that had caused a slight accident by the side of the road. Who would call it in? The Belgian MPs. I went about my daily life in the Belgian occupation zone. My children went to a Belgian school for the children of the occupying military force in Rösrath. On 21 July (Belgian National Day), I accompanied the

Ambassador to a Te Deum — orchestrated by the Belgian army — at Cologne Cathedral.

In Berlin, the premises and German staff of the Belgian mission had been requisitioned by the Belgian government since 1945. We would gradually put an end to this towards the end of 1967—1968, that is, over twenty years after the war.

During my stay in Bonn, I went once to Berlin. Leaving West-Berlin, I went to East-Berlin. The contrast between this side of the city and West Berlin was striking. A consumerist society in one half of the city, socialist stoicism in the other. Upon nightfall, I would go for walks in one of the forests on the border between East and West with a colleague posted in Berlin. Beams of light swung around in wide circles from the East German watchtowers. I moved ever closer. The beams stopped, bathing me in a pool of light. My colleague told me not to move. The East German police were known to shoot without warning.

Axel Springer, press magnate and publisher of the daily, Die Welt, bought a building by the wall in the centre of the city. He installed a lit-up billboard there, which was clearly visible in East Berlin. The East Germans did not respond to the permanent provocation; they did, however, block off access to the street opposite.

In 1965, Germany was still suffering from the aftermath of the war. The Federal Republic of Germany (FRG), which had its provisional capital in Bonn, was formed from the former British, American and French occupation zones. The German Democratic Republic (GDR), which founded its capital in Pankow, was made up of an area that had formerly been Soviet. The West did not recognise the latter as a state.

Austria was detached from Germany and, by the State Treaty of 15 May 1955, renounced from participating in an alliance.

Finally, Berlin (surrounded by the German Democratic Republic) was divided into four military sectors (United States, Soviet Union, Great Britain and France).

Belgium was allocated an occupation sub-zone within the British zone, which still housed our troops. In Berlin, our military mission became a civil mission.

I participate in meetings to establish the regulations that would apply to certain aspects of the lives led by Belgian soldiers while in Germany. We agreed to apply German law in the event of any soldiers fathering children, which meant fathers had to provide maintenance to any such children while these children remained with their mother. Many former Belgian soldiers, who had long returned to their villages and had fully immersed themselves back into their marriages and family life, thus received an order to pay child support for their German child.

History was seen from a different perspective in each country.

What were Belgium-Germany relations like after centuries of wars, interdependence and participating in central empires? The economic interests of the countries had been woven together very tightly over the years, mainly due to the presence of businesspeople of German origin having been in Belgium since the Middle Ages and the significant role of the Rhine as a means of transport between the Basel and Antwerp.

Belgium accepted both a political and military reconciliation with Germany. To avoid starting a new war, Belgium entered into the various treaties concerning European unification (European Coal and Steel Community, European Economic Community and Euratom) and the Western European Union (WEU). It agreed to Germany joining the North Atlantic Treaty.

How was Belgium viewed from across the Rhine? As it was from Paris or The Hague. It was the lost province that maintained close ties and a common language. This attitude was highlighted by the use of German as the only language in my dealings with the Auswärtiges Amt (Ministry of Foreign Affairs).

Upon my arrival in Bonn, I paid visits to the various people I knew I might need to be in touch with for my work: this was customary, and a custom that allowed me to get to know certain people, as well as to make myself known.

Being, among other things, responsible for the press, I paid Gunther Diehl a visit, a brilliant diplomat who had been head of the press at the Auswärtiges Amt before becoming Information Minister (and grey eminence) to Chancellor Kiesinger. He spoke at length about the problems faced in Germany and of memories from his time in Belgium. He had been posted to my homeland during the war (and was a particular admirer of our painters emerging from the école de Laethem).

Before accepting his appointment as Information Minister, he asked Paris if the French government opposed it. In Paris, he had been the intelligent, enthusiastic associate of German ambassador Otto Abetz during the war. The French pandered to him, pretending not to know anything about the matter. The French Services must have a thick file on him, just waiting to be opened...

The shadow of the former Chancellor Adenauer hovered over German politics like the statue of the Commander. As Oberbürgemeister (Lord Mayor) of Cologne, he opposed English occupation several times. Having become chancellor, he anchored the FRG to the West by being a founding member of the European Communities (ECSC in 1951, the Treaty of Rome in 1957) and, later, by getting the FRG accepted into NATO (1955). He signed the Élysée treaty of 22 January 1963 with de Gaulle, cementing the friendship between the two countries.

I attended a congress held by the CDU (Christlich Demokratische Union or Christian Democrat Union). Adenauer alone received applause. Chancellor Erhard, Minister of the Economy in Adenauer's government, "father" of the German economic miracle, achieved only meagre amounts of success.

Upon the death of Queen Elisabeth of Belgium, a registry of condolences was opened at the embassy. We were all assigned our turn to greet those who came to sign the log. Adenauer came while I was on duty. A tall, impressive man, his entrance was stiff. He sat down, signed the registry in large handwriting and then left without saying a word. It was his remains I would salute while accompanying my ambassador a few months later.

A second character played an essential role in the chancellor's entourage: Dr Arthur Rathke. Spokesman of the CDU, the party in power at the time, Rathke was, in fact, the veiled leader of the party. A brilliant mind, a doctor and an excellent historian, he introduced me to distinctive German quirks and the history of each region. As Adenauer and Erhard's man, he wasn't a fan of Kiesinger.

One man with an important standing in the CDU was Professor Weizsäcker, a brother of the famous scientist and President of the Evangelical Church Assembly. He had a significant moral influence both in Germany and within the CDU with his broad humanist culture. I admired the deep sense he had of the responsibility held by his country as well as the moral role it played. He would later go on to be elected President of the Federal Republic of Germany.

Important positions in Foreign Affairs, the press, business and the legal field were held by a group of young Germans at the time. This group would meet very often (two to four times a month), always in the evenings. I was invited in, joining the group as the only foreigner. And there was nothing to it. We would meet at around 8 pm for a few glasses of Rhine or Franconia wine and a few records. We would dance, chat about state affairs, and sometimes, they would say a lot. I kept my mouth shut and listened. At around 11 pm, a quick fried egg served sunny-side-up would bring the evening to a close.

What were the major points of interest when it came to German political and economic life?

The legacy left behind by the country's Nazi period. Hitler's decade in power traumatised Germany and radically changed its citizens' way of life. Having been democratically elected by universal suffrage, Hitler demonstrated how to use the democratic system and transform it into a dictatorship.

Nazism opposed socialism which, in 1914, demonstrated its idiosyncrasies by voting in favour of war in various countries. Hitler rejected communism, a socialism with a central leadership in Moscow managed by communist parties. He was, instead, developing a new form of socialism: socialism on a national level. This would mean rejecting anything that was not German. In doing so, he moved closer to the path walked by Mussolini, a socialist who was aware of the nationalist outbursts of the Italian population, instigated by a frustration caused by the Allies' refusal to grant them the compensation requested after the 1914—1918 war.

According to Hitler, the term German took on the traditional sense of "Deutschtum", which includes all German-speaking countries.

After the war, certain measures taken by Hitler against the traditional right-wing were still being applied: an example was compulsory primary education in village schools. Other measures were not: the ban on student societies, which were predominantly influenced by their alumni, had been lifted.

> *Student societies, some of which had strong religious roots, regained their strong influence in the running of the country. Alumni who operated in the same circles would help each other. I saw this in action at a (white tie) event held by the most prestigious student society in Germany (formerly that of the Kronprinz). I only met two students there, those who were hosting the event, mixed in among a world of ambassadors, politicians, lawyers and businessmen whom I interacted with daily. This deep level of intimacy and this close network created between old and new members of the same circle made it difficult for a foreigner to break into the German world of business.*

Without daring to say so, the Germans remembered being equal to aryans – or nobles, and therefore to the country's ruling class.

The military remembered the honourable place it had once held in society. I could feel its unyielding longing for Hitler's army uniforms. The current army uniforms were ill-fitting. The Germans called them "pyjamas".

The Jewish question always called Hitler's political and economic judgment into question. The abominable annihilation of several (six) million Jews (mainly in Poland, Ukraine, Austria and Germany) allowed the middle class to occupy the positions they had previously held. In the short term, at least. Their disappearance was, however, catastrophic for Germany in the long run. The German-speaking minority of Jews is among the most intelligent. Notable figures that fit this category and have left their mark on the history of humanity include Karl Marx, Rothschild, Freud, Einstein, Mendelssohn etc. This minority was engaged in research and new technologies, thanks to the support provided to them by Jewish banks. With the demise of this population, the economy and this research would lose their momentum.

> *My Israeli colleague told me that he would pay frequent visits to groups of young Germans to talk about the devastation caused by the last world war. At the end of each meeting, he would have private conversations with one or another of those present. One day, a German youth turned to him and said: my father was an SS officer, what can I do to make up for what he did? I imagined the anguish this young man must have felt and the shock his question must have been for my colleague and came to the conclusion that it must have been an incredibly intense interaction for both parties involved.*

The German government must be given credit for agreeing to take responsibility for its Nazi past. Steps taken include: refusing to hire people who had a significant position in the Nazi regime, including Holocaust denial in the Penal Code, banning wearing Nazi uniforms or signs, modifying school books where the 1945 defeat is presented as the liberation of Germany from a criminal regime, and accepting responsibility for the atrocities committed by the Nazi regime.

While Hitler hated the upper-middle class, he did not make the same mistake as Stalin of eliminating it. Quite the contrary, in fact, he gained their confidence in restarting the economy by placing large orders on behalf of the state. He also created state-owned companies like Volkswagen, demonstrating another side to his leftist views.

> *I was shown photos in which this upper-middle-class was posing alongside Hitler himself, although these photos were only produced in private gatherings.*

To the Germans, the military adventures they had embarked on did not seem to have a specific long-term goal. Hitler had annexed Austria, part of the Deutschtum, but he limited himself to occupying other countries. Why? What would have happened if the US hadn't declared war? An unending occupation? Would that even have been possible? By occupying several countries at once, Hitler announced a thousand years of prosperity for Germany but took no measures to ensure them. By examining Germany's position, as drawn by Adenauer within the European Union, the Germans therefore concluded that a skilful negotiation policy would provide Germany with more influence in Europe and the world. Hitler's policy of military adventure, which was intended, above all, to erase the humiliation it had faced in 1918, had no future.

The end of the war affected almost every German family with its brutality. Large cities were systematically bombed. The country was occupied for many years and divided into three (the German Federal Republic, the German Democratic Republic and Austria). Seventeen million Germans escaped from the Soviet zone to Western zones, thus leading to different religions coming to live alongside each other in the small cities (since Luther, German subjects had adopted their prince's faith — "cuius regio, eius religio").

Despite its defeat, Germany did not rebel, choosing instead to enter into an alliance with the victors: the Western and Soviet nations. But was this a choice or a necessity? The West tends to think that the Germans accepted this system freely, in spite of themselves and of the Soviet regime – as demonstrated by the fall of the Berlin Wall and the annexation of the Democratic Republic by the German Federal Republic. Personally, I think the Germans decided to abandon all political adventurism, for the time being, focussing instead on economic development.

To avoid civil servants being able to use a Superior Orders defence as a means with which to avoid being held guilty for their actions — as was often the case in Nazi Germany — the government decided that any civil servant who held a position of responsibility (i.e. if they had been a director or higher) may request to be relieved of their office during any period within which they did not agree with their minister's policy. Thus, this temporary leave would be granted with a full salary and the right to return to their position in the ministry at a later date. I knew one diplomat who was very pro-Strauss and so asked to be granted this leave when Willy Brandt rose to power.

Although certain decisions made by Hitler continued to be applied,

Adenauer and his successors rebuilt a new nation by abandoning fundamental Nazi ideals.

First, that of a dictatorship. The government threw itself into implementing democracy – one that was closely associated with American-style democracy. A great closeness was established between those in power and the press. One that made them appear equal.

Germany gave up on the aggressive xenophobia it had once engaged in, directed mainly towards Jews and gypsies. The Germans did, however, retain a latent xenophobia that stemmed from Hitler's period of power, fuelled by their innate feeling of superiority over other peoples as well as the unity the country had finally achieved under Hitler ("Ein Volk, Ein Reich, Ein Führer", One People, One Nation, One Leader).

The Allies broke down links between big industry and the state. The German government did nothing to rekindle these connections.

Churches, which had been abolished by the Nazis in their crusade against the right, began to reappear,

Adopting certain concepts that had been central to the Holy Roman Empire, within which the idea of decentralisation was key, the Allies imposed a federal structure on the Germans without establishing a real capital that could bring together all the country's forces. Bonn was considered a temporary capital with no future. The only power it housed was political power. Financial power (Bundesbank) was concentrated in Frankfurt am Main, while the economic centres were in the Ruhr area (in decline) and the Stuttgart and Munich regions. Cultural life took place in West Berlin, Düsseldorf and Munich, as well as Vienna and Salzburg, which were also part of the Deutschtum.

Legally, the country was divided into Länder (states), two of which were the cities of: Bremen and Hamburg. Each state had its own constitution. Half the tax income earned in each one went to the federal state; the highest proportion in Europe. Each state has its own regional bank. Their policies covered everything from the police and education to the environment, construction, welfare and retail. The federal government coordinated and harmonised between the states, a role that grew as time went on.

Federal legislative power was divided into a Bundestag, or Federal Parliament, whose members were elected by universal suffrage, and a Bundesrat, or Federal Council, made up of government envoys from each state or region. As elections in the Länder took place at varying times, the majority party in the Bundesrat could change several times during a single Bundestag legislature.

Germany was one of the few European countries with no linguistic minority. Although it has been divided up many times throughout its history, the entire country shares a very important cultural element: the Deutschtum. The "Deutschtum" refers to a politico-romantic notion of the German Nation, which encompasses both its language and its rich culture.

Proponents of the idea mainly see it as referring to East and West Germany and Austria, where the main German newspapers have specific editions, but also German-speaking Switzerland, Alsace and German-speaking regions of Belgium. While stationed in Bonn, the only incident I had with the German authorities concerned the German press, which used unethical methods to break into our German-speaking regions, in particular by accepting small, low-cost ads.

A country marked by the virulence of its religious wars; Germany decided to settle the problem by allowing the religions to live alongside each other in peace. As a general rule, the North is mostly evangelical and the South Catholic. The evangelicals follow Luther's teachings; he translated the Bible into German, thus singling the German language out as the language of God. The religion of the Germans was therefore the true religion and the construction of the Protestant cathedral in Berlin at the end of the 19th century, which is almost on a par with Michelangelo's plans for Saint Peter's Basilica in Rome, serves to symbolise Germany as the centre of the Protestant world. All these ideas were very present in the conversations I had with these Germans.

Luther's attack on the papacy became symbolic of a struggle against a foreign power. It was his actions that formed the origin of German culture being seen as unique (and therefore superior), as several Germans would point out to me. This, in turn, was the first step towards the nationalist theories rife in the 19th and 20th centuries.

The German economy provided for a capitalist system different to that employed by the Anglo-Saxons: Sozialmarktwirtschaft, or social market economy, which is characterised by two basic principles. First of all, the dynamism of the economy must rest on the market with the greatest freedom of operation, primarily targeting prices and wages. Next, the functioning of the market cannot govern the entirety of a country's social life alone. It must be balanced by a social requirement that is, theoretically, established and guaranteed by the state. The German state therefore fit the definition of a social state.

With the memory of the terrible devaluation faced in the 1930s still fresh in their minds, in 1945, the Germans wanted monetary stability. As the Bundesbank succeeded in maintaining the value of the Deutsche Mark, (2 DM = €1), the currency became the core factor of German economic success. To cast doubt on the Deutsche Mark is to cast doubt on the entire system devised in 1945, which is also to doubt Germany's ability to prove that, despite its defeat and countless destructions, it could hold its head up once again and exact its economic revenge.

The economy was managed by consensus. Within large companies, Mitbestimmung, or co-determination, allowed workers and employees to take part in company operations. This system increased the competitiveness of the economy and made it possible to involve employees in integrating immigrant workers. Belgian unions, the Federation of Belgian Enterprises and the Belgian government studied this policy closely.

The German economy had a narrower public sector than the French, although it was still larger than that of both the United States and the United Kingdom. It was a culmination of the Länder banks and government participations into approximately 80 companies, participations that were often inherited from the Third Reich. All of this meant that the government could finally exert a considerable amount of pressure on the sectors to which it gave out subsidies.

The German economy was the most industrial among the large states, providing 40 percent of the country's GNP.

> *During my stay, I learned that Krupp was not a company: its operations depended entirely on the Krupp family themselves. Given the family's contribution to the German army's glory, no bank has ever hesitated in providing the family with any funding they may have requested. I also learned that Mr Abs, a very influential creditor who presided over the destiny of the prestigious Deutsche Bank, wanted to put an end to this. He denied a loan requested by the Krupps' business manager, Mr*

> *Beitz, and made it known. Without further ado, the other*
> *banks immediately stopped lending to the Krupps. Mr Abs*
> *then placed conditions on the loan requested, wanting the*
> *Krupp business to be incorporated and requiring a percentage*
> *of any future shares. In doing so, he forced the Krupps' hand.*
> *Several companies were founded in order to carry out all the*
> *operations in which the Krupps had been involved. Mr Abs*
> *had won.*

Unlike the Anglo-Saxon system, the three main private banks in Germany participated in managing the companies of which they were shareholders. The three banks were Deutsche Bank, Dresdner Bank and Commerzbank.

Traditionally, risk financing has always been provided by Jewish banks. Among the main Jewish banks, Oppenheim and Wartburg were the only ones that reopened after the war in Germany. The same could not be said for the Edmond de Rothschild Bank.

Germany marked the centre of European classical music. It was the birthplace of truly great composers. From as early on as nursery school, German children learn to hold a flute and have music lessons. My daughter, who was at nursery school while in Germany, was no exception. Every German city, even those that were only medium-sized, had an opera house and a concert hall. Nothing dared to be mediocre, and I very much appreciated the artistic rivalry between the cities.

One summer, I went to one of Wagner's operas in Bayreuth. The theatre, which had been designed by Wagner himself, differed from existing Italian-style theatres, where spectators went to see and be seen. There were no decorations, no dressing room and no foyer. The seats were particularly uncomfortable. In short, everything was designed to bring the spectators closer to the drama. It was a revolutionary concept for the theatre at the time. The piece was exquisite; the protagonists played by the best international actors. Both the staging and performance of the singers were highly praised in the press.

The Salzburg Festival, in contrast, was dedicated to Mozart. Although the city was in Austria, culturally, like Vienna, it was considered to be a part of the Deutschtum. There was a lighter, more international atmosphere than in buildings with similar architecture, for example, the small baroque church of Wiese in Bavaria.

The hippie movement came about in 1968 as a way to rebel against society. The Vietnam War, the new standards of sexuality established thanks to the contraceptive pill, the arrival of huge amounts of drugs, violence and racism were all ingredients that went into writing a new musical: "Hair". The comedy premiered off-Broadway in 1967 and was an instant hit. The main songs spread around the world. The musical crystallised the new generation's every fear and aspiration. It was translated into German and performed in Düsseldorf to large audiences. The smell of hashish and other drugs would hit you as soon as you rounded the corner into theatre street. The anti-establishmentarian aspect of comedy was the common thread that bound this population together. The movement's success in Germany served as a marker for the fear felt for the future, one that was also present in the US.

When it came to mealtimes, the Germans had a limited choice of dishes. Game was a speciality, made exquisitely so that the meat was tender and well-seasoned. Their wines were the product of extensive study, their knowledge sourced from a deep understanding of oenology.

Germany was also the cradle of many philosophical currents. I went on a pilgrimage to Heidelberg, a city I was very fond of on the banks of the Neckar. It's the home of one of the oldest universities in the world, the beauty of the city having made it one of the most important centres of German romanticism. A large number of leading writers have stayed in the city, examples being Achim von Arnim, Clement von Brentano, Hölderlin and Goethe.

I had to go on a mission to Bad Kreuznach, on the banks of the Rhine upstream of Bonn. The Burgomaster welcomed me upon my arrival and took me to see the Protestant church where "Karl Marx, doctor of philosophy, and Jenny von Westphalen, without occupation", daughter of Baron von Westphalen, had been married.

He also took me to a small hill, relaying that the Americans had fenced it in with barbed wire in 1945 to contain hundreds of German war prisoners. Under strict orders from General Eisenhower, with nothing to shelter under, the prisoners had dug relatively deep holes in the ground, lying inside and covering themselves with paper to protect themselves from the weather. Some holes collapsed, burying their occupants alive. Food was not allowed, and they all died of starvation.

The stories of this very dark chapter of American occupation contrasted sharply with the welcoming air of the beautiful spa town, with its park, its hotels and its public baths. Although this barbaric treatment is condemnable, however, it was obviously incomparable to the Nazi policy applied to the millions of people summarily executed in concentration camps, like Dachau, in Bavaria, or other important camps like Auschwitz, in Poland.

Last, but by no means least, Germany houses a host of superb museums with exhibits on the most diverse of subjects: from the Alexandre König Museum of Zoological Research in Bonn to the Pinacotheque in Munich and the Berlin and Cologne Museums. These places are home to beautiful works that testify to the extent of the country's cultural wealth. The Krupp Museum in Essen exhibits the Krupp family's impressive contribution to German victories (the Franco-Prussian War of 1870, 1914-1918 and 1939-1945 wars).

Johannes Wasmuth, an extraordinary man who was barely able to write or speak, held public sales of drawings done by his classmates in the street when he was a child. As an adult, he managed to get the permission of the Bundesbahn (German Railways) to use the old ballroom in Rolandseck station — the terminus of the Cologne-Bonn railway line located south of Bonn, which had fallen out of use.

It was in this 19th-century room, where the Kronprinz had once danced, that he would come to hold exhibitions of work by German artists like Graubuner, Uecker, Kokoschka, Martha Argerich, Hans Richter and Walser. People would flock to each opening. Each time, Wasmuth would borrow clothes from his friend, one of the socialist leaders, so as to appear well-dressed.

Wasmuth told me that he had acquired a picture of former Chancellor Adenauer, painted by Kokoschka. A picture he gave to the Bundestag. He also founded the "Arts & Music" association and maintained close links with Stefan Askenase, Marcel Marceau and Yehudi Menuhin, who lived in flats within the station.

*Queen Victoria of England, Emperor Wilhelm II and Prince
Otto von Bismarck were all present at the inauguration of
Rolandseck station. Bernard Shaw wrote about the station.
Guillaume Apollinaire wrote several of his poems there. Upon
Wasmuth's death, the building was modified by New York
architect Richard Meier, thus becoming the Arp Museum.*

Contemporary German literature and philosophy are also quite rich,
although it is often difficult to detach these subjects from the legacy left
by the Nazi period and its consequences. Popular novelist Günter Grass
has become the conscience of socialist ideas. Konrad Lorenz's book, "Das
sogenannte Böse, zur Naturgeschichte der Aggression" (So-called Evil: on
the natural history of aggression), in which he masterfully describes the
similarities between animals and humans in terms of aggression, had an
important impact on the German intelligentsia, which was still scarred by
guilt for the Nazi aggressions.

Each day the newspapers would provide something new in the area of
industry, research, literature or culture. The German intelligentsia, which
was often multilingual, had reached far and wide, travelling around the
world intelligently. Many students, the leaders of tomorrow, would set
off on adventures to the most remote countries in their Volkswagens.
This intelligentsia built many links with other cultures, allowing these
relationships to continue developing quietly in the background.

When it came to their export policy, the Germans rarely emphasised
the word "German". Internationally renowned companies would sell their
products under their own names. The culture they would be linked to
would be Bavarian or of the Rhineland, not Prussian but from Berlin.
Wines would bear the names of the region they originated from. This
attitude, which was intelligent branding for the outside world, is often
badly accepted within the country itself, mainly among young people who
were born after the war and are proud of what their country produces.

Later, while I was stationed in Warsaw, I would travel to the USSR.
While in the city of Samarkand in Uzbekistan, central Soviet Asia, I met
two young East-German organ builders. They had gone to practise their
trade in the Muslim country. They were furious that Moscow had rebuilt

Leningrad (Saint-Petersburg) but refused to allow them to restore the Prussian palaces.

Every year I would go to the carnival in Cologne, specifically for Rozen Montag (Rose/Shrove Monday) — the day before Mardi-gras (Shrove Tuesday). Unlike Mainz carnival, which was more political, carnival in Cologne revolved around more general themes. It was an amazing event to be a part of, a break in the strict life led by German families where everyone let loose, singing, dancing and drinking. It was a real release. There are even those who claim that nine months after the carnival, there is a sudden peak in the number of births registered in Cologne.

The other popular event in the country is a series of Weinfesten (wine festivals) that take place throughout August. The harvest leads to festivities spreading from village to village along the Rhine, in which everyone drinks a few sips of new wine, dances and eats in makeshift taverns. The atmosphere is one of wholesome enjoyment.

Now that I have described certain recurrent features of German life, I will turn my analysis to some political problems that may be of interest.

The first event worth noting was the rise of the NPD party (Nationaldemokratische Partei Deutschlands or National Democratic Party of Germany). It was quickly labelled a Nazi party by the nostalgic romanticism of its militants, who wore Nazi uniforms and performed the salutes compulsory during Hitler's rule. I set about conducting a comparative study of Hitler's former NSDAP party (Nationalsozialistische Deutsche Arbeiterpartei or National Socialist Party of German Workers) and the NDP. They coincided in several ways but diverged in others.

First, Pan-Germanism. The main goal was to re-establish unity between all the German territories: "Germany has a right to the territories within which German people have established themselves for centuries. We are not debating the right any people may have to their own native country, but we are claiming this right for our country with the same fortitude. Being prepared to give it up destroys the defence of the right to life of the German people ("Lebensrechte der Deutsche Volkes"), in terms of public international law". This program included the reunification of Germany within its 1937 borders but did not exclude re-establishing the Reich within the borders established by Hitler (which included Austria).

Next, racism and anti-Semitism. Without openly advocating for these, both these beliefs were implicit in the paragraph dedicated to foreign aid. The NDP opposed all payments made abroad, for whatever reason, as these did not serve Germany's own interests. In addition, development aid was required for education and technical aid above all else.

Third, the economic agenda. This opposed the entry of foreign capital into the country and the sale of German companies to foreigners. German workers were given priority over foreigners. The economy had a duty of serving the state and the population. Agriculture had to be independent.

Fourth, the NDP wanted to do away with the aftereffects enacted in the aftermath of the war (trials of Nazis, etc.) and restore the honour of the army and military service (Wehrdienst ist Ehrendienst — military service is an honorary service).

Fifth, the state and society must be organised in a manner that respects the natural authority of true democracy and the personal freedom of citizens to make their own choices. It must produce a feeling of general interest and give everyone their due. Germany was in dire need of a state in which "being" was better than "appearing".

This manifesto successfully harboured less virulence than Hitler's policies and its authors did not operate on the diabolical scale of the Nazis.

The refugee problem was also a determining factor. Many were forced to leave Silesia and Pomerania after the areas were annexed by Poland. Others fled the East-German regime. In all, 17 million Germans (more than a quarter of the country) formed a powerful pressure group that opposed the agreements made by the Allies in Yalta and Potsdam, as well as any future agreement established along the same lines. In addition, as they scattered throughout the FRG settling in small towns and villages, they ended up contributing to abolishing certain taboos, therefore helping to build a more homogeneous nation. Reinforcing the homogeneity found throughout Germany was the unexpected and paradoxical effect of it having been divided in the first place.

What was the foreign policy employed in Germany?

It is important to note that Germany's foreign policy was an important factor in its domestic policy. They had to be studied alongside one another.

The cornerstone of their policies is the observation that Germany lost the military war in 1945. It then lost the ideological war with the collapse of the NSDAP. Germany thus decided to win the economic war and hold onto its security. This decision was implemented post-haste. That is why, when I arrived in Germany, the cornerstone of its policy was Westpolitik — policies geared towards the West, focused on relations with the European Community and NATO. The Germans were part of several groups within which they had built international bilateral relations.

The United States was an important ally, operating as a bulwark against communism and the Soviet Union. Having been victorious in 1918 and especially in 1945, they nevertheless defended Berlin while the wall was being erected and helped Bonn rediscover a path towards friendship with its neighbours. Relations became strained during the 1960s, mainly for financial and economic reasons. The Americans, plagued by an increased deficit in foreign trade, asked the Germans to contribute to the cost of keeping American troops in Germany. Then, to protect the dollar from falling, the Americans asked the Germans to buy treasury bills. It was not until July 1976, however, that a solution was reached.

Then, there were the three states Federal Germany impacted most, due to its conduct during the 1939—1945 war. Poland, France, and Israel, as the representative of the Jews. I have often wondered about German repentance, whether it is opportunism or conviction. The Auswärtiges Amt didn't provide me with any answers.

> A woman I met confirmed this ambiguity. She was an artist who had been exiled from, now Polish, Silesia. *"I accept that the Poles be given Silesia and Pomerania as a means with which to repay our debt and as compensation for the territories the Soviets had taken in the East of their country. But why can't I go back to my birthplace without fearing being insulted, even stoned? Why has my parents' grave not been maintained? Why am I not allowed to tend to it?"*

Finally, the other European countries, which were now its allies: the United Kingdom, Benelux (occupying nations) and Italy.

Once the alliance had been entered into with the US, Germany's European policy, as implemented by Adenauer, became the cornerstone upon which German policy was built. This European policy helped

Germany break out of its isolation after its 1945 defeat. Germany has, at times, been questioned by its partners, although baselessly; the latter remaining fearful that the former would withdraw from the European Union.

Thanks to the quiet strength of the Deutsche Mark (2DM = €1), Germany showed a direct economic and financial interest in building up Europe of which it was the driving force thanks to cleverly conducted economic and financial policy. The member states of the EEC (European Economic Union) proved to be a very receptive hinterland for their products. The country's political and economic tradition was not, however, one that promoted openness to foreigners, resulting in the EEC having to take strides to combat certain protectionist tendencies.

The USSR was the enemy because it occupied East Germany (the Germans were more concerned with Russian oppression than with the country being split "in three": the FRG, the GDR and Austria)

> *It was rumoured that by the time the German authorities became aware of the prime positioning of the Soviet Embassy, which was located on the banks of the Rhine, above the general telephone cable which ran from one bank to the other, it was too late.*

The USSR's satellite countries, which were a part of Europe, made up the former political and economic hinterland of Germany. The USSR feared political collusion between them and Germany that would aim to take back their pre-war borders. This was why the USSR focused its propaganda on Eastern Europe, by describing the Federal Republic Germans as vindictive Nazis.

Relations with France were particularly versatile, due to centuries of alliances and wars, cultural rivalries and those forged on the basis of scientific research. Since Napoleon, France has never managed to defeat Germany alone; Germany has only been defeated by a coalition of states.

If their conversations are anything to go by, while the Germans relied on the Americans to guarantee peace, they saw France as a fearful yet demanding lover who prided itself on its technological prowess. And that being the case, how could they not follow their neighbour?

With the implementation of the Marshall Plan, the United States asked all European states that were receiving aid from the former, to cooperate in all areas. This idea was revolutionary in a Europe scarred by centuries of war. Europe complied and got a taste for this new level of peace. The continent's collective fear of the USSR was an important additional incentive for them to get along. The idea of a community of states coming together around France and Germany is what eventually resulted in the signing of the Treaty of Rome, which marked the foundation of the European Economic Community.

While Jean Monnet and Robert Schumann were undoubtedly the co-founders of the economic communities, it was Charles de Gaulle who should be credited with having sealed the friendship between France and Germany, through the Élysée Treaty in 1963. Thanks to this treaty, General de Gaulle imposed a French reconciliation with Chancellor Adenauer's Germany, therefore bringing an end to French hesitations. This treaty has proven to be one of the most positive contributing factors in constructing a unified Europe. It established a small structure within which frequent meetings were held at different (political or administrative) levels of both states.

Since 30 June 1965, France has applied the 'empty chair' policy within the EEC, following a proposal by the Commission concerning common agricultural policy. Belgium feared that Germany would follow the example set by France and do the same. Fortunately for us, during my interviews with various German officials, I noted that both the CDU and SPD (Sozialdemokratische Partei Deutschlands or Social Democratic Party of Germany) governments demonstrated exemplary loyalty to both the EEC and the Atlantic Alliance.

While Belgium was fundamentally happy to participate alongside the Netherlands, Luxembourg, Italy, France and Federal Germany in constructing a European Community, there was an underlying feeling that the balance among the Six was unsatisfactory. A feeling which could, in the long term, become a risk factor to the Community as a whole.

This is why Belgian diplomacy, under the impetus of Foreign Minister Pierre Harmel, sought to bring Great Britain into the European Community, starting in early 1967. Harmel considered that *"the golden rule that should be implemented in the diplomacy of small countries in the community is to maintain an equal balance between their three bigger neighbours in order to always find allies against the hegemonic tendencies of one or the other".*

Charles de Gaulle, President of the French Republic, opposed this move. He said the time wasn't yet right. The British still had to overcome their economic crisis. Harmel confided in Kohl, who was a member of the Bundestag at the time, that he feared that "a Europe of Six would become too small for a too-large Germany". Harmel's appraisal received positive, while discreet, approval from my colleagues at the Auswärtiges Amt. Their old reflex of keeping a low profile had remained in place since 1945.

Given the neutrality of French policy, the Belgians feared that Germany would seek a new foreign policy. De Gaulle seemed to fear losing his position of leadership in Europe more than the EEC itself breaking up. This leadership would go down in French history — the only ones capable of contesting it being the British and their American allies.

To facilitate the entry of the British without the French vetoing the move, Harmel, who thought the Germans had lukewarm feelings towards growing the Community, wanted to multiply the links between the United Kingdom and the Community. The WEU (Western European Union) seemed like a good place to start, as it brought the British and the six members of the European Communities together. Brandt told Harmel that he was reluctant to consider a solution that did not involve France. Harmel then proposed trade arrangements between the candidate countries and the EEC, but the French refused.

Two important events took place in 1968; the May 1968 student revolt in France that destabilised the country, and the invasion of Czechoslovakia by Warsaw Pact troops. The entire process of growing the EEC, and even the basic functioning of the community, came to a standstill. Harmel proposed a discussion be held within the WEU on foreign policy, defence, technology and currency.

However, the WEU was an intergovernmental body, which could lead one to believe that Belgium was demonstrating its agreement with the Fouchet plan, a French plan that provided for intergovernmental cooperation for foreign policy. Harmel took the risk of making this proposal due to the simple fact that he thought the British becoming a part of the Community was worth the sacrifice. The French refused. They believed this strategy would give the British means with which to control the EEC and to consider the WEU a court of appeals for Community decisions. The Germans informed me that they would rather not publicly agree with the proposal, preferring instead to fall in line with the position the French had taken.

General de Gaulle rebelled against NATO. He believed that France had to recover "a normal situation of sovereignty without reversing its membership in the Atlantic Alliance". In other words, France left NATO without losing its position in the Atlantic Alliance. This meant that the French troops in the FRG were no longer under the authority of NATO. Helmut Schmidt (SPD) and Franz Josef Strauss (CSU, Christlich-Soziale Union or Christian Social Union, the CDU's sibling Bavarian party) approved of de Gaulle's point of view. They hoped for a better political balance within NATO. A discussion began between the French and Germans as to the status of French troops in the FRG. I followed negotiations closely, noting that if a bilateral agreement was established, this would be with great difficulty. Legally, it would have to stand outside the new agreements concerning Allied troops in the German Federal Republic.

The Auswärtiges Amt thought General de Gaulle's policies were rather fanciful: in 1963 he had suggested that he and Erhard lead Europe together, he then decided to open up to the Third World and, finally, entered into an agreement with the Soviets that had an anti-German undertone. Neither the Germans nor the Soviets took General de Gaulle seriously.

The Socialists had long been the opposition. Towards the end of my stay, however, Willy Brandt became their leader as well as the Minister of Foreign Affairs in a coalition made up of his party and the Christian CDU ("Große Koalition"). The German diplomats resigned themselves to him being accepted into the Auswärtiges Amt.

> *My German colleagues, who were unfamiliar with Brandt's*
> *ideas, read his name as "Brand Gefähr", or: fire hazard.*

His arrival, however, caused less disruption than the German diplomats had feared. Some even discovered that they themselves were socialists. They examined the "Bad-Godesberg programme" (1959), first with scepticism, then with interest. Within the programme, the SPD renounced several of its postulates, advocated for an economy with no nationalisation whatsoever, a strong army, for an understanding to be entered into with the church and for the communist way of managing the state to be condemned. Unlike the Communists, it would accept that the world of finance, economics and religion be separate from that of the government. The role of the former burgomaster of West Berlin, Brandt, was beginning to take on a new light, and he was able to speak to the Soviets without abandoning his positions.

> *While attending an SPD congress, I noticed that a general in uniform, a Lutheran bishop and a Catholic archbishop were all seated next to important party figures in the gallery, as well as some businessmen. In short, enough to reassure a bourgeoisie, who was afraid of seeing the emergence of a party that had been neglected since the end of the war and stripped of its revolutionary, anticlerical and anti-militaristic clothing.*

The interest of certain diplomats in the Bad-Godesberg programme, especially when it touched upon "relations with the communist states" divided the ministry.

For Adenauer's followers, who were also supported by Kiesinger and Diehl, the FRG had to content itself with its Westpolitik and wait for the situation in the East to change so that it could pick up the pieces of what was left of the Soviet empire. The missed opportunities for reconciliation, especially with a sour Poland, had been too numerous to count since the end of the war.

In Brandt's opinion, the FRG needed to broaden its horizons and put together a Weltpolitik (participation in world affairs). Egon Bahr, a brilliantly intelligent man who became head of the planning department at the Auswärtiges Amt, was put in charge of executing this plan. It was to be extended in three directions.

The first, Westpolitik, was to be a continuation of Adenauer's western policy.

The second was aimed at other countries, mainly in Africa, Latin America and Asia. Brandt went there on discreet trips so as not to irritate the Western allies. I followed this policy closely thanks to my contacts in

Foreign Affairs, as he inaugurated a new deal with non-Western countries through the sheer scale of the aid provided. Germany had lost its African colonies in 1919, and as a result, was no longer seen as a colonising power. Brandt provided important contributions to the continent. The same went for Latin America, where large numbers of German emigrants had settled (Buenos Aires, for example, has a huge German population). Germany also held an important position in relation to Asian countries. Germany and the US were the only two peoples whom the Japanese respected. China and Southeast Asia also had significant German populations. German traditions dated back a long way in the Middle East, thanks to the country's old friendship with Turkey (Germany has a large Turkish workforce, some of which has since returned to Turkey), as well as links with Iran, Iraq, Egypt, etc.

The third, which was geared towards Eastern Europe, Ostpolitik (eastern policy), was complicated because it interfered with the German question. It also brought with it a danger of the government facing a backlash from eastern refugees. Brandt's involuntary ally was the Minister of Defence, Gerhard Schröder, who had been his predecessor in the Erhard government.

This policy had been carefully thought out and planned and, in the contact I had with the Germans, I noted their precise knowledge of the towns and villages in Eastern Europe and their respective social and economic problems. It is thanks to this detailed knowledge — which I followed with interest in any contact I had with the Auswärtiges Amt — that my German colleagues were able to provide proposals that met the real circumstances faced in each location.

The basic premise was the stance adopted in relation to the Yalta agreements. At this meeting, the three leaders ratified the minor differences to important territorial modifications made by the Ribbentrop-Molotov agreements of 1939, among other things, as well as compensating both Poland and the USSR with large sections of previously German land. These agreements were imposed on different states. Germany, which had been defeated in 1945, was forced to accept the conditions. The other states, however, involuntarily found that they were, in fact, siding with Germany.

It was precisely this ambiguity that the Soviet government feared, as any collusion between Germany and the other countries to obtain a border revision would result in the position of the Russians being rendered more difficult. To try to avoid such circumstances, Moscow would continually refer to the threat of Germany seeking revenge when talking about federal Germany. Furthermore, these same countries held it against the British and the Americans for having accepted the demands made by the Soviets in Yalta and held them responsible for the difficulties faced at the time.

The Auswärtiges Amt was aware of this position. A lot of skill would therefore be required to establish an Ostpolitik without sparking fear in Moscow. The economies of the members of the Comecon were also worsening, and the USSR was beginning to run out of steam trying to keep them afloat. German economic aid could be contemplated if provided under very strict conditions.

It was Schröder's CDU that initiated the Ostpolitik by sending a "Friedens nota" (peace note) out to all nations in April 1966. This correspondence explained the peaceful aims sought by the German government's policy. It had been written for the communist countries. The other countries were aware of this, and therefore the Allies, which included Belgium, did not respond. (In diplomatic terms, a note verbale is a document written between the Ministry of Foreign Affairs and accredited diplomatic missions; a note is a document without the usual polite expressions used in a note verbale.)

Only the communist European governments responded, by listing their grievances vis-à-vis the Federal Republic of Germany (the German Democratic Republic, which was not recognised as a state by Bonn, did not receive the note). The answers provided were used as a basis for the Ostpolitik's founding documents. Schröder carried out an analysis and decided to enter into discussions with the governments that seemed most accommodating to begin with. Romania, a former ally of the Third Reich, was first. Negotiations resulted in an agreement being reached. We would later come to realise that it was Moscow that had chosen Ceausescu's Romania to stand at the forefront of relations with the West.

Czechoslovakia turned over a new leaf with Dubcek (1968) coming into power, a leader who brought a breath of freedom into his country. The country was next in line after Romania. It raised the contentious nature of the thorny issue of the nullity *ex tunc* (since they had been signed) of the 1938 Munich

Agreements. It was, however, ready to put this aside as long as Germany granted Czechoslovakia the loans it needed. These Munich Agreements, which had been entered into between Germany, France and the United Kingdom, granted Germany the Sudetenland, which was primarily inhabited by Germans. Annulling the agreement would mean all the measures taken by Germany following these agreements would also be annulled.

An abrupt end had to be brought to this contact with Czechoslovakia. The Soviets learned that the governor of the Bundesbank was in Prague to discuss a loan Czechoslovakia wanted to take out. They immediately accused the Czechoslovak leaders of colluding with the "revanchist Nazis". This accusation became the official pretext for the Red Army and its Warsaw Pact allies to invade the country.

Germany was able to listen to Czechoslovakian radio broadcasts, which advocated for the country's new ideas relating to freedom and democracy. These same radio waves also resounded in nearby Ukraine, leading the Russians to fear an uprising from the peoples of the Soviet Union, who were under their control. They therefore decided to stage an intervention.

The Soviet troops advancing rapidly one weekend in mid-August caused panic in Germany. German colleagues of mine who lived on the right bank of the Rhine asked if they could stay with me in the event of a Soviet invasion.

The new CDU-SPD government then rose to power.

Upon entering the Auswärtiges Amt, Brandt noted that Chancellor Kiesinger was opposed to an Ostpolitik conducted outside the CDU, the only guarantor — according to him — of German integrity. His strongest supporter, if not Kiesinger's herald himself, was his Minister of Finance, E. J. Strauss.

Brandt also noted that the FRG had lost its Eastern partners. During his first few days at the Auswärtiges Amt, he had, admittedly, signed the agreement with Romania, thus stealing the outcome of Schröder's negotiations from the latter. Brandt nevertheless wished to carry out the Ostpolitik. As a means with which to pacify Kiesinger and Strauss, he demonstrated that his Ostpolitik followed the same approach as that followed by Schröder.

However, he also changed the policies applied to the Eastern countries. While opening up to a policy of reconciliation with the least hostile countries, he opted to attempt to enter into an agreement with the USSR. He believed that the key to a successful Ostpolitik was Moscow. An agreement could only be entered into with Moscow's allies if one was made with Moscow itself. This was the spirit behind the "Bahr paper", the document written up by Bahr as a basis for negotiations.

Brandt therefore made his proposals to the Russians, and Moscow responded in Autumn 1968. Secret interviews would follow, as well as the exchanging of notes. In Bonn, only the Americans, the French and the British were informed. At the Auswärtiges Amt all I received was general information relating to non-violence, assuring me that Belgium had nothing to fear. A leak brought discussions to a standstill, as the Russians believed that Bonn had been playing both sides. The notes that had been exchanged were published and were surprising due to the vague nature of their content.

Despite this setback, the Soviets and the Germans resumed contact, as they both felt that an agreement could be reached. Soviet priority was ensuring Germany consecrated the status quo in Europe. The USSR's allies were dissatisfied with their alliance and eager to take back the territories the USSR had taken from them in 1945. They saw federal Germany as a providential ally. To the relief of the Soviets, Brandt decided he would play no political role east of the Oder-Neisse.

The Germans, on the other hand, were eager to join the communist club. In the East, Germany was seen as a wolf breaking into the communist sheep pen. They accepted the seemingly innocent cultural, commercial and economic policies they encountered. This penetration, which the USSR accepted in order to ease the strain on its economy, allowed the Germans to demand that the Potsdam agreements be abided by. This demand excluded the imposition of both the formal and legal change in the current eastern border between the Federal Republic of Germany and Eastern Germany pending a reunified Germany signing a peace treaty. Both parties accepted the other's propositions without modifying their own, in terms of the borders stipulated, thus establishing the underlying ambiguities of the Moscow agreement.

Sensing, as only a Pole could do, that an agreement was emerging between Bonn and Moscow, Gomulka, the first secretary of the Polish Communist Party, delivered a speech on 17 May 1969, in which he reached out to Germany yet again. Brandt, whose attention was focussed on other problems, seemed to ignore this speech, seemingly putting off responding. The Auswärtiges Amt informed me the text was being studied.

It was thus decided that I would depart for Warsaw. The day I was given the news, in July 1969, I was invited to an intimate crayfish dinner at Rathke's. Diehl and Weizäcker were among the attendees. Towards the end of the dinner, during which we devoured over two hundred crayfish between ten of us, I announced that I would be leaving for Warsaw. They congratulated me and drank to my new post. The records started spinning, getting us all on our feet. It was then that Weizsäcker told me how heavy he believed the debt Germany owed to Poland to be: "it will take a lot to pay it off. We're ready to accept the responsibility of what we did to the Poles, but Poland must also remember that we are a country that has beautiful pages of history." Rathke confirmed Weizsäcker's sincerity.

As the only foreigner at this dinner party of CDU leaders, these feelings of shame expressed by the heads of the CDU with regard to Poland moved me. I left Rathke's apartment carrying with me the certainty that the CDU would support the Kiesinger-Brandt government in any policy that would establish a reconciliation with Poland. I was oblivious to the fact that as little as three months later, the election would make the CDU the opposition, leading it to condemn Brandt's Ostpolitik.

The day after I was appointed as counsellor to our embassy in Warsaw, when I knew only my Ambassador had been informed, I received a call asking me to transport personal items to Warsaw. I said no, wary of the call being some sort of trap. But how did this person, whom I did not know, know I was leaving?

I stayed with the Ruhfus family for a few days before I left Bonn, while my furniture was being packed up. They were German diplomats I had become close to. Rolf Pauls, the Ambassador of the FRG in Washington, was also staying with them at the same time. I met Pauls upon his return from Israel, having been the first German Ambassador to the country, and a brilliant one at that. Landing in Israel, graffiti on the walls reading "Raus Pauls" (out Pauls) quickly informed him that the reconciliation between the two countries had been on paper only. As a former senior officer of the Wehrmacht, during his stay, he paid very close attention to the Six-Day War. "They used our Blitzkrieg tactics," he informed me. When he eventually left the country, he was accompanied to the airport by the entire Israeli government, an honour rarely granted to a diplomat and proof of a true reconciliation.

We talked about Poland. He had spent time there in 1939 as an officer of the German General Staff. At the end of the conversation he wished me luck and then, remembering that he had been the architect of Germany's reconciliation with Israel, he added: "perhaps I will be the first German Ambassador to Warsaw". His wish was not granted. This conversation was all the more interesting as, in Germany, the Nazi period was considered taboo, and nobody spoke of the Blitzkrieg tactics nor the period of Polish occupation. Mine and Ambassador Pauls' paths would cross again several years later when he invited me to a dinner in Brussels, held in his honour on the occasion of his departure as German representative to the Atlantic Council.

From 1954 onwards, the FRG renounced their atomic, biological and chemical weapons. This surrender was specified several times. However, these specifications did not stop us at the Embassy from identifying several ways in which these weapons could be kept without violating the terms of this agreement. By manufacturing them abroad, for example. Strauss, the German Defence Minister, is said to have visited South Africa several times for this purpose. The FRG's involvement in disarmament agreements is therefore one of the more important points in Western diplomacy. In terms of nuclear weapons, in particular, it wanted Germany to become a member of the Treaty on the Non-Proliferation of Nuclear Weapons. I quickly realised that this would only be possible once the Defence Minister, E.J. Strauss, had left the government. This was, in fact, the case. In January 1967, I learned that the Germans wanted to build a plutonium purifier.

That was when I left the country; one that had undergone immense change during my four-year stay in Bonn. This new Germany, which had been designed by Adenauer and which blossomed under Brandt, therefore stepped into its rightful place in the world, calmly yet firmly. The economy was robust, and the new generation was slowly shedding the shadow cast by the infamous decade; though they were unaware that they still stood in this shadow.

V

WARSAW

(1969—1971)

Spaak had been talking to Rapacki, the Minister for Foreign Affairs of the Polish People's Republic, about reducing forces in central Europe from as early as 1963. Years later, Pierre Harmel would work on developing the same line in relations with Eastern Europe, proposing a possible 'détente'. Following his example, Pierre Harmel also came to reflect on relations with Eastern Europe and a possible easing of policy. While at war with Vietnam, the Americans approved this initiative, given its political rather than military angle. On 16 December 1966, the Atlantic Council decided to conduct a deep reflection into the future tasks undertaken by the Alliance.

Harmel, meanwhile, suggested to the Poles that the dialogue initiated between Spaak and Rapacki be resumed. He was invited to Warsaw in September 1964. The first contact between the two ministers was positive, which led them to decide to see each other annually from then on. Rapacki went to Brussels in November 1967.

In December 1967, the Atlantic Council adopted the Harmel Report. It largely advocated for détente. The three tasks assigned to the Alliance were: to ensure the collective defence of the Atlantic area, to reduce East-West tensions and to achieve peaceful, just, long-lasting order in Europe, combined with the appropriate security guarantees. This was an important development for the Alliance and, depending on how politics evolved in Europe, the West would either advocate for détente or defence.

In March 1968, the Belgians and the Poles began to draft a plan for the partial but progressive disarmament of Europe. Harmel also discussed the possibility of economic and industrial cooperation. The Eastern European countries thus informed Harmel that a détente would only be possible if the Federal Republic of Germany recognised the German Democratic Republic and the Oder-Neisse German-Polish border.

The Atlantic Alliance met in Reykjavik in June 1968. It presented the Russians with a proposal: that a study of the possibility of parity in reductions – between East and West – be conducted, particularly in central Europe. It would not be until five years later that Mutual & Balanced Force Reductions (MBFR) negotiations would begin. However, thanks to the spirit of détente, the Treaty on the Non-Proliferation of Nuclear Weapons was signed by the Eastern, Western and the majority of third-world states.

On 21 August 1968, Warsaw Pact troops invaded Czechoslovakia. The Détente policy was thus exhausted. It was a significant setback. Moscow blamed the FRG and Harmel's "detrimental" détente policy, which "concealed the Atlantic bloc's sinister policy and tried to pass off an instrument of war as an instrument of peace".

> *The Atlantic Council, which met before the break of dawn on the day the invasion took place, realised all they had to go on was a map of pre-war Czechoslovakia.*

Despite these events, in April 1969 the Council reiterated the policy advocated by the Harmel plan with its two branches: defence and détente. Harmel would then specify, in line with NATO's other foreign ministers, that the goal was still to reach a regional security agreement as per the UN Charter. This "objective cannot be achieved now and shall not be achievable until the German question is settled within the framework of a peace treaty". The German government was very aware of this preliminary condition, and so launched its Ostpolitik.

When I left Bonn for Warsaw in July 1969, I made a note of this development in East-West relations, specifically the German government's "Ostpolitik".

Relations between Belgium and Poland have always been good. The November revolt in 1830s Poland kept the tsar busy, allowing the English and the French to establish Belgian independence despite the tsar's warnings. Many Poles went to work in the Belgian coal mines, including Edward Gierek.

As I crossed the German-Czechoslovak border, which was also part of the Iron Curtain, I noted the immensity of the gap between East and West, between greyness and opulence, between a police regime and a Western regime.

What I found in Eastern Europe differed immediately from my expectations. What I had been taught about communism at university seemed detached from this reality.

> *I was chatting to the communists one day while I was there and took pleasure in saying that Poland was a dictatorship.*
> *"What? Is ours not a popular democracy?"*
> *"But think about it," I said, "do you not have a dictatorship of the proletariat?"*
> *Silence ensued.*

In Warsaw, my accommodation was paid for by the Belgian government. The house was old-fashioned, not particularly attractive, and small. The buildings on the other side of the street still bore the scars of the terrible battle of Warsaw, in the shape of bullet holes littering their façades.

The embassy was located in the Palais Mniszech. The building, which was built by Grand Marshal Mniszech in 1714—1730, was immortalised in 1779 by Bellotto di Canaletto as a splendid painting. Destroyed in 1944 during the battle of Warsaw, it was bought by the Belgian government which, in turn, had it completely rebuilt. The facade was reconstructed according to Canaletto's interpretation. The offices were spread along the ground floor. The Ambassador's residence was on the first floor. The strain of the Cold War meant both the ambassador's office and mine were permanently locked. I would find myself turning my key in the lock each time I went in or out of my own office.

We were always spotted on the street. As we drove past sentry boxes – of which there were many — I would note that the sentries would take their phones out to report on me having passed them. When I had to discuss anything delicate with the Ambassador, we would go for a walk together in the small park across from the embassy. Every time we did so, a man pretending to be drunk would approach us. Was he wearing a hidden transmitter? We always spoke Dutch just in case, in an attempt to make what we were saying more difficult to decipher.

My house was riddled with microphones. One day, our maid, a Polish woman who had lived in Belgium, told me about the problems her family had faced in the North during the mutinies. When she came back the next day, she had two black eyes and was covered in bruises. She would gladly stay an extra half hour every day except on Tuesdays. Was that the day she would report to the police?

What was the point of this level of spying? A colleague who had talked to his wife about financial problems was approached by someone offering to help. Another, who took an interest in antiques that were prohibited for export, was granted silence in return for sending certain documents. And so, the unhappy man was caught in a vice which would gradually be tightened.

I myself have never exchanged my Belgian francs on the black market. I was, however, aware that the official zloty was worth two Belgian francs, whereas on the black market a Belgian franc would get you two zlotys. The difference was considerable. In Brussels, the human resources department calculated the living extra allowance based on the black-market value of the zloty. It refused, however, to buy these same zlotys to supply them to the Belgian members of the embassy.

The climate was harsh, temperatures rising to over 30°C in summer and dropping back down to -30°C in winter. As Warsaw is on a plain, the temperature variations from one day to another were significant – as much as 20 to 25°C. After a heavy snowfall, the women would clear the streets with large wooden shovels at 3 am. Snow would be shovelled from the road towards the pavement and from the pavement towards the road, forming a wall half a metre wide and two to two and a half metres high. This wall then became a barrier between the road and the pavement. When it came to crossroads, the wall would be removed to allow pedestrians to cross.

Maurice Béjart arriving, along with his troop, shed light on two different visions of the world. A first disagreement took place before the troop arrived due to the Poles wanting to sell seats at high prices. Béjart opposed the move in the name of his democratic policy. When he left Poland, one of the best Polish dancers followed him; the next day I was summoned to Foreign Affairs, where I was lectured sternly: so, we welcome Béjart with open arms and he thanks us by taking one of our best dancers. I replied: a dancer joining the best ballet in the world, what an honour it must be for that Polish dancer! Today is a great day for Poland. Silence.

I examined Polish internal politics, the first point of which was Silesia. It was the most developed region of Poland, but were the Poles harnessing everything the region had to offer? The Germans answered this question with disdain: "You'll see what they've done to our beautiful Silesia! They should be ashamed!" Unconcerned, the Poles were proud of the province, which produced almost half of the country's exports (coal, sulphur, metallurgy). Gierek, the first secretary of Silesia who then became the first secretary of the party in 1970, gained fame thanks to the good press focussed on his leadership of the region. The official figures registered in Poland were, however, less telling.

Like Alsace, the region was made up of a mixed, bilingual population. The choice of which language to speak was a complex matter: Polish to show that one was Catholic, German to appear Lutheran. Sometimes tax matters would be dealt with differently, or one group would be granted certain facilities. In short, as Ambassador Dobrowolski told me during one of the many interviews I had with him at the Ministry of Foreign Affairs, the Silesians felt German in Poland and Polish in Germany.

What was their legal status?

According to the Bonn government, over a million Silesians were German nationals. The Poles' numbers differed somewhat, estimating the number of Germans in Silesia to be barely a few hundred. Dobrowolski explained that, in 1945, the Polish government had executed the Potsdam agreements scrupulously, by expelling the Germans.

Furthermore, industrial investments were being made to update production methods. Silesia would soon become a pilot region, much to the dismay of the intrinsically Polish regions of the country. The region was also producing good engineers, and it was said that the Germans were covertly taking over the country: wasn't "Zygfryd" a Polish version of Siegfried? The Germans were unpopular enough for their departure to be demanded. The government refused to take such action.

Silesia's geo-economic fragility must also be noted, as the region was still dependent on Germany for its communication networks. A motorway connected it to Berlin, it had rail links to the German network and a waterway (the Oder) ending at the port of Szczecin (Stettin). This explains the Poles stealing Szczecin for themselves. Subdued by the Allies, the Germans gave it up without a fight. It was only when the Soviets allowed the Germans within their borders to form a state that a problem would arise. This problem was settled somewhat ambiguously: the Treaty of Zgorzelec (Görlitz), of 6 July 1950, placed the border in the position granted to it according to the Potsdam agreements. The Frankfurt Declaration (1951), which defined the physical border, established its real location.

The official position taken by the Ministry of Foreign Affairs denied the existence of the Szczecin problem. In actual fact, every time the East Germans considered that the Poles were rebelling against them, they would raise the question of Szczecin, sometimes claiming it, as per the Potsdam agreements, sometimes proposing that it be made a free port. When the Poles requested Soviet support, Moscow would play the sphinx, not taking sides. The Poles would be left with no option but to bow to the demands of the GDR.

I. Krasicki, the journalist, told me that Adjoubei, Khrushchev's son-in-law, had put a proposition to the Poles: if they gave Germany Szczecin, the USSR would give Poland Lwow (Lemberg) and Wilno (Vilnius). Gomulka refused to move the country's western border, and the proposal was left on the shelf.

As I left Silesia, I would seek to determine to whom the region legitimately belonged. The Poles in the region, born after the war, or the Germans, whose ancestors were buried in cemeteries that were now overgrown with nettles?

Did it not, therefore, belong to the Poles now? Shouldn't the Germans agree to turn the page and let the dead bury the dead?

The second crucial point was the Pole's vassal position vis-à-vis the USSR.

As far as I could detect, the USSR was certainly present in both Polish politics and the military, but discreetly so. The links between Moscow and Warsaw ensued from the tangled connections between the two peoples. Up until Catherine the Great's rule, Orthodox Russia had lived in fear of the Roman Catholic Poles.

The Poles, in their union with the Lithuanians, who possessed the Ukraine and Belarus, formed the largest state in 17ᵗʰ century Europe. Polish troops beat the Russians repeatedly until the tsar, finding himself in critical circumstances within the walls of the holy city of Zagorsk, emerged victorious after a long siege. Russian operas sing of the Russian victory over the Poles to this day.

> *When I visited Zagorsk, having established that I lived in Warsaw, the official Intourist guide asked me to remind the Poles that the Russians had defeated "those Catholic dogs".*

When Catherine the Great rose to power, there was a change in Russian policy. The Czarina got along with Frederick II. She made peace with the Turks, which in turn allowed her to reduce Russia's military presence in the south, giving her full power to do as she pleased within Europe.

Very quickly, the enlightened despots, Frederick II, Joseph II and Catherine II, fulfilled the fantasy of the Russian tsars: annihilating Poland by butchering the population.

It was not until the end of the 1914—1917 / 18 war that Poland would resurface as a state.

In 1939, Stalin would resume Catherine II's policy, entering into an agreement with Hitler to get rid of Poland by dividing the country up. After the war, Stalin refused to return a large part of the territories taken in 1939 to Poland. It was therefore a slightly altered version of the 1939 German-Russian Polish border that was adopted in Potsdam as the Polish-Russian border, the same one that was then further established in a bilateral Polish-Soviet treaty.

Faced with these power politics, the Poles, who had become losers since the reign of Catherine the Great, cursed the Russians, heaping insults upon them. They accused the Russians of physical brutality, of abducting their eastern provinces and of ignorance in the fields of philosophy, religion, literature and music. They sought to demonstrate that, compared to their barbarian neighbours, Poland remained the figurehead of Greco-Latin civilisation in Eastern Europe.

To these susceptibilities, it is worth adding that neither rationalism nor the Age of Enlightenment permeated the Orthodox world — Catherine II's influence in this area was very weak in Russia — resulting in the country evolving very differently from the Catholic and Protestant world.

Well-aware of the susceptibility of the Polish, the Russians let them talk. They even allowed the Poles to pursue a "Polish socialism" which involved numerous departures from their doctrine. They accepted the privatisation of four-fifths of their agricultural sector and small businesses, as well as the presence of the Catholic Church. They created a Catholic "Pax" movement using Soviet funds. The movement controlled a large part of what was printed by the Catholic press, forcing the cardinal to weave between a doctrine he kept too resolutely, and what his aides aimed to achieve. A brilliant man, a man capable of great intellectual balancing, the Jesuit in charge of these relations was expelled from Poland at the request of the Cardinal.

Living under this illusion of partial freedom, the Poles sought to influence Moscow. They called themselves the best connoisseurs of the Russians and the most populous of their allies.

In the intimate game that was Polish-Russian relations, the Poles certainly provided Moscow with fairly good knowledge of the West. Poland maintained contact with a diaspora of 6 to 10 million Poles in the United States, Germany, France and Belgium, who regularly sent money back to their homeland.

The most important advantage the Russians held over the Poles, however, was the cynicism of their leaders, which far outweighed that of the Poles.

The second advantage was the Iron Curtain. Forcibly imposed by Moscow, the curtain condemned the Poles — and the other allied countries – to remain allied with Moscow, their only important economic partner.

The third advantage was the fact that the Russian police were able to take advantage of the Poles' police obsession and their taste for secrecy to establish a police network that was both imposing and effective.

> *The Russians used the old police sheet system put in place by the czars; seemingly the best in the world. The Poles followed their lead.*

Ultimately, Poland was an important military challenge for Russia due to geopolitical and strategic factors. The country's ideology only came into play in the extent to which it contributed to consolidating the military system adopted.

When these advantages were combined with the strength of the Red Army, they far exceeded any advantage the Poles had over the Russians. That is, an active Polish minority in the USSR and an unspoken collusion with the peoples under Soviet occupation.

It should be added, however, that the Poles thought the Russians were unable to defeat them alone; the 1921 Polish "victory" over Russia was still well-remembered. Russia had only ever defeated Poland with help from its allies: Hitler in 1939, and Roosevelt and Churchill in 1944—1945.

How was Poland structured?

Most of the members of the political bureau lived in Warsaw, except for Gierek, for example, who lived in Katowice. There, he was part of a decision-making body that served to issue orders sent from Moscow. I do not believe that Moscow established regular direct links with the party's regional offices. The Politburo was divided into regionally represented clans.

On a regional level, the party was modelled on administrative divisions (voivodeships) led by a first secretary – generally an important member of the Politburo, responsible for the main decisions taken by the voivodeship.

The police were put at the disposal of party leaders, as a means through which to exercise their power. These actions reflected the flow of ideas and the circles formed within the Politburo, which often engaged in underhand practices, though less brutally than they had in Stalin's time.

The leaders also used medicine: after all, it was easier to lock up a political enemy due to mental illness than it was to put them in prison. A doctor in Krakow was said to have assembled a superb collection of antiques thanks to the money he made issuing declarations of insanity.

The Polish army had a long and glorious history. It considered itself to be the guardian of Poland. Sometimes it pursued its own policies. Ever proud, it survived the Katyn massacre of its officers by the Russians. In 1945 it was rebuilt from the Anders' army — which came back from London — Polish resistance fighters and Polish troops who had been incorporated into the Red Army. The Poles had to give up leading their army, surrendering it to a Soviet.

When the Warsaw Pact troops invaded Czechoslovakia to break the anti-communist insurgency in 1968, the Polish army was forced to participate in the invasion. Aware of public opinion, Gomulka was able to obtain the rapid repatriation of his troops to Poland. The Poles refused to forgive their officers for participating in the invasion.

The Polish economy was structured according to the Soviet regime, at least in part. When he rose to power, Gomulka managed to convince the Soviets to allow the privatisation of agriculture. For the peasants, who had first been expropriated by the Germans in 1939, and a second time by the Communists in 1945, possessing land became a symbol of resistance. Only around ten percent of the land remained as kolkhozs. In addition, these peasants were granted a preferential regime, which meant that nobody dared oppose this population. Some of their plots of land were no bigger than a few ares. The rest of the economy was carefully planned out. This system, which operated according to its internal logic, allowed the Poles to create a state-of-the-art steel industry around Krakow.

One night, I crashed into an unlit cart full of straw as I rounded a bend in the road. My Polish colleagues informed me that I was lucky. I was a foreigner and could assert my innocence. The agricultural lobby in the country was so powerful that, had they been in my shoes, they would have been arrested.

How did this economy work? Through five-year plans that were broadly outlined every five years and then specified annually. What would these plans involve? Three elements; the quantities to be produced, which could be calculated from information received from all the companies in the country; the standards, which would also be gained through requests filed to all the companies; price fixing. This last point was the most difficult to understand for a Westerner who was used to considering a price to be something arrived at through a culmination of economic, financial and fiscal elements.

These capitalist notions did not apply in the least.

The government, considering social concepts as the standard against which items were measured, set prices for basic necessities very low (basic food, housing, clothing, etc.). High prices were set for non-essential goods. A bed manufacturer, for example, sold their produce at prices that seemed ludicrous to any Westerner, who would be left asking: how do they pay for their raw materials, and pay employee wages ...? With money they got from the bank, would be the answer they received.

Purchasing a small Fiat Polski would set you back twice the price it was manufactured for in Turin, paid upfront even though the car wouldn't be delivered until two or three years later. Why would people need a car when public transport worked so well?

> *Despite the public authorities being guided by this reasoning, the classy thing to do at a dinner party would be to accept a glass of wine, as that meant you had a chauffeur. The ultimate sign of class, however, would be to politely decline the wine, "because I've got my car outside."*

The slipping of the socialist economy in the 1990s was not a result of it being an inherently bad system, as the Western media likes to paint it. On the contrary, in fact, their leaders built factories that contained the latest technical developments to demonstrate their leadership skills to the world. They still saw themselves as being on the cutting edge of technology. But how? A Westerner would diagnose this as an absence of competition, whereas a socialist would accuse the country's leadership of gentrification, of not paying enough attention to the needs of the masses and to technological evolution.

The country's diet included occasional seasonal fruits and vegetables — lettuce from Easter onwards, exquisite strawberries and raspberries, broad beans, apples and pears. In the autumn, families would go out joyously to pick mushrooms in the undergrowth. In winter, we would eat root vegetables (carrots, potatoes, etc.), as well as cabbage. Red beetroot would find itself made into barszcz soup, which dates back to pagan times.

Sernik, on the other hand, would provide the most delicate sweetness — a cheesecake that had been served to King Stanislas himself. A bakery in Warsaw sold them, and it was always packed. The drink of choice was wodka, or "exquisite little water", which came in numerous varieties.

As soon as I arrived, I had to go to Majdanek (Maïdanek), in the outskirts of Lublin, to represent Belgium at the inauguration of the third memorial to the concentration camp. It was the first time I had come into contact with the Polish Politburo. Gomulka, a small, suspicious, quiet man stood at its head. When he rose to power in 1956, he had just come out of an internment in a villa on the outskirts of Warsaw. He then became the most popular man in communist Poland. Almost everyone in Poland shared this point of view and were not afraid to say it once he had fallen.

Gomulka's power had, in fact, been weakening since 1967 and his main rival was his neighbour in Majdanek: Mieczysław Moczar. Why? The Jewish question. The stakes? Power.

I think a brief history of the Jewish question in Poland could be of some use here. When Poland took in the Jews who had been expelled from Spain and the Holy Land five centuries prior, it forbade them from running for the highest offices of state. Up until 1939, Jews lived in Jewish villages or towns like Lodz or Kazimierz. They made up around ten percent of a population of 32 million, which was probably the highest density of Jews in any European country. Their lifestyle was built around their customs and religion. They spoke a language that was somewhere between Yiddish and Hebrew and, despite having spent centuries in Poland, spoke Polish poorly. This meant they were not assimilated, circumstances that were not mirrored by Jews living in Western Europe. They hated the Polish nobility — the only section of the population with access to power. It was the Polish nobility who elected the king.

After the partitions of Poland, these Jews became Prussian, Austrian or Russian. In 1917—1918, when Poland was reconstituted, however, they felt more Jewish than Polish. They marvelled at the audacity and success of the Bolshevik revolt, not because they supported Marxism, but because it led to the fall of the aristocratic class. The Polish nobility was immediately aware of this shift: Jewish quickly became synonymous for Communist.

When Hitler rose to power and proclaimed that the Jews were communists, the Poles quickly began colluding with the Germans. In

1934, Pilsudski, who ruled Poland, signed a non-aggression pact with Nazi Germany. Reichsmarschall Göring would go hunting in Poland. The Poles and the Germans would flirt behind the backs of the Jews and the Communists, and of the French and the English.

Germany's about-turn, a certain stiffening of Poland and Moscow's cynicism all took the French and the British by surprise on 1 September 1939. From the start of September onwards, Germany occupied its half of Poland while Russia occupied theirs under the Molotov–Ribbentrop Pact.

In the part occupied by Germany, the Germans began by bringing in Jews whose names they gained from their many informants. They would later kill them in camps like Oswiecim (Auschwitz) and Majdanek. Meanwhile, in the Soviet half of the country, the Jews were enacting their revenge on the aristocracy and, being good communists, taking up key positions. The 1941 German invasion of the Soviet area only allowed a very small group of high-up Jews to flee with the Soviet troops. The others, who were left to the Germans, would meet the same fate as the Jews in the German section.

When the Soviets returned to Poland in 1945, they were followed by men from the Lublin Committee, which included Jews. Although there were only a few thousand left in the country, the Jews held a large share of power. In Foreign Affairs, for example, 30 percent of the diplomats were Jewish.

It was then that, little by little, anti-Semitism began to develop in the country, coupled with anti-Sovietism. Moczar, who chaired the Veterans Association — the Zbowid — which brought together all the veterans, became aware of this feeling. The Six-Day War (1967), in which the Soviets stood against Israel, seemed like the perfect springboard from which to seize power at the expense of the Jews returning from the USSR. In a violent speech, he accused those who wore "grey capes", in reference to the old tsarist army uniform, of replacing the Poles by preventing Polish policy from aligning with the USSR's. He demanded that they be expelled from Poland. The Politburo accepted the request.

Thus, by positioning himself as pro-Soviet, Moczar would deprive the USSR of its Polish Jewish allies. He demonstrated that he was, in fact, very Polish.

These evictions took place in spite of First Secretary Gomulka (whose wife was Jewish). The Jews were given a matter of days in which to leave the country, without their personal effects. Their passport, which was valid for three months, specified that the holder was not Polish.

These wandering Jews, who were sometimes excellent Communists, tried to contact the Party in either Rome, Paris, Bern or Copenhagen. They were shut out. They formed dissident communities, which were generally made up of the best scholars, generals and diplomats: thinkers Gomulka's Poland had never had access to.

> *A Dutch colleague of mine, who was in charge of Israeli interests, informed me that I had to issue an Israeli visa to any Jew that had been kicked out. Several Poles with not a single drop of Jewish blood tried, in vain, to sneak into this widespread expulsion.*

Having conducted a successful exodus of the Jews, Moczar sought to seize power. Fortunately for Gomulka, the Czechoslovak crisis (1968) — which took place just in time — gave Moscow the pretext it needed to withhold its support of Moczar.

In order to appear more Polish, Gomulka allowed the Jews to be openly criticised. This did not extend to Israel, except when referenced in stereotypical official speeches, as although the Poles were readily anti-Semitic with regard to their own country, they were Zionists when it came to Israel. Wasn't the Six-Day War a victory against the common enemy, Moscow, Egypt's ally?

The role of the Catholic Church, and in particular of Cardinal Wyszynski, was also very revealing. Not wishing to embarrass Gomulka further, the Cardinal decided not to side with anyone in terms of the measures taken against the Jews. He thus avoided a crisis of conscience among his Polish flock, who were traditionally anti-Semites.

> *I found myself in the midst of an altercation with some Polish officials at a soirée one evening. I blamed them for the expulsion of the Jews. They replied: "the West is never happy. The Russians stopped the Jews from leaving, and the West complained; we removed them, and the West complained.*

> *What is it the West wants?" I replied that there had to be more freedom: that those who wanted to stay could stay and those who wanted to leave could leave.*

When the subject of the German atrocities was touched upon, the Poles would readily describe a "martyred Poland", citing the number of Jewish deaths. They would add that the German defeat of 1945 is what had saved them, as the next step would have been the elimination of the Poles. This Polish arithmetic explained the accusation I would later hear coming from exiled Polish Jews that there had been anti-Jewish collusion between Germany and Poland.

Being Catholic and Roman were core aspects of Poland's identity. This evidence guided the Russians. Catholicism was not only tolerated but was an important part of the Polish political spectrum. I began to see the extent of this when Gierek rose to power in December 1970. He had only succeeded in doing so because he had gained unanimous approval from Moscow, the Polish Communist Party, Cardinal Wyszynski — the Primate of Poland — the army and the administration (in that order). The way in which Gomulka had risen to power followed the same pattern.

The Polish Catholic Church was the most fervent in Europe: it was intimately linked to Polish history. It could be characterised by its patriotism and its total absence of class prejudice. It readily put itself forwards as the Catholic outpost stationed between Orthodoxy — or Communism in those days — and Protestantism.

During the wars of religion, Poland became Protestant in an act of treason against the Crown and out of sympathy for the Prussians and the Swedes. It was from the fortified Catholic abbey of Czestochowa that Polish Catholics regained power and that Prussians and Swedes were expelled. This victory served as proof that only a Catholic Poland could be independent.

When the "Republic" was established, the Primate of Poland was appointed ex officio regent upon the death of the King, until a new King was elected. Collective Polish memory remembered the communist regime as a hiatus in Polish history and the cardinal as the guardian of a free Poland. Cardinal Wyszynski, defender of the Church of Poland, was imprisoned in a monastery in 1953 and released upon Gomulka's arrival, in 1956.

The Church played an important role in Polish-German negotiations. The Polish episcopate, which assembled in Rome during the Second Vatican Council, responded to 1 October 1965 Memorandum of the German Protestant Church, on 18 November 1965 with a Christian opening to Christian brothers. The Polish government immediately accused the episcopate of taking over state affairs, and of doing it outside Poland.

The cardinal was unaffected by the accusation. He contacted the Vatican Secretary of State and asked him to reconnect the bishoprics located in the former German territories to the Polish episcopate. The Vatican, which was under pressure from the German government, only accepted the appointment of bishops as apostolic administrators in May 1967. These would be attached directly to Rome. Despite numerous, repeated requests, the Cardinal was unsuccessful in bringing these bishops into the Polish episcopate. The Vatican claimed that the decision could only be reassessed once the country's international circumstances had changed.

The Vatican was, in actual fact, awaiting ratification of the Treaty of Warsaw before it could consider this clause fulfilled. This decision resulted in acidic comments being made by the German CDU, which believed — with good reason — that the Treaty of Warsaw had done nothing to alter any borders.

While the town of Nowa Huta ("The New Steel Mill") was being built near Krakow in 1949, the Communist authorities built the most efficient steelworks in Europe. The city was to be a centre where daily life and working relationships were carried out according to a Marxist perspective. It was therefore a town within which the architecture, living conditions and the general atmosphere were designed to generate a prime example of communism.

The Poles rejected this model. They wanted a place of prayer. They erected a cross in the central square. The authorities issued a demolition order. They were then forced to approve the construction of a church in 1967. One man was busy observing and measuring the depth of Christianity in the region — the Archbishop of Krakow, Karol Józef Wojtyla (future Pope John Paul II), who was familiar with the workings of communist public life. He was eager to hold Christmas midnight mass outdoors in Nowa Huta in temperatures -10°C. The communists took note of him, aware of the power of his personality. They thought he could serve as a good counterweight to Cardinal Wyszynski. They took action in Rome, and Wojtyla was appointed cardinal. Unfortunately for the communists, the two cardinals got along well, and they could not play them off against each other.

"Religion is the sigh of the oppressed creature, the heart of a heartless world, and the soul of soulless conditions. It is the opium of the people." This was the opinion held by Karl Marx. Was it also that of the Polish leaders who, while on the run, would go to mass and have their children baptised in obscure, remote villages?

When I arrived, I paid several visits to my colleagues in Foreign Affairs. In the tradition established within the Cold War, one visit upon arrival was considered enough. Any following visits would have to have a specific purpose. These visits followed the ritual of an hour of conversation over a cup of coffee. I didn't feel the ritual was enough and went back to see my colleagues with the simple aim of maintaining contact with them. I couldn't help noticing their inquisitiveness, but managed to create a fairly relaxed working atmosphere, nonetheless.

The start of the Polish-German negotiations worked in my favour. They revolved around two points: the Oder-Neisse border and the repatriation of Silesians wanting to move to Germany. For the Poles, this meant firmly establishing its western border, especially in the event of a German reunification. For the Germans, it was the price they had to pay to regain a cultural and economic foothold in Poland. The Poles asked me about the Germans. "We haven't had any relations with West Germans since the war, and you've just come from there: what can you tell us?"

The Polish delegation for the negotiations with Germany was made up of a troika. Deputy Minister Winiewicz stood at its head, assisted by Ambassador Dobrowolski, Deputy Director for Federal Germany, and Czyrek, Director of the Planning Sector.

Dobrowolski followed the bilateral nature of negotiations, Czyrek was in charge of coordinating the multilateral aspect.

Józef Winiewicz, the head of the delegation, was a very skilled man. Having been a far-right journalist before the war and Polish Ambassador to

Washington after the war, he became Deputy Minister of Foreign Affairs and member of the party.

On my first visit to Dobrowolski, I was questioned extensively about Germany under Bonn. I noted that the experienced diplomat before me had an almost physical fear of the Germans. All he saw in them was revenge and the Nazis. I explained that our Embassy in Bonn kept a close eye on those matters. We had more reason to fear them than the Poles. We were the FRG's neighbours and did not have the luxury of the shield put up by the GDR. And even so, we hadn't found anything. Even the NDP, whose manifesto I had personally compared to Hitler's NSDAP's, was closer to French poujadism than it was to the NSDAP.

Poland should celebrate, rather than criticise, Germany's membership of NATO and the EEC. Good economic health and a controlled military were the best ways to safeguard against a new NSDAP gaining ground.

Without a hint of scepticism and, I do believe, a certain sense of relief, Dobrowolski took note of the impressions I had gathered of the leaders of the CDU and the Auswärtiges Amt.

Then, Dobrowolski explained the offer Gomulka had made on 17 May 1969, that the FRG recognise the Oder-Neisse border through means of a treaty.

I left his office under the impression that the Poles were in favour of this agreement, but did not know their partner well enough, their files on the latter containing very little information.

A few days later, I paid Ambassador Böx, head of the German trade mission, a visit. He held a challenging position in Warsaw. All his mission boiled down to were basic commercial agreements. From his point of view, the offer made on 17 May was rendered meaningless on 21 July as, in his second speech, Gomulka also required the GDR to be formally recognised.

As we began talking, Mr Böx assured me that we could speak openly, as the mission, and his office in particular, were regularly checked by German security services. While reading Der Spiegel two weeks later, I came across an article about the Germans finding a network of microphones within the mission, which had been placed behind the radiators. Furious, the Germans sent a 220-volt charge into the wiring,

*which must have caused significant damage. The Poles
retaliated by throwing acid at a member of the German
technical mission in the street.*

German elections were held the following weekend, marking the end
of the CDU's reign.

I would see Dobrowolski and Czyrek shortly after. They did not
breathe a sigh of relief with the SPD's (socialist party) rise to power. There
was no denying that the CDU was imperialist, and its ally, the CSU even
more so. But the SPD, Czyrek would tell me, had a very nationalistic
old guard. He would tell me that one of his friends was surprised by the
nationalist, anti-Polish words spoken by one of the other prisoners at his
stalag, Kurt Schumacher. He would add that this trend was dying out, but
only very gradually, within the SPD.

I discussed the legal aspect of the treaty with Czyrek. What about the
Belgian-German border rectification treaty? he asked. The treaty dealt
with mutual cessions of territory along the German Fagnes railway. The
Poles saw the Belgian-German treaty as the Western counterpart of their
Oder-Neisse treaty.

I replied that the two treaties could not be compared in such a
way. Germany's western border had not been reshaped by the Potsdam
agreements on one hand, and on the other, the treaty was of mutual
interest when it came to rectifying the borders involved. The Belgian
government was well-aware of the fragility of their agreement,although
it was signed in agreement with the countries holder of the « reserved
powers ». Belgium entered into the agreement nonetheless, as it knew it
could rely on the honesty of the FRG. Bonn thus became the co-guarantor
of the border challenged by Hitler.

The Netherlands, Austria and Switzerland have since signed similar
border rectification agreements.

It's worth adding that the Zgorzelec agreement between Poland and
the GDR did not lead to any territory being ceded to Poland. It merely
established a border. The USSR never formally agreed to it. The USSR-
GDR (art. nine) and USSR-Poland (art. five) friendship treaties are vague
enough to contradict each other.

I got no reaction whatsoever upon making these remarks. Had they not been studied? Had I managed to make the Poles aware of the fragility of the friendship treaties they had entered into with the USSR and the GDR? The treaties were seen as the cornerstones of their foreign policy.

It was obvious that Belgian interest was geared towards ensuring the success of an Ostpolitik — which shook certain eastern dogmas — on the one hand, and avoiding a "Rapallo" by maintaining a certain vagueness surrounding the German borders with the East on the other.

Leaders of the Treaty of Warsaw parties met in Moscow in early December. Czyrek informed me that they had discussed negotiations with the FRG and that Poland had succeeded in establishing that GDR recognition would not be required as a prerequisite.

A green light from Moscow had Gomulka increasingly freer and freer from Berlin. Berlin's bitterness towards Warsaw, however, would only grow over the following months.

A fortnight later, Dobrowolski and I discussed Poland's Northern borders. I asked him why Poland was not asking to have them recognised. That is, Poland's northern border in ex-German Pomerania.

This conversation had to be reported to Gomulka as, during a speech, he had asked the FRG to recognise the country's western and northern borders. This request was never repeated, and the negotiators did not recognise the borders. Did they want to lock in their borders following an intervention from the GDR, for fear of Warsaw, or did the Soviets refuse to let Bonn become the guarantor of the Soviet-Polish border? Personally, I think it was because a light had finally been shed on the fragility of the agreements concerning the Polish borders.

The Poles really were afraid of starting negotiations. Who were those German negotiators anyway? And what a lack of tact to send this Duckwitz, who we knew belonged to the old NSDAP!

I set about trying to soothe the atmosphere. Duckwitz was, admittedly, a member of the NSDAP. As such, in his position as secretary to the German Embassy in Copenhagen during the war, he had been forewarned about the Jews being rounded up. He wasted no time letting them know as much. This allowed them to flee to Sweden. Cynically, I pointed out that even an anti-Semite could not deny Duckwitz's courage and non-conformism. The skilled man certainly had a deep understanding of the Polish problem. What I did not share, however, was that while I had been in Germany, Duckwitz had told me something he had said to Brandt one day: "The SPD lacks a propagandist and isn't gaining visibility: he needs a Göbbels."

So Duckwitz came. The anxiety began to dissipate. The meeting was poignant. Little was said during the first meeting, but Duckwitz certainly won over the hearts of the Poles. Polish diplomats were now at peace; journalists and economic figures reassured. "He understands us," they would tell me.

At the second interview, everyone spoke more directly. The Germans were ready to recognise that the border "was" the Oder-Neisse but asked that the Silesians be granted some breaks. Böx was delighted. The Poles agreed to erase the entire paragraph recalling the suffering of the last war, requesting that no mention be made of the 1945 German expulsion: a sinister barter between the living and the dead.

Meanwhile, Chancellor Brandt went to Erfurt, having been invited by Wilhelm Stoph, the Prime Minister of the GDR. The unpopularity of politicians in the GDR was particularly evident to Brandt, who was the only one to receive a huge round of applause. The Poles rejoiced *in petto*. Berlin also got the impression that Warsaw had the wind in its sails and even feared an agreement being reached between Bonn and Warsaw at its expense.

East German Foreign Minister Winzer was sent to Warsaw to set things straight. Before he had even left the airport, he made a point of reminding the Poles of the Warsaw Declaration, which had been signed when the Iron Triangle had been constituted, in 1967, due to Romania having suddenly become insecure. The declaration required both Poland and Czechoslovakia to consult with Berlin before entering into discussions with Bonn.

If they were to consider the GDR's weight in the Warsaw Pact, Winzer's words at the airport should have frightened the Poles. They didn't. Jedrychowski even replied that the Iron Triangle was a way of making the socialist countries cooperate even more closely on an economic level, something the GDR was trying to avoid. The MSZ was quiet yet sly: there was no Winzer-Jedrychowski meeting, and Winzer went for a walk around the town. Furious at having been played, he went back to Berlin.

The fifth session took place on 23 July, the day after Polish National

Independence Day. Dobrowolski hoped this would be the last meeting. Poland was ready to ease Silesian immigration but did not want to be forced to do so. It was unwilling to authorise German emigration to Poland, as this would mean opening the country's doors to the Germans returning to Silesia en masse.

Dobrowolski's expectations were met, and the text was agreed upon. Winieswicz made his way back to Moscow to be granted a green light and came swiftly back. Duckwitz told him to wait to hear the outcome of the trip taken by Scheel, the German Minister for Foreign Affairs, to Moscow, with the aim of signing a German-Soviet agreement. This agreement was negotiated in parallel to the Polish-German negotiation.

The Poles let the Germans and Soviets initial their agreement before the one made with Warsaw, as they already had an agreement. They thought standard procedure would be to sign the Treaty of Warsaw before the Treaty of Moscow in order to emphasise the specific "reconciliation" angle of the Treaty of Warsaw.

In the meantime, it would be necessary to set a date for the agreement to be signed, and for this to be done quickly. Bonn turned a deaf ear. The end of July had come; the Poles fully trusted Bonn, and especially Moscow, to set a date. They were so confident, in fact, that the country's leaders — including Winiewicz – went on holiday, though not before hosting Pierre Harmel.

As the question surrounding the German borders was almost settled, his trip was made with the intent of pressuring the Poles to approve the start of the Conference on Security and Cooperation in Europe (CSCE) along with the other members of the Warsaw Pact. His efforts were made in vain.

Three days later, it was announced that Brandt would be going on a trip to Moscow the next day. News of the Moscow Treaty being signed on 12 August 1970 fell like a sledgehammer in a deserted city. The MSZ despaired. The situation felt like a betrayal. Bonn and Moscow became suspects of only God knows what. The reaction served as proof that the scars left by the 1939 partitioning of Poland had not yet fully healed.

The MSZ pulled itself together and declared that it was not ready to sign, claiming that important points still had to be discussed. Negotiations were adjourned. Polish honour had been saved.

What was going on that summer? Cardinal Wyszynski was making plans to celebrate the fiftieth anniversary of what laymen call the Battle of the Vistula on 15 August. God and his followers in Warsaw called the event the Miracle of the Vistula. Our Lady of Sorrows, the Queen of Poland, appeared, thus stopping the Russian Communists at the gates of Warsaw. No one spoke of Weygand and Pidulski.

The Polish episcopate reminded its leader that miracles were no longer taking place in Rome. The only result of a sermon held on the subject was to compel the government to take action against it. The primate replied that he was ready to give his life for the cause. The government informed him that if he delivered his sermon, catechisms would be banned in schools, loans granted for the construction of churches would be cancelled and tax arrears demanded. Upon seeing that it would be the church and not the Cardinal himself who would be punished, he backed down. On 15 August, he went to Czestochowa amidst several tens of thousands of pilgrims. It was a particularly impressive sight, as the cardinal held his mass on the ramparts of the fortress. Pilgrims who had been transported from all over Poland on special buses gathered around him.

On 16 August, he was in Warsaw, at the re-inauguration of the Jesuit church. A large crowd gathered. I was not allowed in, so I stood outside with the rest of the assistants. He gave a two-hour sermon, talking at length about the role the Virgin had played in the life of the city of Warsaw. There was no mention of a miracle.

As I walked through the central park in Warsaw one day, where swarms of mischievous squirrels lived, two of them took it upon themselves to climb up my trouser legs. Remembering the joke where they wonder "shall we eat in or take away?" I shook my trousers, to the despair of their new inhabitants.

That summer, relations between Bonn and Warsaw intensified. Ambassador Emmel, who replaced Böx at the head of the German trade mission, held daily meals attended by very high-level German and Polish visitors: politicians, trade unionists, businessmen and members of the art community.

These Germans came together to renew their traditional ties. The Poles requested aid from the Germans to revive their languid economy. They offered to accept German loans, joint ventures and subcontracting work, asked German specialists to come and share their technical knowledge and sent their technicians to study in Germany. In short, they redirected an important part of their economy.

The demands made by the Polish were so vast that it was impossible for the Germans to fully satisfy them. They answered that they were prepared to cooperate in any way possible, but that any cooperation must take place according to the laws of the market. This reference to the laws of the market irritated the Poles, who argued that the Soviets were granted loans with conditions more favourable than those on the market. The Germans held their position.

> *Polish cultural life was intense and centred on both Polish and Western authors and artists. The Chopin competition was a revelation. While my knowledge of Chopin was limited to stiff imitations by Rubinstein, Westerners and Russians, I discovered the Poles' romantic interpretation as I watched the competition. Professor Ekier was one of the best musicians. He was an exciting man. Every Sunday, his pupils would perform in the 19th century house where Chopin was born, in Zelazowa Wola. The window next to the piano would be left open, and the general public would stroll through the garden as the notes hung in the air. It was a wonderful event, and the young girls couldn't help but let their emotions get the better of them.*

The Polish government refused to cooperate on one point, prohibiting its workers from leaving the country to work in Germany as foreign workers. This idea went against their socialist vision. Unemployment was non-existent in Poland, which meant no workers were available to go over anyway. The Poles came to regret the doctrinal rigidity imposed by Moscow eventually, however, as they lost out on an important source of foreign currency coming into the country.

Another limit imposed by Moscow: the FRG could not become a more important trading partner than the USSR. A wise precaution taken by Moscow because, in as little as a year, the FRG went from bottom of the list to second place, second only to the USSR in all the USSR's allied countries. Ostpolitik marked the return of Germany to its hinterland, though it was not allowed to participate in politics.

The Federal Republic of Germany immediately became very active in the cultural field, as up until then any German cultural influence in Poland had been driven by the GDR and Austrian embassies. Many contacts were made, scholarships granted, and cultural events organised.

However, alongside an almost euphoric development of trade, economic, financial and cultural relations, the mood was growing steadily more sombre when it came to politics. The Poles suddenly came to the realisation that their position, as seen from Moscow's perspective, was the same as that held by the Germans in Berlin. They found they had been seated at the children's table; told they should be seen and not heard.

But neither Ulbricht nor Gomulka accepted Bonn and Moscow dealing with all the matters exclusively, leaving them on the side-lines. Stoph, the East German Prime Minister, came to Warsaw at the end of September and agreed to establish economic cooperation with Gomulka. They even discussed getting rid of several contentious lawsuits, in particular those regarding transporting materials from one country to another. The springtime rift that had been caused between them was therefore closed once again.

The Poles turned a deaf ear when it came to Bonn. For them, the Treaty of Moscow did not trigger the Treaty of Warsaw *ipso facto*, as the former looked to the future by prohibiting settling disputes using force, while the Treaty of Warsaw aimed to erase the past and reconcile the two peoples.

The Germans immediately took advantage of this point of view. The nature of the Treaty of Warsaw was, of course, entirely different, which was why it had to be consecrated by the Four Powers exercising responsibilities in Germany. The Treaty of Moscow did not require the same conditions to be met; the three participating differently in the latter. The humanitarian side also had to be consecrated with the right to "family reunification" being reaffirmed, a euphemism used for Silesian emigration.

The Poles started off rejecting the motion, though they later agreed to discuss it, provided the texts were external to the treaty. Germany accepted and negotiations came to an end with the Winiewicz-Duckwitz discussion in Bonn.

> *Meanwhile, the Chinese and American ambassadors in Warsaw had been holding regular meetings in one or other of their embassies since 1970. They refused to be hosted in Polish establishments to avoid any information being leaked to Moscow. We got very little information from either side. The meetings aimed to ease tensions between the West and the communist states, finally culminating in a meeting between Richard Nixon and Mao Zedong in China in February 1972. The ambassadors also negotiated the points to be included in the "Shanghai Communiqué", which marked the end of hostilities and normalised relations between the two countries. However, it was not until the "Joint Communiqué of 17 August 1978" that diplomatic relations were established between the two governments. In addition, the People's Republic of China was admitted to the United Nations – instead of the Republic of China (Taiwan) — in September 1971, thanks to the US. It was also granted the right of veto it held in the Security Council.*

Upon his arrival in Warsaw to initial the treaty, Scheel, the FRG's Minister for Foreign Affairs, would call it into question. Legally, the treaty could not prejudge the peace treaty or diminish the rights of the Four in Germany as a whole. Calling into question the "gentlemen's agreement" entered into when negotiations began, he added that the agreement could not legalise an injustice such as the expulsion of millions of Germans.

This position irritated Poland, as they had been assured that the finalised text had been agreed upon in Bonn, a few days earlier. Unaffected, Scheel joked about the matter, as the Poles had done in July. He also wanted to prove that he was gaining something too, and all thanks to the new discussions that had arisen.

To mitigate the negativity caused by his questioning of the agreement, Scheel went on a conciliatory visit to Auschwitz. The press picked up on it and reported on the visit positively.

And just then, de Gaulle died. A mass was held in the cathedral and was attended by Scheel and the German delegation. Among them was Achenbach, the deputy leader of the Liberals, a notorious former member of the NSDAP and former assistant to Abetz in Paris during the war. Because of his past, the other five members of the Common Market challenged Bonn when they named him Commissioner to the EEC. We also refused to allow him to become President of the European Commission, and there he was, at a requiem held for de Gaulle in Warsaw, as a part of the German delegation, no less!

An agreement was finally reached.

The Treaty of Warsaw was made up of three points.

First of all, the Treaty of Warsaw on the normalisation of their mutual relations. Article one stipulated that the western border of Poland "is" on the Oder-Neisse (there would therefore be no recognition). Article two stated that they would restrain from the threat of violence or the use of violence in their mutual relations. Article three stated the ways in which they could cooperate, and Article four specified that the treaty would not derogate from any existing agreements. There was therefore no mention of the Potsdam agreements, which soothed Poland's nerves. As far as Poland was concerned, these agreements did not definitively establish the country's border as being on the Oder-Neisse.

The second point of the Treaty of Warsaw was copies of the letters sent to the French, British and US Embassies in Bonn, by the Auswärtiges Amt, pronouncing that the Treaty of Warsaw would not affect any rights held by the Allies. Ambassador Emmel brought a copy of these letters to the MSZ the day before it was to be signed, telling me to "note Poland's acquiescence" to the notes. Dobrowolski would tell me that Poland did not consent, rather had been "informed". This was a point of some ambiguity between the interviews.

The last part of the Treaty of Warsaw related to "family reunification" (Silesian emigration). Scheel requested that a document be drawn up exchanging the departure of Germans from Poland for the Oder Neisse affair. After all, hadn't Adenauer got Moscow to release prisoners of war in his day?

Poland agreed to accelerate Silesian departures. However, as the number of emigrants already amounted to several thousand each year, the Poles did not want to bind themselves to such an agreement in writing. They agreed to discuss the subject nonetheless, and even drew up a declaration, all the while stipulating that Poland did not commit to anything and would not sign anything. The German delegation drafted a text that would later be typed up.

The text was discussed and corrected on each respective side of the table, and an agreement was reached. The Germans typed up the new terms and gave the Poles an original, keeping the other original for themselves. The Germans' enthusiasm for typing had allowed Poland to navigate the entire encounter without writing a single note, as Dobrowolski would tell me later.

And so, the second ambiguity in the agreement was established. One that curiously reconciled Poland's desire that nothing should be written on the subject, with Scheel successfully returning to Bonn with a written document.

Needless to say, the Polish press limited themselves to publishing information about the treaty – failing to mention the exchange of letters with the three powers and the declaration on family reunification. The German press, on the other hand, published the treaty in full.

A few days later, on 7 December 1970, Chancellor Brandt came to sign the Treaty. He asked to go to the Warsaw Ghetto Heroes Monument and found it was particularly difficult to get his request approved. After having shed a tear as he signed the treaty, he dropped to his knees suddenly in the ghetto. Having shown himself to be a tough negotiator with Moscow, he proved he was also human, and one filled with a sense of responsibility for Germany's actions towards the Jews. The anti-Semitic Poles dared not say a word, and the photo of Brandt kneeling in the ghetto did not find its way into the Polish press.

As December came around, Gomulka believed he was at the height of his glory. After the turmoil caused by the signing of the Moscow Treaty in July, the events that had taken place in the autumn brought a sense of euphoria back to the country. Poland was showing itself to be worthy of its place in Europe, having taken legal steps to get what it wanted from Germany. And doing so successfully. Hopes ran high when it came to the latter providing economic and financial aid and – inwardly, at least – the former hoping to be able to count on the latter for political support. This success was achieved without annoying Moscow. Not even Berlin's feathers were ruffled. The feat of strength had been achieved, and Gomulka was entitled to his feelings of happiness.

The Treaty did not change anything fundamental from a legal perspective. It allowed the Germans to participate in Polish life, and they did so easily and efficiently, economically, commercially and culturally.

Unfortunately, nothing new emerged in the short term. The government's euphoria was opposed by a discontent felt by the general population, who were unhappy with the economic fortune they had been granted.

Gierek, who sought power, used this dissatisfaction, organising demonstrations against Gomulka from October 1970 onwards. Gomulka ignored them, believing he was invincible. He boasted as much and, once Brandt had signed the Treaty, decided to apply the new price increases to basic necessities, as had been decided by Comecon, in early December. It was the straw that broke the camel's back. Workers in Gdansk (Danzig) and Szczecin (Stettin) rebelled, creating a real 'soviet'.

Gierek took advantage of the panic caused by these events to narrow the gap with Warsaw and attempt to take power. Gomulka called on the Soviets for help, as the army no longer answered to him. Doing so, however, proved to the Soviets that the old man was no longer in control of the country, leading them to replace him with Gierek.

To make this transfer of power legal, Gomulka was examined by a doctor who declared him unfit to perform his duties. Shortly after that, Polish doctors asked for a raise, threatening to cure Gomulka if it was not granted. Gierek also managed to get rid of Soviet Ambassador Aristov, who was pro-Gomulka, having him replaced by a Belarusian diplomat.

I had two strange experiences at the Soviet embassy. The first was at the beginning of November, on the anniversary of the October Revolution. The Embassy's rooms were full, and the entire Polish Politburo was present. The second was the Soviet Ambassador's farewell reception, which barely five percent of the same crowd attended. The Polish party leaders only sent their second strings. It was proof that even a Soviet Ambassador could be boycotted.

The Polish party was quick to back Gierek. Working in his favour would have seen Gomulka's ascetic policy abandoned, as well as bringing the promise that dignitaries would be granted the right to a dacha — as their colleagues at Comecon had been.

The Primate acquiesced on one condition: that Gierek committed to respecting the country's constitutional freedoms. He even declared as much in the pulpit. The Cardinal's secretary told me that the prelate did not hold Gierek's qualities as an intellectual and statesman in high esteem. He did not, however, want to cut himself off from the latter completely, as this could provoke a Soviet reaction.

As for the army, the "heir to the royal army" was eager to take a step back from internal politics, only beginning to back Gierek in February.

When the time came for me to leave Poland (September 1971), Gierek still hadn't been accepted in Gdansk and was particularly unpopular in Szczecin, where there were still limited, though frequent, revolts.

Poland had been living in danger from the communists since December 1970. I said as much to the Polish officials who acquiesced in noting the appearance of the new workers' power. The Poles were very careful when it came to proving to the Soviets that this revolt was not a consequence of the Treaty of Warsaw. No Russians were troubled, no anti-Russian speech delivered.

But Poland wanted change. Moscow sent strict instructions that the government did not follow.

One morning, Czyrek asked me to come and see him as quickly as possible. I got into my car and meandered through the streets of Warsaw alongside tanks and armed soldiers. The atmosphere was heavy, the sky grey, the snow black and omnipresent. The shops had all been looted. I walked into Czyrek's office. He wasted no time in telling me the two points on his agenda.

Firstly, he had information to share with me. If a power (while he didn't name it, we both knew he was talking about the USSR) launched an attack on Poland, an army of a million soldiers and partisans would be raised within 48 hours. I was careful to take good note of this very important piece of information so that I could pass it on to my government.

> *This point was very important when it came to Polish defence tactics. It meant that if Moscow were to intervene, an endless guerrilla war would ensue in which the Poles would take full advantage of their many forests, by hiding in them. Oddly enough, if one were to assess the forces involved, it seemed obvious that any Soviet intervention would end in a Russian victory. History, however, proved otherwise. Moscow clearly did not want to risk it.*

Secondly, he had a question to ask me. What would NATO do under such circumstances? I answered that I did not have the authority to answer on behalf of the Alliance, but that I would pass the question on accordingly. In my personal opinion, separate to any position that may be taken up by the Alliance, I believed it would not do anything, just as in Czechoslovakia in 1968. From a human perspective, I found it was particularly challenging to provide this diplomat, who I meet with regularly and with whom I had established strong links, with the answer that if he were to call for help, we would not react.

> *It was obvious that providing any aid would trigger a major conflict. How could troops be sent to Poland without marching through East Germany, where so many Soviet divisions were stationed? How would they get through Czechoslovakia, a country that had barely recovered from being under Moscow's rule, without initiating a conflict with the Soviets? The only option left was a hazardous path traced through the Baltic, where the USSR had their Kaliningrad naval base.*

I had had no answer from Brussels. Then, everything calmed down. The Treaty of Warsaw began to take effect. On 3 September 1971, the Berlin Agreement was signed. I hardly ever saw Dobrowolski anymore, as the main file had been closed.

My meetings with Czyrek, on the other hand, were becoming more frequent due to the multilateral dimension of Ostpolitik and the rather slow negotiations taking place on the subject of holding a European security conference. Within this discussion, the Poles essentially operated as Moscow's couriers. They would put forwards an idea Russia implicitly agreed with and examine how the West reacted to it. Then, either the idea was deemed to be good, thus becoming a Russian idea, or the Poles were accused of having launched proposals lightly. The Poles accepted the thankless role they had been given. Poland's own position was to multilaterally recognise the existing borders and the renunciation of the use of force in European relations. Czyrek confirmed the existence of a right, one that had been applicable in 1969, and more precisely up until at least 1971 — allowing the USSR to intervene in any country with a socialist regime.

A few days before I left Warsaw, on 15 August 1971, Nixon's government surprised the world by severing the link between the dollar and gold. As I met my Polish colleagues and those from other Eastern European countries, I could see they were distressed. Are you not happy? I would ask. Marx had predicted the end of capitalism would arise from its internal contradictions. Quite the contrary, they were dismayed. Why? Aren't you paid in dollars? They would ask. I answered that I was paid in Belgian francs. They told me their salary was paid in dollars from the moment they went abroad. Nixon's decision depreciated the dollar and, as a consequence, their wallets.

A fortnight before I left Warsaw, Prince Radziwill passed away in his own home, which was on the outskirts of the city. I knew him personally, as his son had married Nicole de Schoutheete, who was also Belgian. I gave her a call. She accepted my offer to drive her and her children to church, as her husband had gone ahead in their car to make sure everything was set up. The church was small: the pews had been removed, and the crowd was so dense that we almost muscled onto the catafalque several times. A priest took photos from the pulpit. As we made our way out into the cemetery, Nicole told me that her mother-in-law wanted to walk behind the coffin. She asked me to take care of Mrs Onassis (former Mrs John F Kennedy). She had come from her Greek island, along with her sister, who was married to the brother of the deceased. I took her in my arms because she was afraid of the large crowd. People were not even glancing at her. This crowd had only come to pay homage to the "prince", one of the survivors of the Katyn massacre and a hero for many. We were not even able to make it into the cemetery, as the crowd formed a solid barrier. A man who had perched in a tree above the grave fell in it. The priest, who was wearing a chasuble, made his way there with great difficulty. We turned back: a tram stopped, and we both got in, hitching a ride back to my car. I had lunch with her that day. Her personality and presence highlighted her femininity. Intellectually, she was fascinated by the trip Mr Nixon had planned to China.

It was certainly an interesting way to conclude a post in a communist country.

I managed to gather several impressions from the two years I spent behind the Iron Curtain. The first was that the communist regime had had a remarkable contribution to the development of industry.

However, convinced that an excellent investment was being made, no steps were taken to modernise it. This was also a Poland that was beginning to stumble over the values it held dear, seeking its true path. And lastly, it was a country where family relationships and friendships were still deeply important to the population as a whole.

VI

PARIS

(1971—1974)

Being appointed counsellor to our Paris embassy, the city where I had gained my degree, felt like a homecoming of sorts. Life had an intense quality there. Upon my return, I could not help but notice that many things had changed. The number of theatres had decreased, and cultural life was starting to fade away. The majority of the plays performed were translations of plays written by foreign authors. (Did this demonstrate an openness to all that was foreign or the weak nature of French writing at the time?)

In sports, a brand-new version of the Parc des Princes was built in Paris and inaugurated in 1972. Belgium received high praise in France thanks to Eddy Merckx, who won his fourth Tour de France in 1972 and his fifth in 1974. The *Diables Rouges* were lagging slightly, though they managed to rank in the Group stages of the World Cup. Their fame in France was still very much intact.

France still ranked as one of the top countries in the world when it came to its culinary prowess, but fast food and sugary drinks had managed to take root to a surprising degree in a country so fond of its traditional homemade dishes. The spirit of Édouard Manet's "luncheon on the grass" had been lived out, and a quest for efficiency and speed had become omnipresent. A compromise was reached in the concept of a business lunch held over good food.

I settled into Paris, moving into a flat on the left bank of the Seine near the Pont de l'Alma. The Embassy offices, which had been acquired by my father, were located at Rue de Tilsitt, on the Place de l'Étoile. They were in one of the marshal buildings surrounding the (round) square. I had a view out onto the Arc de Triomphe and, every day at around 6 pm, would hear the *Sonnerie aux Morts*. The desk I was given had previously been my father's.

Home politics in France was far from simple. Since the French Revolution, the country had lived in a state of constitutional instability. If the constitutions brought about as a result of the Revolution were added to those drawn up by the two empires, two monarchical regimes, the Commune, the Vichy regime and five republics, a total of fifteen constitutions had been implemented over two centuries.

This instability was also reflected in everyday life. French parliamentary tradition had always favoured a multiplicity of parties, though they were still grouped into right and left-wing. It seemed that the trademarks of French political life had come about as a result of these contradictory forces.

The first was the inability of the right — which saw itself as the representative of state authority in politics, the economy and culture — to accept the consequences of the French Revolution. Among these, the most important advocated for liberalism, that is to say, bringing an end to the state's tight hold on the economy.

The second was the inability of the leftist workers to accept they had been somewhat defeated in the French Revolution.

The circumstances within which they operated were unclear, creating a significant amount of tension in labour relations. This, in turn, led to frequent striking. Reaching a consensus was seen as a weakness, striking as a strength.

Within the nebula of French power, two influential groups occupied prominent positions: the Jewish community, with its banks (Rothschild, Lazard, etc.) and business; and the Protestant community, which, while discreet, was very present and grouped around established Protestant banks (Hottinger, etc.).

Geographical tensions must also be added into this picture, which is now beginning to come into focus. France is split in half by the Loire.

Populations south of the Loire rejected certain aspects of French life, examples being the 1914—1918 and 1940—1945 wars, which were seen as Northern Wars. Since Napoleon, the South had lived peacefully except for when it had been under German occupation, from late 1942 until the Liberation of France.

Yet another rift must be added to this fundamental divide, this time between Paris and the rest of France. A rift that had been sought since the Fronde. Centralising the country's leadership was a means to avoid it disintegrating. Paris had not only become the location upon which the government was centred, but French, the language, spoken between Paris and Touraine, had also been imposed as a national language. The other languages, Occitan, Flemish, Breton, Walloon, Alsatian German and Savoyard Italian all came to be regarded as regional dialects by the Parisians.

Having feared they would find themselves in a hostile capital since the 1870 Commune, Right-wing governments placed Paris under direct governmental control. The *mairies* (councils) within Paris became mere satellite centres. Civil power was placed in the hands of the Prefect of Paris and the police, who were also charged with maintaining order.

Paris developing into an essential centre for all decision-making quickly led to a problem developing: transport for workers in the city. The government had decided to only build a select number of motorways leading into Paris. Living in Paris itself and avoiding the traffic jams forming in the suburbs therefore became somewhat of a luxury. The lack of accommodation in the city also pushed the price of accommodation up. It was therefore the wealthy population who lived in the centre. Right-wing candidates would always win in these undersized electoral districts.

The suburbs, on the other hand, welcomed lower earners. Paris gradually found itself becoming a right-wing island surrounded by a large red suburb made up of oversized electoral districts. It was at this time that the government reinstalled the Paris Town Hall and Jacques Chirac became the city's first mayor.

France's industrial philosophy dates back to Colbert, who had applied the concept of state-owned companies. The French right has always held this concept dear, even finding itself agreeing with the employed leftists on this point. It was thus due to the influence of both the Anglo-Saxons and the European Commission that France would be asked to change course. The latter would apply every means possible to curb the decisions made by the Commission. The large national companies were privatised, but each would become a shareholder of the other, leaving only a small percentage of the shares on the stock market from the very beginning. The directors of these companies were chosen by the invisible shareholder, i.e. the state.

During my stay in Paris, the French President was Georges Pompidou. While he was Prime Minister under de Gaulle, he implemented the General's key strategies in matters of industrial policy, which were guided by two main ambitions. Firstly, developing all the industries necessary in order to construct a French *Force de Frappe*, with the broad purpose of gaining independence and national grandeur. Then, adapting the French economy to meet the standards set by the country's international competition due to the borders being opened at an accelerated pace, as per the Treaty of Rome and GATT agreements. Georges Pompidou's government would apply this policy by pursuing major industrial projects with a specific focus on launching the Concorde project and implementing a nuclear power sector in the country.

Going on to be elected president in 1969, Pompidou continued this policy, becoming the champion of French industrial development. He prioritised communications, building the high-speed train network (TGV), modernising the telephone and building motorways, including those that can still be seen in the city centre, like those that run parallel to the riverbanks in Paris.

He was also the first post-war president of France to leave physical traces of his presidency set in stone, having transformed the Les Halles district into a centre for contemporary art. The Centre Pompidou, built by Enzo Piano, became its central element. Under his presidency, some rooms of the Élysée Palace were also remodelled in order to accommodate contemporary art.

France dreamed of matching Germany's industrial power. Pompidou painted a picture for his fellow citizens based on the prospect of a society as egalitarian and prosperous as Sweden's, "but with some added sunshine".

It was a substantial project, especially given that 85 percent of French people born in 1945 lived out their entire lives in the village where they were born. Common EEC agricultural policy condemned hundreds of thousands of small farms to be absorbed into larger units. This forced farmers to emigrate to industrial centres. The dramatic expansion of the French economy as a result of this shift led to a dramatic change in the way of life of the French population. It also provided a measure of the revolution that has taken place in the minds of the people.

Pompidou liked to boast about having been raised in the country and his down-to-earth approach. He was also, however, one of the brilliant minds to come out of the great French tradition of "normale sup." (one of the most selective and prestigious higher education institutions in Paris). He was only pro-Europe out of necessity and did not appreciate the supranational aspect of the European structure.

However, like his predecessors — de Gaulle in particular — he understood that the Franco-German alliance and the Treaty of Rome, which created the European community, made up the two main pillars of French policy. Why? The French believed that treaties allowed them to hold the reins of European leadership. Without defying Germany, they believed they had managed to maintain a subordinate relationship with the former. This explains the need they would express from time to time to show off their nuclear force. The Germans had a rather different view...

Shortly before my departure, I found out that Mr Pompidou was seriously ill and, in February 1974, that he would not make it past March. He died on 2 April 1974.

> *A colleague of mine from the Quai d'Orsay very kindly informed me that my private telephone was being tapped (as it had been in Bonn and Warsaw): I felt reassured because it meant the Quai thought the conversations I was having were important...*

While I was in Paris, I was put in charge of political relations. It was not an easy task as we did not always agree with French policy. The Belgians in Paris focussed their attention on our bilateral relations more than on a daily review of French domestic policy. This was also the case for our embassy in The Hague. In Warsaw, the embassy was aware of 90 percent of relations. In Paris, it only had access to a small proportion.

Before getting into our relationships, I would like to point out a few other diplomatic activities.

The first important event was establishing diplomatic relations with the People's Republic of China, which had finally been admitted to the United Nations thanks to the United States. Before I arrived, Robert Rothschild, our Ambassador, had negotiated the agreement with his Chinese colleague. After it had been signed, invitations were exchanged with their respective Embassies.

I followed the implosion of Pakistan on 6 December 1971 closely, watching as it became Pakistan and Bangladesh, as well as Indira Gandhi's anti-Pakistani policy. Once Bangladesh had been recognised as a country by the Belgian government, I was appointed Belgian interlocutor for Bangladeshis. Bangladesh and France had already exchanged diplomats. I set about initiating Belgian-Bangladeshi relations with my Bangladeshi colleague in Paris. The jute problem was the only thing we were concerned about, as it was one of Bangladesh's major exports. Belgium imported the product for most other European countries. The reciprocal opening of embassies between Brussels and Dhaka led to my role being abolished.

At last, I turned my attention to following the evolution of European space cooperation.

Negotiations that did not concern the French government were also taking place in Paris. The most notorious were the secret negotiations entered into between Mr Kissinger, the American Secretary of State, and Mr Le Duc Tho (an important Vietnamese politician), with the aim of ending the war in Vietnam. On 27 January 1973, one year after Nixon's visit to China, the talks between Le Duc Tho and Kissinger led to a cease-fire agreement being signed.

My relations with the Quai d'Orsay and the Élysée were focussed on our bilateral relations.

The first subject tackled was the French approach to European affairs.

French behaviour towards Europe was complex. On the one hand, the government understood how necessary it was, on the other, this Europe had been built despite France's deepest reservations.

The party most opposed to Europe was the French right. Thanks to a poll I managed to get my hands on, I was also able to see that the left-wing Communists were the most fervent Europeans.

Among those who supported Europe, one man was of particular note: Jean Monnet, the tireless pilgrim who knocked on every door and did what he could to put pressure on the governments.

Credit for having persuaded France to join the European adventure goes to Robert Schumann, Minister of Foreign Affairs of France, Alsatian by birth, German-speaking and a devout Catholic.

In France, the idea of Europe came up against the underlying inclinations of the French right.

First of all, Gallicanism, a doctrine based on defending France from the Vatican, was the successor of a middle-of-the-road policy adopted since Louis XIV, which was somewhere between obedience to Rome and Protestantism. These ideals were particularly present within the minds of the traditional right. The policy regarding the construction of a European community would oscillate between accepting the decisions made by Brussels and rejecting them.

Then, the republican tradition, a somewhat vague expression, was used to define the legacy left by the French Revolution. It could be used to refer to a certain form of atheism within the Christian tradition, the acceptance of the ideals of freedom, equality and fraternity, a "certain idea of France", as General de Gaulle would call it, without specifying that it was a way in which to meticulously scrutinise the nation's sovereignty, etc. Like the Gallican tradition, it opposed outside interference and fed easily on the fear of the unknown; the refusal to discern what was happening elsewhere.

Thus, the big, generous idea that was Europe was hindered by disgruntled souls, successors of their countries' pasts.

A country of warriors, France had a superb military tradition. While the army was seen as acting rather than speaking, never expressing its own point of view, several French soldiers have played an important role in history, nonetheless. Since Napoleon, there have been the note-worthy Foch, Joffre, Pétain and de Gaulle. The latter two even ruled the country at one point or another. Others have been men of legend like Lyautcy, de Lattre de Tassigny, Massu, etc.

With this impressive line-up making up its ranks, the country only experienced two major military defeats: the Indochina War and the Algerian War against the FLN. A very important Franco-Anglo-Israeli defeat during the Suez Crisis in 1956 should also be added to this list.

What were the consequences of these defeats?

De Gaulle succeeded in restoring his army's bruised pride by providing it with nuclear weapons. He believed that even his small number of bombs would achieve complete deterrence. Taking into account these different elements, the French government continued building its European policy with Germany. They sought to avoid starting a new war. They were building a European community. The agreement reached with the Germans was thus established in the Treaty of Rome. While France and its other partners accepted the plan to launch into this European adventure, Germany requested that a new reading of the treaties be carried out in the event of a reunification. The request was approved. Germany's position was, therefore, not final.

De Gaulle then implemented two further policies that seemed to contradict each other. The first was the Franco-German treaty, providing for close cooperation between the two countries in many areas. Allowing for numerous ministerial meetings, it was also the engine that drove the European community.

The second was placing nuclear warheads on medium-range rockets in Alsace, that is, beyond the reach of the Iron Curtain. Why was Alsace chosen as the location for this, and not, as the Germans would ask, the former French zone in Germany where the French still had troops? Because France wanted to maintain a position of power over Germany.

However, stuck in an uncomfortable position between a lack of enthusiasm for building this vision of Europe and the conviction that the only way to maintain an alliance with Germany would be precisely to build this supranational European body, France found the freedom it needed, allowing its wildest dreams to come true amidst the international monetary turmoil of 1971—1972.

Seen from Paris, this disruption of the international financial order was interpreted as follows. Like Belgium, France was using a double exchange rate in 1971, using different rates for commercial and financial transactions. This situation was complicated by Nixon's decision to sever the link between the dollar and gold. France, like Belgium, ended up establishing a single exchange rate, agreeing to participate in limiting conversion rates between European currencies. Monetary Europe thus seemed to become more united.

A French merchant bank's research department told me that
the price per ounce of gold should rise from $32 to over $350:
the estimate seemed unrealistic at the time. Time, however,
has attested to the accuracy of the study.

The exchange rate between the United States and France led to intense discussions taking place. In 1965, General de Gaulle had criticised the "exorbitant privilege" granted to the United States and therefore the dollar, the international reserve currency. This was down to the "seigniorage" the United States benefitted from, by forcing foreigners to pay for goods or services worth the equivalent of the dollar reserves they held. The United States was earning about $12 billion a year in seigniorage revenue.

In 1971, the trade deficit, unemployment and inflation caused by the Vietnam War led to the decline of the dollar. President Nixon suspended the convertibility of the American currency into gold. To avoid a further fall in the dollar, Nixon also froze prices and wages for three months.

The Bretton Woods (1944) agreements therefore faced in-depth modifications. To prevent the dollar from devaluing, the Americans asked that European currencies be revalued. Giscard d'Estaing, the French Minister of Finance who had just devalued the Franc, refused, arguing that the general public would not understand. On 17 and 18 December 1971, an agreement was reached by the Group of the Ten at the Smithsonian Institute in Washington, following a Franco-American agreement in the Azores reached on 13 and 14 December. This new agreement created a new dollar standard, in which it was devalued by around ten percent when compared to European currencies. A 2.25 percent trading band was applied to the six States within the Community. The decision followed a choice made by the Benelux States in 1971, displaying yet another example of their pioneering policies. They had established an almost fixed parity between themselves while remaining united with the German Mark.

In March 1972, the French alerted the Americans to the fact that they believed Washington was not carrying out its share of the Smithsonian Institution agreements. Meeting with its European partners, France proposed a more European-focussed monetary policy. It was then that Europe set up the European Monetary System (called the "currency snake"), in an action driven by both the French and the Germans. These came to be known as the Basel Accords: banking regulations that created an area of monetary stability within Europe. The tolerance for currency fluctuations was thus reduced to 1.25 percent each way. (April 1972)

Europe began to define itself in monetary terms when compared to the United States. It was at this time that the French attempted to set up a more international and less supranational European approach to foreign policy.

For Belgium, the stakes were high. Precisely what were we dealing with?

An international Europe would be a Europe where each State retained its sovereignty. These states would then be able to make the joint decision to create a tool that allowed them to set an agreed-upon pace at which to develop their foreign policy. In other words, nothing would prevent the French and the Germans, and even the Italians, from implementing a policy that had been agreed upon with the other states. This Europe was disadvantageous to the EEC's three smallest states: the three contained within Benelux.

A supranational Europe entrusted a Commission with the role of proposing policies and executing them once they had been unanimously approved (or approved by a qualified majority of its members). These decisions were then binding for the six members of the EEC, even if the decision had not been made unanimously. In the event of this decision being infringed upon, the country in question would then be brought before a Court of Justice. This Europe restricted, eliminated, even, traditional sovereign rights.

The second point that interested us was the way in which the concept of foreign policy was defined. The Quai d'Orsay, that is, the Ministry of Foreign Affairs, favoured the international route over the supranational route, considering that the problems relating to dollar / European currency relations were unconnected to the Treaty of Rome. I reread the Treaty of Rome carefully and was unable to detect measures relating to either coordinating foreign policy or monetary policy.

No one questioned the exclusive competence of the Commission in matters of foreign trade. It was, therefore, within this framework that the Americans requested that customs tariffs be lowered and freedom of access to the European market was discussed for American products.

I asked whether common agricultural policy was also a part of this international cooperation. The response I received was evasive, though it was not a firm "no". France had no interest in abolishing common agricultural policy, which it found was largely beneficial to the country. Euro-American agricultural relations, however, had been poisoned by mutual accusations levelled over the subsidies granted to farmers. Allowing the Americans to negotiate with each state independently would result in policies in line with those adopted in the weakest of the six European states. This was unlikely to benefit France.

These conversations led me to believe that the French were seeking to squeeze the Treaty of Rome into a very tight corset. This would allow them to deal with as many areas as possible under the terms applied to international cooperation.

However, the need for cooperation started to become apparent from 1970—1971 onwards. The first two areas subject to closer consultations were the Middle East and the OSCE (Organisation for Security and Cooperation in Europe).

The idea was far from new. In 1961, de Gaulle had instructed Christian Fouchet to design a project. The "Fouchet plans" of 1961 and 1962 proposed a confederal, rather than supranational, model of political cooperation between the Six. The Belgians, who were backed up by the Dutch, rejected the plan (17 April 1962), because it conflicted with the European defence plan contained within the Atlantic Alliance.

In 1970, the Six adopted the Davignon Plan, which was focussed on the possibilities and conditions of cooperation between the countries, relating to their foreign policy. It provided for half-yearly ministerial meetings held before the Commission.

Following this report, Harmel would reflect on the possibility of growing and deepening European communities. In May 1972, Belgium formulated its ideas in London, then in Paris. What did the country recommend? Embedding the Economic and Monetary union, scientific and technological policy and defence and foreign policy into the European Community. Refusing to split the Council. Limiting the duration of the presidency held by each member state to one year. Defining the legal personality Europe would adopt as a confederation. The Belgians would have liked a federation but knew its partners would refuse to accept the term. Monthly meetings held between the Foreign Ministers in order to provide the Director-Generals for Policy with directives, in close collaboration with the Commission.

The talks held in London went well. The British opposed the French idea of a political secretariat in Paris.

The discussions held in Paris were much less positive. In October 1971, the Quai offered me a permanent Secretariat, which would potentially be established in Brussels along the lines of the Fouchet plans. This permanent secretariat would have been responsible for coordinating the foreign policy of the member states.

Pompidou suggested to the Germans that this secretariat be founded in Paris so that the French language would take precedence.

In addition, Mr Pompidou sought to strengthen his position within Europe by calling a referendum on the Treaty of Brussels of 22 January 1972, allowing four new members to join the European Community: Great Britain, Ireland, Denmark and Norway. 61 percent of voters voted in favour.

It was at this time that Gaston Eyskens and Pierre Harmel met with Mr Pompidou (5 June 1972). I was responsible for setting the visit up. The main subject to be discussed was European cooperation in foreign policy and the French proposal for a political secretariat.

I got in touch with the Élysée and the Quai d'Orsay. We needed this political secretariat in Paris. "All it will be is a secretariat filled with translators and typists. If you want, we could allow Mr Davignon to run it". The proposed body did not include members of the Commission and was deliberately placed outside the supranational sphere of the Treaty of Rome.

As I dug further, I noted that foreign policy was referred to in its broadest sense. The Commission would continue to deal with "current matters" following the procedures set out in the Treaty of Rome. France saw no reason why it should add to the powers granted to the Commission any further.

During the lunch held for our delegation, Pompidou expressed an interest in Belgium's proposals for economic and social union. He said he was ready to continue cooperating in diplomatic matters despite the recent negative attempts that had taken place concerning the Middle East. He advocated for European independence from the United States and establishing the political secretariat in Paris. He found the British to be unsupportive but welcomed the positions taken by the Danes and the Irish. He proposed that economic and monetary cooperation, which were considered to be external to the Treaty of Rome, should be established in Basel, the international financial centre and seat of the Bank for International Settlements, which would also make it possible to include Switzerland.

The Belgian Ministers, who wanted these powers to be assigned to the Commission specifically, replied that they did not share France's views.

After lunch, Mr Pompidou took on a more threatening tone as he announced that a Summit Conference for enlargement could not be held if important results could not be obtained.

Eyskens replied that he did not understand why the objectives rested so heavily on the location of an institution. He asked that the meeting of heads of state or government, which was to take place in Paris, remove the ambiguities in order to allow the Community to remain the privileged centre of European economic integration.

On the day prior to the meeting of heads of state or government, held on 19 October 1972, the Belgians met the Dutch and Luxemburgers: they suggested presenting the idea of a European confederation. The Luxemburgers agreed. The idea of the European Community veering away from its American ties concerned the Dutch, who preferred the idea of a federation but knew that by requesting one, they would be undermining the very idea. Having been approached by the Belgians, Pompidou suggested the idea of a Union, as "it does not mean anything". At the Paris Summit on the enlargement of the EEC, the chair, Pompidou himself, put forward the concept of a union. The Belgian delegation had been provided with a report on the future of the European Union by the end of 1975.

Belgium was made responsible for revising the first Davignon plan, which led to the second Davignon plan being created, which was then adopted on 23 July 1973. The proposals gathered within these plans became the first foundations of the European Union's Common Foreign and Security Policy.

> *In practice, a special telex network, Coreu, had been created between the Ministries of Foreign Affairs of the member countries and the Commission. An official was appointed in each Ministry of Foreign Affairs to bear the title of European correspondent. They would be responsible for providing the other European correspondents with correct information. The Coreau network would thus relay information about each interview held between a member state and any third state. The Director-Generals of Policy and a member of the Commission had monthly meetings. The heads of departments met as necessary. My workload at the embassy got considerably lighter as a result, as I no longer had to ensure information was exchanged on our policies. My contacts at the Quai told me they had either met with or informed their counterparts in other departments; they did not need to be informed a second time. Embassies in the member countries thus followed policy and, when relevant, commented on it, through the Coreu.*

As for monetary policy, it had largely been integrated into supranational bodies, which enabled the Euro to be created.

Belgian diplomacy was therefore able to prevent common foreign policy and monetary policy from falling into the realm of pure intergovernmental cooperation. Belgium also added a new facet to the latent tension building within Europe between the big countries and the other powers. The former had reluctantly agreed to give up their autonomy when it came to international relations. The latter, quite the opposite, had begun to participate in the decisions made by the big European powers.

Belgium, having experienced international influence at the end of the 19th century thanks to the expansion policy adopted by King Leopold II, was re-establishing the presence it had once held in distant countries. It was out of the question for Belgium to abandon its European policy, one that resolutely placed international relations in the supranational sphere — where joint decisions were taken in an arena in which it sat in one of the armchairs — in order to go back to an international cooperation policy where it was perched on a white wooden stool.

This fundamental point at which the Belgian and French views diverged, demonstrates, once again, this curious European theorem: for Europe to move forwards, it would be necessary for a German-French understanding to be reached. It would, however, freeze in the event of any friction between France and Belgium, as had been the case back in the days of the European Defence Community. My German colleague, who I kept up to date with developments, turned to me one day and said "you Belgians, you can afford to contradict the French because of your shared language and recent history. We cannot." The British would soon join the Union and were little inclined to supranationality, remaining cautiously outside this dispute. The Italians followed us Belgians, but at a distance.

The Conference of heads of state and government, which decided on whether the United Kingdom, Ireland and Denmark would be allowed into the EEC, was an important step in the development of a European community. The EEC still only had six members. The pact entered into by the first six members was fundamental: it was a question of creating a structure that could prevent a new war from breaking out. The presence of both France and Germany was therefore essential to establishing the treaties that led to the creation of the European Economic Community.

New members were more interested in benefitting from the economic and financial advantages provided by the European Community and, incidentally, from the political aura emerging from it.

France reluctantly approved British membership. The person most opposed to them joining was Charles de Gaulle. His opinion was that the United Kingdom had not felt what it was like to be occupied or faced all the consequences of such an event; it had not seen its social fabric torn and its economy transformed. In addition, de Gaulle saw Britain as the US's Trojan horse within the EEC. De Gaulle's opinion was reinforced by the Bermuda Agreement of December 1962, through which President Kennedy gave the British Polaris missiles. The British accepted them, giving the other European nations no warning whatsoever.

Belgium, a country with close ties to Britain, was in favour of the United Kingdom joining the EEC. The conference, the conclusions of which were agreed upon in advance, was interesting to observe. Chancellor Brandt slept through it, Jens Otto Krag, the Prime Minister of Denmark, did not understand a word of either French or English, and the French busied themselves getting down to business.

Britain, Ireland and Denmark joining the Union, and Norway voting against joining also shed light on old reflexes that had been visible back when religions held more significance. Apart from the six founding countries, all the other countries brought their religious past with them. Thus, the Catholic countries of Ireland, Austria, Spain, Portugal, Poland, Lithuania, the Czech Republic and Hungary, who were all accustomed to an external authority sitting in Rome, were quick to accept a new authority installed in Brussels. The British, who founded the Church of England in order to counter Rome's authority, found it difficult to accept a power that was in Brussels. The Scandinavians and the two northern Baltic states, which also had their own national churches, were no more inclined to grant the Commission important powers. With Greece joining the union, a very old rift would reveal itself once again; one that dates back to a quarrel between Rome and Byzantium. Islamic countries (Albania, Turkey) would also see their Islamic culture countered.

The second important point in our relations was linked to the French defence doctrine.

I had several conversations at the Department of National Defence about the subject.

The basic premise was de Gaulle's decision to create a nuclear force. One that was laughable when compared to the American and Soviet arsenals, but comparable to the British force. The French believed that a few bombs would dissuade any army. France also had nuclear submarines, which were only able to leave their base in Brest at high tide if they wanted to do so while staying below the waterline.

From 1939 to 1972, France was at war. During the Second World War, France spoke through two voices: Marshal Pétain's — a General officer in charge of the daily management of France; and de Gaulle's — the architect of the alliance between France and the Allies, mainly concerning Britain and the US. It was in the wake of this alliance that France agreed to sign the Washington Treaty, also known as the North Atlantic Treaty.

France, however, later withdrew from the Treaty's Organisation (NATO) because it wanted to maintain its freedom to act. France's withdrawal, a decision made by de Gaulle, was based on the premise that the US needed to keep Europe in its economic and military orbit. It was therefore in their interest to ensure Europe was defended either way.

Europe is, indeed, the US's only possible ally thanks to its technological potential, its human capital and its financial means.

France could thus leave the Treaty Organisation with impunity, as it was sure the United States would intervene in the event of any Soviet aggression. This position brought the additional advantage of allowing the French army to be at the disposal of the government in the event that French interests were infringed upon.

I tried to better understand this subject in order to examine the possibility of cooperating more effectively with the French. In April 1972, the French Department of National Defence ruled that the United Kingdom, which was linked to the United States through the Bermuda nuclear cooperation agreements, could not participate in a common European defence. The Department of National Defence was, however, prepared to accept a joint defence proposal. All they received were suggestions that they re-join NATO. France was thus ready to participate in the Bermuda agreements. The Anglo-Saxons, however, did not trust the French.

What were Belgium's interests? After the neutrality policy adopted by the Belgian governments before 1940 had been abandoned, Belgium was keen to see tensions reduced between their two former enemies. Once the European Defence Community (EDC) failed, Belgium trusted American troops to keep the peace between the allies of the Washington Treaty.

The purpose of my visits to the Department of National Defence was to examine the possibilities available for better collaboration between European armies. A first stage could have been establishing a few regiments with an initial military staff. We were still nowhere near the idea of the EDC...

An analysis of the French position led me to conclude that it was no longer as adamant in its refusal to cooperate with Germany and the Benelux states. It would, however, take several years for the Eurocorps, the army corps created in 1992—1995, of 60,000 soldiers trained by France, Germany, Belgium, Spain and Luxembourg, to be established.

In addition to these talks, I was also able to hold several meetings with an American, Mr Stone. He had numerous contacts in French intellectual circles. He seemed to me to be the long arm of Washington in the country. We talked one-on-one, our conversations focusing on Euro-American and Franco-American relations. For the Americans, these were all taking place against the backdrop of the disastrous end to the Vietnam War, American support of the Israelis during the Yom Kippur War (October 1973) and the Watergate scandal. Mr Stone was disappointed in Europe, asking the United States to defend it without providing any substantial financial involvement. France was particularly vindictive.

"Turn the tide," I told him, "suggest that the United States cut itself off from Europe and see what happens." A few weeks later, the Americans made it clear that they could disengage from Europe. European voices immediately spoke up, demanding that American troops stay in Europe. Nixon met Pompidou in Helsinki in June 1973, on the side-lines of the CSCE conference. The former told the latter that the American Congress was neo-isolationist. Pompidou assured him of how important he considered the American military presence in Europe to be. Trust was therefore rebuilt in both the political and military fields. In economic relations, the Americans were beginning to tighten up on their position, now faced with a Europe that was becoming more powerful.

It's worth adding here that while this meeting was taking place in Helsinki, the Portuguese were holding their Carnation Revolution, rising up against the regime put in place by the late Salazar with the aim of proclaiming a Socialist Republic. Soviet ships set sail towards Porto and Lisbon. Back in Helsinki, Nixon intervened firmly with Brezhnev, threatening him, it seems, to send ships to Polish coastlines. The red adventure the Portuguese had set out on, thus came to an end. It served to show the French where the limits of American tolerance lay in the context of the Cold War.

The third important aspect of French foreign policy was its approach to the Middle East.

Once the Evian Accords ended the Algerian war, the French put a damper on the traditionally good Franco-Israeli relations. France officially played the Arab card and, as a result, emerged from Algeria with an important oil and gas contract with the country remaining intact.

The position taken by the French remained ambiguous. Pompidou, who had fond memories of having worked at the Rothschild bank, had a particular fondness for Israel. The Quai d'Orsay was reluctant to maintain good relations with Tel Aviv. Military ships sold to Israel, but kidnapped in Brest, disappeared mysteriously one night. The French Navy did not react.

In February 1972, the French agreed to buy the Mirage jets sold to Israel, but that had been embargoed. Incidentally, I found out that it would be Dassault Belgium that would deliver the spare parts needed for the Mirages already in Israel. Neither Paris nor Tel Aviv mentioned this agreement.

> *I greeted Mr Ben Nathan, the Israeli Ambassador, at the presentation of New Year's greetings at the Élysée Palace: Israeli sailors had just received a delivery, right under the noses and beards of the French navy, of the Escorteurs they had bought and paid for, but that had been under French embargo. Ben Nathan showed me his locker room ticket: no. 007...*

In the energy sector, cards were starting to be redistributed. In 1971, the British removed their troops from the Gulf region. The Shah of Iran reacted by declaring that Iran would keep the Gulf secure. Meanwhile, a wave of nationalisations swept through the oil companies in Kuwait, Venezuela, Saudi Arabia, Iran, etc.

In 1971, new agreements were signed, providing increased revenue for oil-producing states. The old order was over, and the oil-producing countries demonstrated that they were capable of understanding and cooperating in controlling production, as well as driving up the prices.

In mid-September 1973, the OPEC countries met in Vienna. These agreements were dead letters to them. They requested that new negotiations be entered into with the oil companies.

On 6 October 1973, when negotiations were about to start, Egypt and Syria launched the so-called Yom Kippur War, or October War, against Israel. On 12 October, the OPEC requested that the price of oil be doubled. On 14, negotiations were broken off with the oil companies as they considered the conditions to be unreasonable. On 15, Israel brought an end to the Egyptian invasion of Sinai.

On 16, the Arab and Iranian ministers, who had since returned from Vienna, met in Kuwait and decided to increase the price of oil by 70 percent, placing it at $5.11 per barrel. This was the first time producer countries had set their prices alone.

On 17 October, once the Iranian Minister had departed, the Arab

Ministers decided to reduce oil production by five percent per month and to establish an embargo against the United States and the other countries that had helped Israel (the Netherlands, then Portugal, South Africa and Rhodesia). The French, who had only just signed the Evian Accords with Algeria, were delighted not to be placed on the list of countries that supported Israel.

While Arab production of oil reached 20.8 million bbl/d in October 1973, in December, it had dropped to 15.8 million bbl/d. Other producing countries, including Iran, seized the opportunity to increase their production. Prices rose to $ 17/bbl/d in December and even as high as $ 22.60/bbl/d in some contracts. The embargo had important psychological effects on both the West and Japan, the economic progress of the 1960s seeming to weaken.

The anti-Anglo-American feelings harboured by the French were gaining strength, aided by the usual French mistrust and long-fuelled by the country having been cut off from the Middle Eastern oil industry, the lack of support from the Americans during the Algerian War and the American veto during the Suez Crisis. It is worth noting that petroleum was the only source of energy not controlled by the EEC.

The Japanese seized the chance to break away from American policy for the first time, by standing with the Arab nations.

The West reacted by holding an Energy Conference in Washington. France was the only country that refused to attend, thus distancing itself from its European partners. It did not want to aggravate the Arab countries, especially not Algeria. The conference led to the International Energy Agency being created as a part of the OECD. Its objectives were to ensure non-discrimination between oil consuming countries, that oil was always stockpiled, etc.

Only a few short months later, the West would be aiding the reign of OPEC (Organisation of the Petroleum Exporting Countries), an organisation made up of the Arab oil-producing countries, Iran, Venezuela, Indonesia, Nigeria, Ecuador and Gabon.

In 1973 the OPEC supplied 65 percent of the oil extracted from the free world (thus excluding the USSR, Romania and China from these figures).

Quadrupling prices allowed the oil-exporting countries to see their revenues rise from $23 billion in 1972 to a $140 billion in 1977. These increased prices resulted in a depression in the western countries (the USA's GNP dropped by six percent between 1973 and 1975). The West came to the realisation that the OPEC countries, drunk with their new power, could interfere in the Cold War by picking a side.

France would later play the Islamist card in Iran by hosting Imam Khomeini. It hoped to be rewarded with good oil contracts in Iran, but to no avail.

France's anti-Anglo-Saxon policy was further extended through its involvement in the Malta case.

The archipelago of Malta is located halfway between Sicily and Tunisia and controls the passageway between the eastern and western Mediterranean. It is therefore the Mediterranean's central lock. Malta has long been under British rule. Since the island gained independence in 1964, the British and NATO's Allied Forces Southern Europe's Naval Force had retained a military base there.

Malta's new government sought to sever ties in February 1972. NATO agreed, its naval command retreating to Naples. Negotiations on the British base, conversely, had become bogged down. While at the Quai, I heard that France was secretly considering taking over from the British and setting up a military base in Malta. I spoke to my British colleague, who had been left in the dark about such matters. The British intervened the next day, and the case was buried, much to the discontent of the Quai d'Orsay. On 26 March 1972, a seven-year agreement allowed British forces to remain at their base. And so it was that this event successfully avoided becoming yet another hindrance to Franco-British relations.

In Africa, the last important element of French foreign policy, de Gaulle succeeded in retaining a certain position of strength in the French sub-Saharan colonies once their independence had been granted. The French troops that remained in the countries were kept on-hand to intervene at the request of the local government. He created the CFA franc regions, linked to the French franc, guaranteeing monetary stability while forcing all transactions with foreign countries to be carried out via the Banque de France. I studied this mechanism, one that hindered our exports to these countries.

Brussels was firmly opposed to any European cooperation, much less belgo-french, in sub-Saharan Africa, particularly when it came to Zaire, Rwanda and Burundi. I got the impression the French were not actively pursuing such relations.

In culture and tourism, the French used the Agency for Cultural and Technical Cooperation (ACCT) which brought France, Belgium, Canada and French-speaking Sub-Saharan African countries together. The Agency invested in tourism and education, mainly in French-speaking Africa. It was one of the instruments the French government used to maintain its stranglehold on its former colonies, as, out of the three western countries, it was the only one providing school materials and investing in cost-shared tourism.

While attending an ACCT meeting in May 1972, I noted that we were paying out but seeing very little in return. I suggested that a few changes be made, towards a more realistic policy. Brussels followed my lead, thereafter creating leadership positions and allowing us to participate directly in French-speaking Africa's cultural development. This move was rendered all the more important by several African delegations approaching me, asking me to counterbalance the imperialist position France had granted itself. Canada shared our views.

During my stay, I was taken to meet French politicians. The most accessible were the leftists in the opposition. A Lecanuet was difficult to connect with; a Soustelle far easier. The most interesting and chattiest person present was Duclos, the Communist Party's second in command. He did not allow what he lacked in height to hold him back from being an excellent speaker and a politician of great stature. I spent three hours in his office, at the Communist Party headquarters located in a bunker on Place du Colonel Fabian. My having lived in Poland and my experience of the communist system immediately elevated the conversation to another level. At one point, the conversation even turned to the party's finances and the financial loss caused by their newspaper L'Humanité. Even if we have to give it up, he said, it would be of no matter, as our real daily newspaper is Le Monde – a communist in neutral clothing.

My time in Paris allowed me to see the true face of French diplomacy in all its light and shadow. A face lined with history. While it managed to achieve exceptional industrial and technological success, it was unable to detach itself from the hazy ideas held dear by its politicians (a certain vision of France, those who had died in combat so that France could live on, etc.). It was a very significant handicap which prevented it from playing a much more important role, as any initiative taken by French diplomacy would raise suspicions due to it seeming to be at odds with the spirit of the age.

I turned the page, bringing an end to my time in France and finding myself in Iran.

VII

TEHRAN

(1974)

"Whether one thinks of Iran as Eden or Garden, The smell of musk abounds there from friend and companion."

Ferdowsi

Having left Paris, I was appointed counsellor to Tehran, a new global centre of power thanks to the rise in oil prices. This time spent in Iran allowed the Orient of my childhood to surface once again, after the castration it had suffered from the rational teachings of Europe and the puritanism of the spheres I had moved in. To me, Islam seemed to be a simple, tolerant religion with a theology as sophisticated as that of Judaism or Christianity. Again, I let my intuition guide me, only then explaining my ideas with Cartesian reasoning so my compatriots could accept them. I reread Xenophon and came to the realisation that mentalities had barely changed at all.

The country was stunning. I got the chance to explore it from top to bottom, roaming through Isfahan and Shiraz. It was unfortunate that I was unable to see it all. The semi-arid expanses were striking and the small villages, with their adobe mosques, charming. Throughout the country, as soon as they had access to any water, however little, the Iranians could be seen farming their land.

The air was very dry in Tehran; the city surrounded by desert. Suffice to say that everything was covered in sand. To protect themselves from it, many women could be seen wearing a chador. In some regions, the traditional garments were brightly coloured scarves worn to protect the heads of both men and women.

Tehran was built up against the mountains, the most affluent neighbourhoods sprawling at their feet. It was there that I found my accommodation, first in a hotel, then in a small apartment.

In the summer, I went climbing in the mountains and stopped in a tchaikana. These were places where one would lie down on low tables to drink tea or eat a chelow kebab. The tables had been placed in a nearby mountain stream. When we felt we were getting too hot, we would dunk our hands and feet in the cold water.

The country fascinated me immediately. I committed to trying to understand it. Unfortunately, the length of my stay in Iran did not allow me to do so thoroughly.

Like China, India, Japan and Egypt, Iranian history stretches back several millennia and is marked by the reigns of emperors and famous warriors such as Cyrus, Darius and Xerxes. The country also has a long history of relations with the great Asian empires. For the past century, the country has focussed its energy on building relations westwards. Iran has, nonetheless, managed to remain an inward-looking empire. It was rare for Iranians to marry foreign nationals, apart from people within a particular section of the bourgeoisie that was able to travel. Historically, Iran has acted as a border, preventing Buddhism from spreading further West, and Christianity further East.

This border was formed by an ancient Iranian religion, Mazdayasna, which then became Zoroastrianism (in approximately 1000 BC). Mazdayasna worship was safeguarded by the self-appointed Magi tribe. The religion even lured Saint Augustine in, before he became a Christian. The Iranian people were not very religious and considered Islam to be a religion forced upon them by Arabic weaponry from as far back as 642. Shia Islam bears traces of the ancient Zoroastrian religion to this day.

A factor considered more fundamental to the country's identity than religion is its status as an Indo-European country, the expansion of Shia Islam having been primarily due to the population's desire to oppose the Sunni Caliphate of Constantinople.

Islam set the pace to which life was lived. The precepts of the religion were the yarn from which the fabric of the country was woven.

> *After Muhammad's death in 632, Ali, his son-in-law, and Hussein, Ali's son who was married to a Persian princess of the ancient Sassanid dynasty, were murdered. The Iranians, Shiites out of loyalty to Ali and Hussein, firmly attached their religion to Persia's glorious past. They opposed the Arabs, who remained Sunnis.*

Because of this double heritage, the Iranians use both the (Islamic) lunar calendar and the (Zoroastrian) solar calendar.

The Zoroastrian feast of Nowruz (New Year) overlaps with the spring equinox (usually 21 March). A fire festival called "Chaharshanbe Suri" falls on the evening of the last Tuesday of the year. Bonfires were lit in each square, and the population would shout as they took turns jumping over the fire. The New Year was also a time in which houses were cleaned thoroughly, from top to bottom. On Nowruz itself, seven items whose names begin with an S were placed on a tray: sabzeh, senjed, sibe, serke, sumac, sir and samanu. In a mixing of traditions, a Quran would also be added, as well as poems written by Hafez and a bowl of fresh cream. On the thirteenth day, the family would have a picnic. The day would be brought to an end with dancing. Iran would come to a standstill for a celebration that lasted as long as a fortnight.

The Iranians were also steeped in the verses of the Rubaiyat by mathematician and poet Omar Khayyâm (1040—1125). Expressing his cynical hedonism in the 11th century, he also verbalised the futility of all human desires in the face of inevitable death and his confusion before a God who had abandoned mankind in a world it did not want. These are the reasons behind the relatively moderate way in which the Iranian clergy condemned the poet.

Renounce, renounce everything in this world: wealth, power, honour.

Veer the steps you take away from any path that will not lead you to the tavern.

Ask for nothing, want for nothing — except for wine, songs, music, love!

A noble, handsome young man, seize a skin, grab a cup. Drink!

But beware! Do not be frivolous; take care with what you say ...

Drink golden wine! It is the only rest for the mind, incomparable balm for the injured heart.

If everywhere you go, you are hunted down by a pack of sorrows, and you feel a torrent of sadness is ready to swallow you whole, cling fearlessly to delicious golden wine. It is the only way you'll save yourself.

Omar Khayyam

In 1781, Agha Mohammad Shah rose to power and founded the Qajar dynasty. The most illustrious members of the dynasty were Fath-Ali Shah, who made great leaps in the areas of the Arts and Humanities, and Nasser al-Din Shah, who gave rise to the first state reforms. Ahmad Shah, the seventh Qajar Shah, left Persia for Europe. In 1925, Reza Khan became king under the name of Reza Shah and founded the short-lived Pahlavi dynasty. He was forced to give his throne up to his son, Mohammad Reza Shah.

One-third of the population was Turkish speaking, descended from the Turkestan warriors who conquered Persia in the wake of Genghis Khan and his successors. Besides this important minority, several other rebellious tribes also called the country home: the Qashqai people, the Kurds (six to eight million), the Baloch tribe, the Bakhtiari people, the Turkmens, the Azeris, the Arabs, etc. This diversity made the country difficult to govern, requiring a substantial authority to oppose centrifugal forces. The use of torture dissuaded the population from speaking out.

Iran's traditional economic forces were the clergy, the bazaar and agriculture.

The clergy followed Shia practices. The religious centre of this branch of Islam is in Karbala, Iraq, and is structured into a hierarchy (unlike the Sunnis). This framework allowed for a standardisation of its doctrine. When he rose to power, Reza Shah removed the ability to enact justice and education from the clergy, establishing control over the revenue received from religious property. He did not, however, secularise the state in the same way as Atatürk had done.

> *The mullahs, religious men who made up the ranks of the lower clergy, were little respected and the stories of the brave mullah Nasr Eddin brought joy to all. Listening to these tales was enlightening, as they illustrated the contempt in which the Iranians held their clergy.*
>
> *Examples include:*
> *- Mullah, have you seen the men queuing up outside your wife's house? You cannot allow that; you will have to divorce her.*
> *- Why? To then queue up with the others?*
> *Another example: the mullah's daughter complains to her father that her husband has beaten her. Nasr Eddin beats her and tells her to tell her husband that the next time he beats the Mullah's daughter, Nasr Eddin will beat the man's wife.*

The bazari, or businesspeople, made up a very old and influential institution. Generally grouped into centres (bazaars), the men's economic activities were all interlinked: from sheep to carpets and butchers, etc. They remained connected to each other via a system that dated back over a thousand years, keeping them up to date at all times. Suffice to say that, as a power, they were important enough to be able to oppose the government. The bazari did not appreciate a new social class forming thanks to the oil industry, one that was favoured by the shah.

Agriculture and animal husbandry were practices that had traditionally been carried out by wealthy families (who owned "villages") and the clergy. These wealthy landowners mastered the practice of irrigation. Rivers provided half of the water required; the rest came from either wells or a system of underground pipes that dated back thousands of years: qanats.

The landowner would appoint members of the village to clean the qanats and wells. Inspired by UN agencies within the framework of the "White Revolution", in 1963 Mohammad Reza Shah decided to implement an agrarian reform, which led to him distributing the land among the peasants. This disadvantaged population did not have the means with which to buy seeds, tools or machines. Following a suggestion from the UN, the shah created cooperatives. Managed by peasants, these operated very poorly. Incompetence and corruption were widespread, resulting in famine. Iran imported certain foodstuffs, such as rice. Along with those implemented as a result of the White Revolution, these measures led to a deep feeling of discontent forming among the population. Khomeini was deported to Iraq after a hate speech was made against the shah.

As part of the White Revolution, Mohammad Reza Shah ultimately began promoting education, providing a system of education for all. This led to many schools and several universities being founded, though the standard of education provided was often poor. When it came to subjects like medicine and physics/chemistry, no teaching materials were used whatsoever as the teachers did not know how to use them.

Concerned by the versatility of the students, the government had the secret police, the Savak, watch them closely. Students, however, no longer found this acceptable and rioted. The shah believed these students to be communists, executing them as a result (an average of three to four per week). The country's academics rebelled further, and the authorities managed to close universities. Those affected by these closures were mostly provincial universities. The University of Tehran, well-known to all the foreigners in the country, who mainly lived in Tehran, was forced to participate in the halo of democracy with which the shah pretended to surround himself.

A generalised lack of organisation and the corruption present in the country made it difficult to practise a trade. Many intellectuals, having studied in Europe or the United States, made their way back to their home countries. What they faced upon their return was an absence of assistants and a requirement to pay sizeable bribes. Junior staff tended to be poorly trained.

All this unrest only increased the peoples' hatred for the shah. The intellectuals who were able to, went abroad. The pungent smell of the end of a reign began to form.

I was invited to a traditional wedding. It was held in the
bride's house. A bride's betrothed is not meant to know who
his future wife will be. He finds out by walking into a room,
where he sees his bride for the first time as a reflection in a
mirror. This is Persian symbolism. The sun shines too brightly,
so we have to look at its reflection, the moon, instead. The sun
is equated to the face of the betrothed. It goes without saying
that this ritual was no longer practised and that the couple
who were to be married were very well acquainted.

Iran's culinary tradition dated back several centuries. It was little-known and delicious. Vegetarian-inspired Persian Zoroastrian food (following the Avicenna tradition) where cold takes energy away, and hot brings energy, was combined with lamb dishes brought by Islam. Cooking was regarded as an evil skill. The population was strictly prohibited from writing cookbooks, and it was not until 1921 that the first cookbook was published. The entirety of culinary arts was based on the theory of moods, of which there were four. These moods corresponded to the four humours: blood/hot, phlegm/cold, black bile/dry, yellow bile/wet.

The country's most popular dish was chelow kebab and abgoosht. Wealthy families filled their tables with an array of delicious dishes.

As for sport, football was the most popular. A stunning stadium had been built in Tehran. To please the powerful Armenian minority, the government had built them an additional stadium.

In 1974, one subject took precedence over all others: the rising cost of oil.

The history of oil in Iran was interlaced with the country's recent evolution, having been subjected to Russian then Soviet, English, and later American influence. Oil, alongside the forces of the clergy and the bazaar, participated in bringing together the funds that would eventually lead the country to evolve.

The story dates back to 1901 with the discovery of oil. Mozaffaredin Shah granted d'Arcy a concession. Oil was of immediate interest to the British and the Russians, both of whom set out to appropriate it.

After the First World War, the British, who were concerned about Soviet influence in the country, sought to gain absolute control. Ahmad

Shah, the last Qajar sovereign, opposed this move. It was at this time that Reza Khan rose to power, becoming shah.

The new monarch strove to modernise his country. Mustafa Kemal's success in Turkey fascinated him. The former failed, however, to impose the same reforms in Iran.

Furious at the drop in income due to the Great Depression, on 26 November 1932, Reza Pahlavi abrogated the concession agreement made to d'Arcy in 1901. A new concession agreement was signed in 1933; one that was more favourable to Iran.

Both Soviet and British forces occupied Iran during World War II (late August 1941). They believed Reza Shah had pro-German inclinations and forced him to abdicate in favour of his young son, Mohammad Reza Pahlavi.

At the end of the war, the Soviets organised a rebellion in the province of Azerbaijan, which had constituted itself as an independent state (November 1945). Soviet troops withdrew in April 1946, and, in June 1946, Azerbaijan was reinstated as part of Iran.

Although these events were not altogether very recent, they still exerted a significant amount of influence on politics in Iran.

Between 1945 and 1950, the Anglo-Iranian Oil Co. registered a profit of £250 million and only paid Iran £90 million in royalties. While a latent xenophobic, particularly Anglophobic, tension could certainly be felt in the country, the situation was becoming steadily less and less stable. Mohammad Mosaddegh, a member of the former Persian imperial family, became Prime Minister in 1951. On 1 May 1951, he nationalised the Anglo-Iranian Oil co.

The British reacted by putting "Plan Y" together, a plan that involved a non-military intervention at the Abadan refineries. The Americans opposed, fearing Soviet intervention. To strengthen their hand in negotiations, the British declared an embargo on Iranian oil. Henri Rolin, a professor at the Free University of Brussels, became Iran's legal representative (and then had a street named after him in the centre of Tehran).

The British were thrown out of the Abadan refineries in September 1951. Mohammad Reza Shah fled to Rome in early August 1953. At the end of August 1953, following demonstrations in Tehran (paid for by the Americans), Mosaddegh resigned, and the shah returned from Rome with the promise of American aid worth $45,000,000. It was the beginning of absolute monarchical power and American influence over the country.

As payment for the part they had played in returning the shah, the Americans received a significant share in the production of oil. The British were forced to accept the establishment of an Anglo-American consortium. An elaborate contract was being drawn up in which Iran, via its new National Iranian Oil Company (NIOC), owned the subsoil. The NIOC entrusted the Anglo-American consortium to extract the oil, further entrusting the consortium with refining it and selling it abroad. The NIOC then sold it back to Iran.

In 1971, the British removed their troops from the Gulf region. Mohammad Reza Shah reacted by declaring that Iran would now become the guardian of the Gulf, backed by the Americans.

Then came the 1973—1974 crisis, during which the Iranians and Arabs agreed to raise the price of oil.

> *Nevertheless, the Iranian government went even further with its reasoning. It did not want to be dependent on oil. After having used a research reactor as part of the American "Atom for Peace" program and having become a member of the Treaty on the Non-Proliferation of Nuclear Weapons in 1970, the shah sought to develop nuclear energy from 1974 onwards. Belgium was called upon but was not selected, as it was the Germans who received the order.*

The cartel of OPEC producers put the West's economy in jeopardy without firing a single shot. The West feared an even more significant fall in its economy and the USSR invading the OPEC-member Muslim countries in force.

The remedy? Funding the Islamists in the oil-producing countries. The fervent Islamists opposed communist Marxism and the regimes already in place. Helping them was seen as a way in which to weaken governments, who would thus no longer dare to take important measures.

1974 Iran was interesting to observe.

With each month of 1974 that went by, millions more came pouring into the budget. What could be done with it? Attention was turned to grandiose projects that had now become possible. The windfall ended up fulfilling the arbitrary nature of power in the country, however, allowing Mohammad Reza Shah to dispense his generosity as he saw fit. The result was the shah maintaining a society split in two: a group of people he made all the wealthier and an obedient mass.

It was at this time that the true nature of the head of state became apparent. The Shah's father, Reza Shah, could neither read nor write when he rose to power, whereas his son went to the Rosey school in Switzerland and met the crème de la crème of the leaders of tomorrow. The school, however, was not able to erase two of the future shah's complexes: his height (or lack thereof) and his humble origins (albeit as the son of a Shah). Money allowed him to assert himself. He hosted royal families, organised the Persepolis festival and banned photos in which his height could be noted. He also established a new protocol under which letters of credence would only be issued to Ambassadors who bowed down before him; it was as they were bowing that a photograph would be taken and published in the newspapers.

From the summer onwards, the coffers were full, the country's debts repaid, and the convertibility of the currency assured. The shah was living in what was close to a state of ecstasy. Her Britannic Majesty's Ambassador, who had made both the sun and the rain beat down over Iran, asked him (almost humbly) for a loan of $ 1.2 billion. He granted the Ambassador's request with a winning smile that drove my colleague close to crazy. The French followed suit without a hitch. The Italians were not as fortunate, as the shah had asked that the peninsula be rid of the Communists (what a cheek, my colleague would say). As for Germany, the shah bought a stake in Krupp.

The sovereign's arrogance manifested itself in several ways. One example was on the anniversary of the shah's return from his exile in Rome. The Queen Mother held a reception at her palace, preceded by an open-air play performed in Persian. The shah, the shahbanou and the queen mother were all seated in fauteuils at the top of the long staircase leading up to the palace. The court was seated behind them on chairs. The diplomatic corps sat on the steps themselves, at the shah's feet. The German Ambassador sat on my feet. No one reacted: oil had won.

Despite this royal arrogance, the Iranians tended to refuse to take responsibility for their own problems. They held the Americans responsible instead. Since the shah had returned to Iran thanks to the Americans, they had settled into the country more and more. Despite this grip on the country, the United States' Ambassador, Richard Helms, former head of the powerful CIA, was unable to comprehend the Persian mindset.

At the Tehran fair, Helms told me that he had been unable to get Iranian customs to release twenty or so award-winning cattle he had brought over to display. The cattle thus remained on the plane, which sat at the end of the runway in over 45°C heat for several days.

When the Iranians, encouraged by Khomeini, invaded the American Embassy, they would find files proving that he had not properly informed the US State Department of the worsening situation in the country, a worsening that had become clearly visible.

From the American point of view, the shah fulfilled two of the country's objectives vis-à-vis the Cold War: guaranteeing a source of oil that was unaffected by the Arab oil boycott and building an army on the USSR's southern border. These two reasons underpinned actions taken by the Americans to buy the army's favour by supplying it with sophisticated weaponry and considering it charged with keeping order in the region. I rented an apartment that overlooked barracks. This enabled me to observe the military. To me, they did not seem to be particularly motivated.

While the Americans were poorly informed, the Soviet Embassy, quite the contrary, was very well informed. My Soviet colleague was fully aware of our IBRAMCO affair. He was helped by the Tudeh party, a nationalist party — though it posed as socialist — which had fairly intimate relations with the Soviets.

The Soviet Union did not hesitate to show its strength when necessary. I saw as much when the shah moved to index the price of the gas sold to the USSR to one similar to the price of oil, as the contract entered into between the countries authorised him to do so. In response, my Soviet colleague raised the question of the status of Azerbaijan. Faced with the threat of the secession of Azerbaijan, the shah agreed to maintain the price of gas. The Soviets also owned a steelworks in Isfahan. My colleague informed me that the volume of gas to be delivered was considered a means of payment from Iran to the Soviets: increasing the price of gas would mean modifying the parameters upon which the price of the steelworks was calculated.

The shah also gained favour with the Soviets by refusing to install American missiles within the country's borders.

The situation remained tense throughout 1974. Fearing he would be overthrown, the shah arrested — and executed — anything that moved. Prisons were particularly harsh, torture ubiquitous. This move gained him powerful enemies, even within the new bourgeoisie he thought he had bought out. Meanwhile, he was also paying off the foreign press (Time, Der Spiegel, Paris Match, etc.) to praise his democratic, pro-Western policies.

The shah had strong views when it came to foreign policy. He was entirely against any international military presence in the Persian Gulf, though he allowed for freedom of navigation. He claimed to have the fourth most powerful army in the world. While relations with the House of Saud, the rulers of Saudi Arabia, were strained, he maintained excellent relations with Sultan Qaboos of Oman. The latter faced a rebellion in the Dhofar region, so the shah sent him troops to lend a hand. Relations were good, though complicated, with Bahrain, a country with a Shia majority where most Iranian emigrants had settled. Dubai held its traditional position in the centre of the markets (both legal and black-market) between the states bordering on the Gulf. The shah maintained reasonable relations with the country. There were, however, disputes over the sovereignty of certain islands at the entrance to the Gulf.

The shah personally monitored purchases of military equipment. The sellers told me they had been impressed by his precise knowledge of the characteristics of the various weapons.

When it came to Israel, he believed that Israel's holy sites could not be left solely in the hands of the Israelis. His relations with Israel were excellent, though kept secret, including a critical Israeli mission stationed in Tehran. During the Arab League boycott of Israel in 1974, he had no qualms when it came to delivering oil to Israel. In public, he attacked the country.

> *The Jewish celebration of Purim is held in memory of the noble actions taken by Ahasuerus, king of Persia, who listened to his wife Esther and saved the Jews from being killed.*

Iran maintained bad relations with Iraq due to the long-standing difficulty faced in Arab-Iranian relations. These difficulties came to be embodied as border disputes. The Shatt al-Arab border, a delta formed by the confluence of the Tigris and the Euphrates, was rather vague. The discovery of oil on both sides of the border was the catalyst that led to it being better-defined. A treaty was entered into under British aegis in 1937. Iran would renounce this same Treaty thirty years later, as the British had conceded all the rivers separating the two countries to Iraq, except in Abadan, where the border follows the thalweg.

One day, my British colleague set about questioning his colleagues in the EEC. Iran wanted to launch an attack on Iraq using tank warfare. The tanks in question had been given to them by the British, and it was the latter who helped the Iranians handle them. Could these handlers interfere in their war? We all answered that they could not. London followed suit. According to the British Embassy, the controllers drove the tanks up to about thirty miles from the combat area and then withdrew. The tanks went no further.

A second aggravating factor was the policy adopted towards the Kurds: the Kurdish population was shared amongst Iran, Iraq and Turkey. Each country was waging war against the Kurds in their country while helping the Kurds in other countries. This was particularly true of Iran and Iraq.

Iran's relations with Turkey and Pakistan appeared to be courteous, as the former was connected to the latter two via the CENTO, a cold war alliance between the three countries, the US and Britain. In actual fact, relations were polite, though unenthusiastically so. Turkey, ever suspicious, had ensured the railway that connected it to Iran went through Lake Van so that the carriages had to be placed on a barge to get across.

What was Belgium's position in Iran?

Belgium's relations with Iran date back to the end of the 19th century. Relations were officially established in 1890. King Leopold II, who at that point in time had no good relations with the business world with interests in Persia, was unsupportive. Despite their king's lack of interest, Belgium managed to exert a certain amount of influence. It was Belgium that inspired the Persian constitution of 30 December 1906. It developed essential sectors of the economy, such as the railways (the old locomotive No.2 is still south of Tehran), glass, sugar, copper, oil, customs and the country's postal service. From 1900 onwards, industrial companies quickly began grappling with the conflicting policies between the UK and Russia, and Persia's social instability. Since then, relationships have grown and expanded to other vital areas.

When I arrived in Tehran, I found a serious situation at hand. The Belgian government and the shah had entered into an agreement that involved establishing an oil refinery near Liège: the IBRAMCO (Iranian-Belgian Refining and Marketing Company). The project involved the Iranian government delivering crude oil to IBRAMCO, which would then refine it and sell it in Europe. However, the agreement between NIOC and the consortium did not allow the Iranian government to sell oil outside Iran. The oil companies believed there had been a breach of contract. The shah cancelled the day before the final agreement, claiming that there had been a delay of 48 hours since he had last had a response from the Belgians. In actual fact, this was probably due to him being under pressure from the oil companies. This action taken in Iran is what led to the fall of Leburton's government in Belgium.

I arrived the next day, and Belgian-Iranian relations were at a standstill. The Ambassador left for Afghanistan, where he was also accredited. I was left in the country, alone and in charge. Not a single Iranian spoke to me. I was unable to go on my first formal visits. I found myself at an impasse.

Although I did not go to Afghanistan, I followed the development of opiate production closely. The French and English governments had controlled its production and sale in the 19th century. Only the USSR had managed to maintain the privilege in the 20th century. The industry had

> *been privatised elsewhere. Western governments encouraged*
> *production by banning it, leading, in turn, to an increase in*
> *prices and income. The same policy was being implemented*
> *as that followed by the American government during*
> *prohibition; one that helped the mafia make its fortune.*

I started building new relationships. It seemed that our economic and political relations had stalled. In that case, I would focus on the cultural. I held concerts that sold out. As the evenings drew to a close, the Ambassador, who had returned from Kabul, would host distinguished dinner guests, among which was the powerful Minister of Court. Our relations had been put back on track.

It was then that a Belgian group presented the Iranians with a proposal that involved collecting gas and selling it in Belgium and Europe. This project was also closely followed by my Soviet colleague. The volume of gas was equivalent to 20 percent of that consumed in Europe.

Several options of how the gas could be transported were explored.

First, liquefaction of the gas, after which it would be transported to the gas terminal at Zeebrugge. This solution was thrown out by Egypt refusing to allow the LNG carrier passageway through the Suez Canal. Sailing around Africa would have required at least a second LNG carrier, making the project unviable due to high costs.

Second, the idea of a tripartite agreement with the Soviets. Iran would deliver gas to the USSR, meeting its needs in the south of the country. In return, the USSR would deliver gas to Belgium. This pipeline project was opposed by the shah, who did not want to depend too heavily on the USSR.

Finally, the idea to transport it via a gas pipeline built through Turkey, Bulgaria, Yugoslavia, Austria and Germany was proposed. Transport royalties and the insecurity caused by the idea of having to go through countries allied with the USSR brought a definitive end to this idea.

Having arrived in Tehran just after the Nowruz celebrations, I left at Christmas time. Iran wanted to spearhead the Persian Gulf states' new energy policy. However, the country had to give up managing their oil to the British, and later to the Americans. It would not be until Khomeini rose to power that Iran would take back the reins of its destiny. The country's entire trajectory was fascinating to follow.

As I left Tehran, I spent a few days in Kuwait, a country I had never visited before. This state, which had lost its primary income, pearls – to Japan's cultured pearls – had since found oil, providing it with new wealth. Spanish-Portuguese rivalries were in full force, and the Catholic Church testified to the presence of a colony of Portuguese-speaking Indians from Goa. The Kuwaiti royal family took the Saud family in when they were in exile, thus creating a bond between these two royal families.

VIII

BRUSSELS

(1975—1986)

I was back in Belgium by the time December drew to a close in 1974. While there, I was appointed to several positions in the Ministry in this sequence: Deputy Head of Eastern European Policy, Deputy Chief of Protocol, Head of Economic Development for North Africa and the Middle East — a particularly dynamic position due to the sheer scale of the contracts landed by Belgian firms — and finally, Head of Economic Development for Sub-Saharan Africa, where I mainly managed debts.

Going back to Belgium, a country where I had only previously lived for some four years between my military service, the 1958 World Fair and my two years interning in Foreign Affairs, I got to rediscover a country whose interests I had been defending abroad for all this time. This allowed me to see the country through a wider lens.

Having lived in societies with regimes different from Belgium's, when I returned to Belgium on leave, I had been struck by how stereotyped opinions were, and how limited the margin for intellectual freedom really was. Ask around, and everyone will tell you they have absolute freedom. No one was aware that Belgian society was being held captive by a gang; by the ideas of a select group of hidden decision-makers. Ideas that were then spread around by the press and advertising campaigns. Yes, they could express their opinions without ending up in a concentration camp, but that's where their freedom ended.

During the Cold War, the USSR, who strived to be a great diplomatic power, sent its notes and letters in Russian, without attaching a translation. The Soviet Embassy in Brussels did the same. When it reached the Foreign Affairs office, this literature was sent straight to the translation service, which operated slowly. One day, the Soviet ambassador complained to Spaak about not having received a reply to a note he had sent. Spaak called his chief of staff, Mr Loridan, turning to the ambassador to announce: "Here is the culprit". "You must punish him," boomed the Soviet. "Are you banishing me to the Ardennes?" asked Loridan.

Doctors, for example, influenced holiday destinations (incentivising fresh mountain or sea air), the diets employed and even the medications taken, by writing technical publications on these subjects. Statistics of pharmaceutical sales by country are instructive in this respect. Cotton is better for your health than synthetic fabric, etc.

These factors are what contributed to my first impression of the country: that it was one where important decisions were made behind closed doors. Only a few friends would be informed.

The second observation was that the Belgians were focussed on the future. They were not afraid of innovation. Even when it came to provincial matters, they would reason wisely, with the full picture in mind. At that time, however, we lacked the daring businessmen who had brought industrial superiority into the country over the previous century. An examination of our foreign trade was enlightening. Though we had by far the highest export figures in the world per capita, almost 70 percent of our international trade was conducted with our neighbours, and barely four to five percent was conducted outside Europe. This was our weakness.

Belgium also had excellent researchers. Historically, Belgium has one of the highest densities of Nobel prize winners per million inhabitants. The Belgians, however, did not like singling out one of their own as being better than everyone else. I had to learn from a foreigner, for example, that a particular professor was, in fact, a world authority. The poorly structured tax system that provided funds for research succeeded in preventing Belgium from becoming the focus of European research.

The third observation was how very open and friendly the Belgians were. They had been equally welcoming to Victor Hugo, Multatuli and Baudelaire when it came to accepting them into their country. It was where Karl Marx had written his Manifesto. In the 19th century, Masonic lodges had had a decisive creative influence on the way in which Belgian policy was managed, particularly in the social sphere. It was through examining Belgian social ideas that the apostolic nuncio in Brussels gained awareness of the colossal mistake made by the Catholic Church: ignoring the new social reality that had come about as a result of the industrial revolution. Once appointed Pope, Leo XIII wrote his encyclical Rerum Novarum. It was also in the melting pot that was the University of Louvain that the Second Vatican Council's main ideas were forged.

My last observation was that the country was divided up into a clan system, which was frequently linked to its municipalities. Little wars broke out within this clan system, either related to politics or the economy. Thus, the far right and the far left waged a mottled, sometimes violent, war for several years.

Political parties certainly held a crucial position in the clan system, acting as the glue that brought clans together. The Christian clan laid claim to the universities of Louvain, Catholic education, the CSC union, Christian parties, hospitals and Christian mutuals. When the University of Louvain split in 1968 (into the New-Louvain University and University of Louvain), an end was brought to an agreement that had been in place since the 1830s, restricting Brussels to the freethinkers. The University of Louvain opened a faculty of medicine in Brussels and created the KUB (Katholieke Universiteit Brussel).

In return, socialists and liberals, which were members of often rival lodges, were very present in Brussels via their two universities, as well as most of the city's hospitals. As for the rest of the country, Antwerp and the industrial regions were home to substantial socialist settlements thanks to their unions and mainly liberal cities.

Carrying over into the economic field, this clan tradition led to a network of competing companies forming without any particular one monopolising the economy. It was an original, human form of economic democracy. The absence of a sizeable Belgian multinational was, however, a handicap, at times; especially when it came to our export policy.

Despite the diversity of languages spoken (Dutch, French and German being the national languages, but also English, Walloon, etc.), the country was relatively homogenous thanks to the proximity between the cities and successful integration of immigrants. It is worth noting that the socialist party, which could mainly be found in the French-speaking part of the country, had succeeded in integrating immigrants thanks to its welcoming policy. This immigration mainly originated from Flanders (the only group with few ties to their ancestral ground), Poland, Italy, Spain, Portugal, Morocco and Turkey. The party managed to make itself indispensable and was rarely excluded from the government as a result.

The creation of linguistic communities with an emphasis placed on the majority language spoken, as well as television becoming more widespread, were significant factors in aiding this assimilation. They allowed the population of Wallonia to learn French and that of Flanders to learn "ABN" Dutch, thus removing the social barrier between those who spoke the national language and those who only spoke the regional dialect. Any inferiority complex the Flemish may have felt in relation to the Netherlands, or the Walloons to France, was thus rendered obsolete.

The Burgomaster of a city was the main figurehead in a country which was, above all, a union of cities. A sophisticated evolution of the power structure was achieved by the imposition of both regional and community executives. Working from the premise that the country's forces would be unsuccessful as a unitary state should they come together, the parliament opted for a federalism that allowed each one to flourish in their region or community. The experience I gained through my various positions demonstrated to me that federalism was, in fact, the policy best suited to Belgium.

It was a simple principle. Matters relating to the population were dealt with by communities. Regions dealt with the rest. The federal government maintained sovereign rights (Internal Affairs, Justice, Financial, National Defence, Foreign Affairs) and certain powers considered to be of national interest, such as health and social security. This model removed the central government's ability to manage many departments considered to be public in Belgium, but which were privatised in other states. These core faculties counterbalanced this system of devolution of power in matters of finance, strictly limiting both regional and community autonomy. Needless to say, this system has been of great interest to several foreign governments, who have examined it with a view to reducing the scope of their central government's powers.

We must not forget that Belgium, as its current borders stand, is the result of a compromise between the great powers who came together in London, in 1830. Each power would have liked to be granted control of the country. The result was a country open to all, but where control remained in the hands of the Belgians. The spirit of this agreement had remained valid and manifested itself in several ways. Foreigners owned most of the three thousand of the country's largest companies: Germans, French, Dutch, English, Americans, even Russians, Indians, Japanese, Singaporeans, etc. These companies, which were often powerful multinationals, were in favour of the decentralisation of non-sovereign powers. They believed that regional governments were weaker than the central state and more accommodating to their particular problems. This same reasoning led these companies to support the idea of maintaining a central government capable of both solving the issues relating to managing the state and opposing any foreign country gaining too much power to the detriment of other nations.

Though Belgium was the second most substantial industrial power after the United Kingdom in the 19th century, it had managed to retain a significant amount of its potential. Its population was richer than most other peoples. It was one of the most important economic connectors in Europe thanks to the Rhine and Scheldt rivers, its motorways and to it having built the densest rail network in the world. Our agreements with the Netherlands made passage down the Scheldt waterway between the North Sea and Ghent / Antwerp a smooth journey. These two ports, as well as the port of Zeebrugge, were all important routes used by several European countries as a means through which to enter and exit the continent: Germany, France, Switzerland, Luxembourg and even the Netherlands.

Finally, while our neighbours (the Netherlands, France, Germany and Luxembourg — for the Belgian province of Luxembourg) considered us to be the lost province, not taking the time to get to know us, Belgium was granted the honour of several international institutions basing their headquarters in the country. Amongst other reasons, thanks to its central position in the knot of European communications. The country acted as the axle of a wheel the Taoists hold dear. Without its axle, a wheel cannot turn.

The logical consequence of this position is that Belgium became a centre of consensus. Curiously, the Belgians are unaware of their status. They do not realise the global importance of Brussels, both politically and economically, and the damage caused to Belgium's reputation by internal disputes between the Belgians.

Belgium has often played the role of a Vestal and guardian of the true faith in Europe. As European Union policy has been drawn up, the sight of the Belgian delegation proposing a compromise that suits everyone and remains in line with European construction has not been uncommon. The Belgians' intimate and impartial knowledge of the problems faced by each state was well-known abroad. My Warsaw Pact colleagues and the British, who had recently joined the European Union, both agreed on the impartiality of Belgian diplomacy.

In commerce, foreigners wishing to export to Europe frequently used the Belgian market as a starting point. The duality of cultures and the population's taste for the good life were the perfect testing ground for foreigners to determine the direction of their future commercial prospection in Europe.

While in Brussels, I married Shirin Malek-Mansour Qajar. Second marriages were fairly unusual in those days, and Father Leroy was very helpful in smoothing over the devilish forces standing against us. He was a renowned friend of fellow Father Teilhard de Chardin's. We had met in Tehran. She was a Doctor of Medicine at the University of Liège, specialising in dermatology. She also discovered a method of treating skin melanomas by stimulating a patient's immunity using DNCB (dinitrochlorobenzene). Her mother was Belgian and her father Iranian, and she was a direct descendant of Iran's former royal dynasty. She had a son, Philippe and two granddaughters, Lara and Julia.

1. Department for Eastern European Policy (1975—1978), Brussels

This department dealt with policy concerning the USSR and the allied countries of the Warsaw Pact. And so, I was placed back in a position where

I dealt with the same matters as when I had first begun my diplomatic career. Now, however, I was armed with the experience I had gained in Poland, providing me with a more thorough appreciation of Soviet politics.

In Poland, I was able to examine the specificity of the country. From Brussels, all the USSR's allies blurred into one, in a fog pumped out from Moscow.

It was the Brezhnev era, and relationships were very static. There was not much going on. I will thus provide a brief summary of all the elements available to me that allowed me to better appreciate the USSR's policy.

Despite the country's large surface area, one constant feature of Russian politics was a fear of being surrounded. This fear could be explained by its borders, which do not open directly onto the world.

It was for this reason that, while it never forgot its messianic spirit, Russia continued to pursue policies of colonisation when it came to its neighbouring countries. This enlargement policy was achieved with the country pushing back its land borders.

The country's political centre of gravity travelled Northwards: first Kyiv, later Novgorod, then Moscow, and finally in Saint Petersburg. The Soviets made Moscow their temporary capital; Lenin, who dreamed of a worldwide revolution, was already planning its transfer to Berlin or Paris.

Russia had developed across two continents, Europe and Asia, without ever fully identifying with either.

What's more, Russia was a totalitarian state facing a Germany unified under the IIIrd Reich. Two continental countries, their central powers, Moscow and Berlin, engaged in a struggle to see who would control the "Heartland" — the central and eastern European states. The war ended, and Stalin emerged victorious. However, Bonn's Ostpolitik meant that the balance of power began to change. Circumstances would be reversed soon enough, with Germany regaining leadership.

In meetings about the USSR held with our allies, we came to discuss the relationship between Russians and non-Russians within the USSR. All those present were convinced that relations were good, considering Russian colonial policy to have been a success. I was the only one to oppose it and made sure to request that the minutes state that I found these relations to be very tense. A trip I took to the USSR towards the end of my time in Poland opened my eyes to the matter. It was in the Soviet republic of

Uzbekistan, in particular, that I saw how high tensions ran; higher than in South Africa. Russia had its colonies trapped in an iron grip.

The Russian agricultural tradition, the "obshchina", meant peasants had a right to land, though this did not implicitly result in them having a right to property. Stalin took up the idea and collectivised the land, eliminating the most successful farmers ("koulaks") and succeeding in wiping out two-thirds of the country's livestock. Since then, agriculture has always been fairly neglected. Adhering to a more industrial, rather than agricultural, model, the farms were large and often poorly managed. Peasants were looked down upon under the Soviet regime.

During these years, the country's production of wheat became insufficient. At meetings with our allies, we identified the problem despite the difficulty posed by Soviet statistics. The data did not provide figures in terms of production, rather a percentage demonstrating the change since the previous year. We estimated that between ten and twenty percent of production had been lost, mainly due to the poor quality of the silos (humidity, rats, etc.) and poor means of transport. These were the factors that led to the Soviets being forced to import wheat. Apart from certain other suppliers, such as Argentina, the United States was the leading supplier. We took a particular interest in this trade because the transatlantic ships were too large for the Soviet port used for importing. To remedy the problem, the wheat would be trans-shipped to smaller boats in Antwerp, which would go on to the port of Ventspils (Latvia) in the Baltic, a seaport that specialised in importing grain and which was not affected by icy winters.

The Soviet companies specialising in shipping problems, those that sold oil and Soviet diamond dealers all came together to form a small, very active Soviet colony in Antwerp. The Soviets asked for, and were granted, permission to open a consulate in Antwerp so that they may assist and monitor this population.

Industry was the tool used for the USSR's economic expansion. The country's remarkable results during the first fifty years of communism had made the USSR a beacon for many developing countries.

Industry was divided into military industry (which covered anything soldiers may need, from satellites to socks – an area granted the highest share of budgetary allocations); heavy industry (provided with the second-highest shares of capital); and light industry (last on the list).

The country's leaders were happy to keep on praising the industrial successes attained. They did not follow the new trend of technological renewal, did not use the influx of capital from private savings and froze the standard of living. To its credit, however, Soviet industry managed some impressive achievements, enabling it to be placed second in the world after the United States. The Soviets' technological assets included both conventional and nuclear weapons (generally installed in the Ural, with its secret or closed cities), its space industry, heavy and light metallurgy, petroleum and petrochemicals.

The road and rail transport sectors were visibly underdeveloped, which, when combined with the problems caused by the weather, created major bottlenecks and contributed to slowing the country's development. It was precisely for this reason that navigable rivers were of such great importance.

Finally, the USSR had a wealth of primary minerals: iron, gold, oil, diamonds, coal, copper, aluminium, strategic metals, etc.

A closer analysis of Soviet strategy led me to note that it was fundamentally different from the strategy employed by Western European countries.

The "third Rome" tradition of Russian orthodoxy having been an essential part of the nation's past, Moscow was given a central position in the world as they knew it. After all, one of the primary elements that influenced the country on a constant basis had been Russian messianism. This materialised as a challenge towards the West. The messianism consisted of a Russian conviction that it had a historic mission to fulfil with regards to Europe. It had been Russia that saved Europe from Napoleon, Hitler, etc. It had been the very same who had defended the Caucasian Christians against the Turks and Persians. Under communism, this spirit then became a will to modify the other countries' pre-existing regimes, replacing them with regimes similar to the Soviet one.

Tradition states that, before he chose orthodoxy, Grand Prince Vladimir carried out an investigation into various religions. He is said to have refused Islam because of the ban on alcohol. He believed that no Russian would agree to stop drinking vodka.

The second element was that, despite the sheer size of the country, it was not a land of immigration like the United States. The USSR was still haunted by the idea of authority becoming dispersed due to its size. This led to it forming a multinational state with Russian ethnicity at its core.

The third element was the fear of being surrounded. This seemed curious from abroad, especially when the size of the country is taken into consideration, until access to the warm seas is considered. Russia had no access to the warm seas and made sure it monitored all access to them carefully.

During the Cold War, the Orthodox Church became an instrument of Soviet policy.

During the Second World War, under Stalin, the USSR had been devastated. It had also been politically strengthened, however, thanks to Stalin's genius.

Stalin was convinced that "the international system" could not be regarded as a guardian of Soviet interests, as it was a capitalist, anti-Communist system. Therefore, any cooperation with the West would be limited to tactical moves, as would any integration into the suicidal "international system". He was wary of the United Nations because it was unwilling to defend Soviet interests.

When the USSR acquired the atomic bomb, it came to the realisation that the old strategies were now outdated and that a war with the United States was no longer possible. This was the reason behind it accepting the "peaceful coexistence" policy. Russia remained suspicious, nonetheless.

Aid was provided to the recently decolonised states in Africa and Asia. The criterion used to judge whether they deserved it was no longer their socialist character. It was enough that they were anti the West. This aid was not considered to be compensation for the damage caused by colonisation, as it was when provided by Western Europe.

Brezhnev was building a conventional army alongside his nuclear army. He remained convinced that the West and Japan were potential enemies, also believing that he would make the Western states more cooperative by projecting greater power. It was a profound modification of Soviet policy compared to that conceived under Stalin.

The Soviet government developed the "Brezhnev doctrine" by which the USSR gave itself the right to intervene, militarily, even, in Warsaw Pact member countries should they opt for a policy that aligned more closely with the West. The first case was the 1968 situation in Czechoslovakia. The second case — though there was no Soviet intervention – took place in Poland while I was posted to Warsaw, the details of which I have already described.

Russia's role within the USSR has varied. The civil war that raged after the 1917 revolution caused ten million deaths. These still haunt the nation's collective memory. Then, Lenin strongly condemned chauvinism and Russian hegemonic culture. Soviet historians explain that Russia was a force of oppression, one to which the proletarian peoples must be opposed.

From then on, each population was encouraged to speak its own language and develop its own culture. This fundamental change in cultural policy led to non-Russians becoming more nationalistic. It was also a source of painful humiliation for the Russians, who were accustomed to using a language spoken throughout their colonies.

The 1939—1945 war was especially terrible for the Russians. Stalin took the opportunity to review relations between Russians and Non-Russians within the USSR and to grant the Russians "elder brother" legitimacy. The Russians backed down once again with the arrival of Khrushchev, "the butcher of the Ukraine". After Khrushchev's departure in 1964, Brezhnev returned to the old equilibrium. National officials sat on the Politburo, and the idea of a centralised state was abandoned. Brezhnev, however, made speaking Russian a preliminary requirement for those wishing to occupy a position of state, coordinating the Politburo to be overwhelmingly made up of Russians.

Since Brezhnev had risen to power (1964—1982), the desire to become the leading world power was no longer a daily concern like it had been in the days of Stalin and Khrushchev. The reign of terror had ended (under Stalin, 7,000,000 were executed, 5,000,000 had died from government-orchestrated famines, and 15,000,000 had been sent to the gulags. It had been the worst genocide of the 20th century). Power was now maintained by corruption or coercion, by encouraging the acquisition or loss of privileges, whether it be banning a person's children from attending university, denying them a passport, or banning them from owning a second home. From a totalitarian regime under Stalin, the regime became authoritarian.

At first, the country's economy continued to evolve. The population increased by 60 million. The administration grew but confined itself to its own interests and distanced itself from its citizens. Building works increased. Consumer goods began appearing (fridges, televisions, etc.), and the population became greedy.

Then, gradually, the country's development started to plateau. The leaders become lax, and a parallel economy was quick to develop — one based on easy money made thanks to party funds. The Soviet mafia, which had been an ally of power since 1917, seized their opportunity and expanded significantly.

Thanks to this mafia, "citadels of power" were created across the country. They felt strong enough to circumvent traditional Soviet rules. I noticed surges of independence in certain republics, in particular in Caucasus and Siberia.

But the Russian economy remained frozen, while the Western underwent its industrial revolution.

During a congress of the Communist Party of the Soviet Union, Brezhnev described the devolution of power within the party.

The USSR's Communist Party stood in the centre, spearheading the transformation of Soviet society, which had been described as socialist, into one that was communist.

The first ring around this party, which was primarily Russian, was made up of the communist parties of the Slavic federated states (Ukraine, Belarus).

A second circle, which departed from the primary principles of the party, was formed by the Islamic federated states (Kazakhstan, etc.).

Then came a third circle made up of the communist parties of the allied states (Poland, etc.).

These were followed by the Western communist parties (France, Italy, Spain, etc.).

Finally, the last circle was made up of the third- world states' national liberation movements, those that had spearheaded their obtention of independence.

The communist parties in Western Europe — mainly those in France, Italy and Spain — seemed to veer away from this idea, advocating for Eurocommunism. On analysis, I noted that these three parties continued to follow the Central Committee of the Communist Party of the USSR's directives, but with a zest of independence — enough to deceive public opinion.

> *During a lengthy interview with my Czechoslovakian colleague, I would come to explain the structural and cyclical problems faced by the Belgian economy. He found it difficult to understand our reasoning due to the vast difference in economic culture between the communist countries and those in the West. The following week, he informed me that he had told his Soviet bloc colleagues about my presentation. They went on to adopt our criteria as a new method of reasoning where our economic problems were concerned.*

In parallel to the Communist Party's rings of power, the Soviet state made sure to share information about particular scenarios with its European allies. Ceaucescu's Romania had just finished playing at having a free election, opening the country up to diplomatic intervention from the Middle East. The Czechs sold contraband weapons to the national liberation armies. The Bulgarians spied on as much as they could via their freight trucks, which were riddled with transmitters and receivers. The East Germans continued to maintain contact with Western socialist parties. The Poles agreed to pitch new ideas on disarmament in Europe and sought to keep track of the movements of goods by sea, thanks to their merchant fleet and their ridiculously low prices.

At one point, I went to Warsaw to prepare for a visit from our sovereigns. I worked with the Poles to draw up a final press release for their visit — a press release that no one read or published except for the foreign ministries. It has since served as a model for other Western visits to Eastern European countries. The exercise was a balancing act between touching upon all the controversial subjects and stressing everything we had in common.

A Catholic priest whose name I do not recall asked to meet with me. He told me that the third part of the Virgin of Fatima's secret was an announcement that Russia had abandoned communism. Christianity would thus gain ground. This information, provided while Brezhnev was still very much in power, seemed interesting, yet illusory. The passing of time has proved the priest right.

Soviet influence on the third-world countries' national liberation movements has resulted in all studies or definitions of the policies towards these countries being attached to the Department of Eastern European Policy.

What are the elements that make up national liberation movements' policies?

Decolonisation. The Second World War was partly fought in the colonies: in North Africa, the Middle East and especially Southeast Asia. A period of unrest followed; one the colonisers were unable to keep on top of for long. The two great powers that emerged victorious from the war, the United States and the USSR, stood against the European forces keeping their colonies. They wanted a calm Europe with no extra-European ambition or warlike will. They left their troops in Central Europe to ensure they achieved this.

The decolonisation that ensued produced a diversity of effects.

Firstly, it was a blessing to European state budgets, which were being used to rebuild their economies.

The former colonies were, however, confronted with the problems implicit to running a state. These countries, having lost their political traditions to colonisation, tended to blame all their management faults on their former colonisers. The Americans supported this point of view, the Soviets even more so as they sought to form a new client base.

The USSR even gave independence movements a helping hand, while the United States remained indifferent. This indifference ceased, however, when the importance of some of these countries dawned on the Americans, either thanks to the products found within them, or their strategic location. It was with this change of heart that the United States conducted both the Korean and Vietnam wars. Their reversal came too late. The USSR's influence was already spreading throughout the Third World.

> *(Mao Zedong said that the world was divided in three: the first world made up of the USA and the USSR, the second world made up of first world allies or like-minded countries and the Third world, made up of countries not linked to the those considered to be first world).*

On the American continent, the USSR succeeded in breaking the Monroe Doctrine, which advocated for the abstention of non-American states in any conflicts within the American hemisphere. These were the crises in Cuba and Nicaragua, and the coming to power of Allende and his pro-Soviet policy in Chile.

In Asia, Afghanistan and Burma came under the communist sphere of influence, as did China and Vietnam, though the latter's links with the USSR were more strained.

In Africa, Guinea, Angola, Somalia, Ethiopia, Mozambique and South Africa's ANC all become communist clientele. The USSR's rewards were less certain to be reaped in this continent, however, leading to it abandoning its positions.

Secondly, these countries rejected European values, which mainly applied to the European quarrel between Western capitalism and Eastern communism. Instigated by Tito, Nasser and Nehru, the countries that were not members of a military alliance regrouped during the 1955 Bandung conference, forming the Non-Aligned Movement.

The Movement's neutral, non-aligned position was then gradually broken down with one country or other aligning itself with the USSR, the United States or a European country.

The main subjects addressed within the Movement were the condemnation of imperialism, colonialism, neo-colonialism, apartheid and the politics of foreign military bases.

In an action that ran in parallel to the political movement, the "77" developing countries convened in Cairo in 1962 as part of an economic conference. In 1964, they managed to create the United Nations Conference on Trade and Development (UNCTAD) within the UN.

The main subjects addressed were those concerning developing countries: economic development, the new international economic order and the balance of payments deficit.

The Non-Aligned Movement, which was born out of a desire to keep its members out of bloc politics, had now merged with the Group of "77": they gradually become a union, in which certain developing countries came together against imperialists, essentially, Westerners.

As more and more of them gained independence, third-world countries demanded that they become members of the United Nations. The organisation thus gradually became dominated by these third-world countries.

Many wars broke out. The vast majority of them were fought by the Third World. These wars required military resources disproportionate to state budgets.

The 1970s was when a third block, the Third World, strove out ahead of the other two, but with different weapons. The oil crisis of 1973 was essentially the manifestation of a triumphant Third World. It was also the beginning of a certain distancing within the Third World between Muslim states and other states.

This new emergence of the Third World also allowed for an appearance of leaders who distanced themselves from the politics of the great powers: of Khomeini's Iran, the Khmer Rouge's Cambodia and the China of the cultural revolution, etc.

The West, led by President Carter, responded openly, using moral arguments: the need to protect human rights, returning to religion, etc. It was also a time in which the West provided aid to Muslim fundamentalism.

2. Deputy Head of Protocol (1978—1981) in Brussels

The Protocol Service managed all foreigners, i.e. 40,000 people to which common law did not apply. This covered diplomats, NATO, SHAPE and EEC staff, and those of other international institutions with headquarters in Brussels. Each of these organisations had signed a "headquarters agreement" with Belgium, which regulated the immunities and privileges granted to them by the Belgian government. These would vary from agreement to agreement.

The diplomatic corps accredited to the King benefitted from the Vienna Convention. The same was true of consuls. Atlantic Alliance and European Union diplomatic corps, on the other hand, had their status regulated by the headquarters agreements.

The work we did was necessary though quite routine, reasonably flavourless except for one or other drug bust involving diplomats' suitcases as they arrived in Zaventem.

The task assigned to the Protocol was to hold Minister's receptions at Egmont Palace as well as arranging official visits.

Foreign guests had to be well-received. They would be met at Zaventem airport. Leaving with a full police escort, they would be granted interviews with the authorities and free meals, and gifts would be exchanged, etc. This all meant preparatory meetings had to be held with the police and the gendarmerie. Meals had to be ordered from the caterer, etc.

As well as these visits, we also had visits from people headed to the European Union's headquarters. Ministers, even heads of state or government, attended certain meetings at which their security detail had to be orchestrated. As well as specific European Union meetings, there were also those of the ACP countries (Africa, Caribbean and Pacific), which were attended by prominent figures from these countries. Belgium frequently hosted opposition leaders to those governments, so special attention had to be paid to the safety of these guests.

> *During coordination meetings held with my colleagues from the other Protocols of the European Union Foreign Affairs Departments, we sought to standardise the rules concerning official visits: state visits, working visits, etc. We also examined the protocol list in each country. It was a reflection of the political importance given to each institution. In Belgium, the presidents of the chambers (representatives of the people) come before the Prime Minister. In the United Kingdom, the Commons speaker was far further down the list than the Prime Minister.*

Following an attack on President Sadat of Egypt, a national funeral was decreed in Cairo. Our sovereign, King Baudouin, flew out for it, as did

I as a member of his entourage. We arrived in a relatively deserted city. The ceremony took place on the site of the attack, the stadium. All the guests were placed in the gallery. Apart from the officials, there was not a single Egyptian. After the eulogy, the army carried the body ceremoniously. All the guests followed on foot in a disorderly fashion. Suddenly, a group of Egyptian soldiers caught up with us, weaving their way through the guests to join the guard of honour around the catafalque. Remembering that it had been a soldier who had killed President Sadat during a parade a week earlier, a buzz ran through those present. Everything carried on without a hitch.

In 1980, the television station, CNN, broadcast 24/7, giving the American authorities a megaphone of astonishing power. Indeed; you could pick CNN up in most countries around the world. While the fall of the Berlin Wall in 1989 made CNN popular, its highest point would have to be the "live from Baghdad" segment during the Gulf War in 1991.

3. Head of Economic Development for North Africa and the Middle East (1981—1984) in Brussels

My previous post in Iran led to me taking a particular interest in this appointment, as it allowed me to take stock of the situation in the Middle East and North Africa.

The main currents flowing across the region at the time were due to Turkish, Arab and Iranian influence, the Palestinians, Kurds and Israelis. Influences from major European powers could also be added to these — from the United Kingdom, France, Germany, Russia and the United States.

Up until 1919, the region had been part of the Ottoman Empire. Its success came from having been able to manage territories populated by different ethnicities and varied religions for several centuries. No other force that has managed to dominate the region temporarily has ruled the Middle East for so long.

Arab nationalism was awoken at the end of the 19th century. It was rooted in the Nahda, a movement formed by different political currents

175

brought together by their support of democracy, the emancipation of women and socialism.

Nahda disintegrated, however, and I noted that new (very varied) ideological and cultural values had taken over. The traditional middle classes seemed to have been marginalised by the new wealthy classes. These new layers, which had mainly gained their wealth from oil, were steeped in religious fundamentalism. They were funded by the video civilisation and consumerist society. They no longer identified with the Non-Aligned Movement.

In summary, faced with the disappearance of their old order, new moves started to appear on the Middle East's game board. The Zionist dynamic had a mighty army. Palestinian Authority was beginning to emerge. A robust, stable power was established in Syria. Power granted by oil and fundamentalism were asserting themselves. Religious renewal brought about a revival of religious thought. It was encouraged by both European and American capitals, who saw it as an antidote to communism.

After the turmoil faced between 1973 and 1975, during which the West shuddered, relations between the West and the Middle East took a turn.

On the one hand, the West accepted higher oil prices. Economists considered the new price to be equivalent to the cost of oil in 1945, in real terms. This sudden increase in wealth generated important contracts for the West and resulted in Middle Eastern leaders viewing the capitalist system as more attractive than an agreement with the USSR.

On the other hand, in order to ensure that none of these present or future governments either turned to the USSR or decreed a new increase in the price of oil, the West funded the Islamist movement in the oil-producing countries, thus weakening their governments. Several ambassadors and ministers asked me when we were going to stop financing the Islamists.

Islamism, therefore, seemed to be the solution rather than the problem. This was a dangerous game, a fact we would learn further down the line. In the short term, it was a winner. This Islamism found its roots in an in-depth study by literary thinker Sayyid Qutb "In the Shade of the Quran". In it, he explains how miserable lives in western societies are. According to him, despite their economic productivity and scientific knowledge, they face a divide between material excellence and spiritual demands. This division leads to a poor distribution of wealth, creating hatred, misery and fear of the unknown. Man is never reassured. There is also a weakening of moral values which can only lead to the destruction of material prosperity. Qutb adds, however, that Islam is open to other ways of thinking, but only if the laws imposed by God are accepted. He rejected any circumstances under which more influential men created rules for other men, as this would be to deny them of their freedom. Finally, the Islamist movement presented itself as pious and charitable.

These were the thoughts that haunted my new interlocutors.

> *I was quite surprised by the workings of the council that presided over the various mosques in Belgium. This council was a meeting of plenipotentiary Muslim ambassadors. I proposed this system be altered and the running of the mosques entrusted to Belgian Muslims, basing my proposal on the argument that the other religions in Belgium — Catholic, Protestant and Jewish – were managed by Belgians. My proposal was rejected because "there had been no problems".*

The Arabian Peninsula saw its financial resources increase from ten billion to a hundred and sixty-three billion dollars between 1972 and 1983, thanks to the increase in oil prices. This income, one that was not generated from work, concealed both economic and social problems thanks to the well-being it created.

Created in 1981, the Gulf Cooperation Council (GCC) grouped Saudi Arabia, Kuwait, Qatar, Bahrain, the United Arab Emirates and Oman together in order to promote the development of common foreign, military, social and economic policies.

From 1970 to 1980, the three leading players in the question of oil were the Shah of Iran, Algeria's President Boumédiène and Libya's President Gaddafi. However, the main pillar was Saudi Arabia.

From the coming of the Prophet Muhammad in the sixth century until oil was discovered (1933), no event had taken place within the country that had resonated on an international level. It had never been colonised by the West and had no state tradition, in the modern sense of the term.

Since then, Saudi Arabia had evolved. The installation of the "oil civilisation" had set in, in this country where a fundamentalist, austere variant of Sunni Islam reigned: Wahhabism. The result was one of the most explosive cultural shocks of the century. Under the reign of Faysal (1964—1975), oil revenues increased from $ 0.5 billion in 1964 $ 27.8 billion in 1974. (For comparison, in 1974, German exports amounted to $ 90 billion). In a bid to maintain the influence of Islam, Saudi Arabia built one thousand five hundred mosques around the world.

Faysal got along with the two other Sunni Muslim, anti-communist, religious states: Morocco, whose sovereign was descended from the Prophet, and Pakistan, a nation born from India to ensure Islam was respected. The role of their leaders was eased by the disappearance of secular Nasser and secular Sukarno from Indonesia. After the fire of the al-Aksa mosque in Jerusalem, an Islamic meeting was convened in Rabat, and a permanent secretariat created. Faysal thus became the charismatic Muslim figurehead, replacing Nasser. And thus, an end was brought to both secular and socialist influences.

Faysal and the Saudis shared a love of religious Puritanism, progress and dynamism with the Americans. They also had a common phobia: communism and Soviet expansion. Faysal added that, for him, Zionism was nothing more than a product of communism, and that communism was a vast plot put together by international Judaism, aiming to destroy ethics and ways of life so that they may take over the world. Israel was therefore created as a product of Soviet invention.

Finally, for him, American aid to Israel was forgivable, because it was the result of work done by the powerful Jewish lobby in the United States. If it had not been for this lobby, they would have received no help. This reasoning is quite common among Muslim leaders. It allowed them to keep the esteem they held for the Americans intact. This admiration was combined with the fact that this country (like Germany, which they also admired) had no colonial relations with the Arab world, as well as the US seeking stability in the countries where they invested (Saudi Arabia, Morocco, Jordan). Conversely, the Soviets were accused of destabilisation, despite the aid they provided to socialist regimes.

The revival of Islam was primarily due to the Saudis, who were great providers of Islamic funding. Funds flowed through the Muslim World League (an NGO created in 1962) of which the Secretary-General was

Saudi, the Organisation of the Islamic Conference, organised by Saudi Arabia to counter the Arab League, then dominated by Nasser, and the Islamic Development Bank for infrastructure projects.

There were also "private" networks, such as the Dar al-Maal al-Islami Trust in Geneva and the Dallah Al-Baraka Bank, which financed the "Afghan" networks made up of Arabs who came to fight alongside the Afghans. Finally, Islamist education was provided at the Islamic University, founded in Islamabad in 1980. It educated the fighters who had gone there from Afghanistan.

The pace of the Saudi economy was determined by oil revenue. If the price of a barrel of oil changed as little as $1, it would mean a $2 billion difference in income.

It was therefore a particularly exciting period to observe, as Saudi Arabia's public and private finances were in excellent condition, allowing us to gain many contracts. Few problems were encountered.

I organised Prince Albert's visit to Saudi Arabia and Oman. There were one hundred of us in the entourage, and I had requested an Air Force plane to transport us. Our contract-gathering operations were fruitful, and several disputes ended up being settled thanks to the prince's presence. The difference between each of Saudi Arabia's cities was striking: Jeddah was open to international trade; Riyadh, a capital in the middle of the desert; and Dhahran, a city of oil, where everyone bore arms. The general atmosphere was astonishing, varying between extremely wealthy princes and the appalling poverty of foreign workers, who were contained in camps set up next to their places of work.

Justice was served by one or the other prince who would go to a village and hold a *majlis,* or court of justice. Everyone would attend to air their grievances. The verdict would be rendered on the spot, and then carried out immediately: a hand cut off for theft, beheading for a severe crime. Two to three hundred beheadings took place per year. There were few prisoners and no appeals.

At the time, an average wealthy family owned up to six or seven motor cars, which would be upgraded annually. The weekends, which lasted from Thursday noon to Friday evening, allowed many Saudis to make their way out into

*the desert where an often-embroidered tent would be erected.
They would relax, surrounded by a large number of domestic
staff: a sheep or goat kebab would be served with dates,
rice, etc.*

Saudi Arabia built petrochemical plants to compete with the European petrochemical industry. It held seven percent of the world's installed capacity. The Saudis asked me to open our market up to their products. Before I gave them an answer, I sent the petroleum federation a detailed note. I held an information meeting with the leading oil companies present in Belgium. The answer was no. The Belgian and European petrochemical industry had a production overcapacity of 20 percent. The Saudis breaking into the market was a particularly unwelcome idea. This was the answer I provided them with. They were happy to hear as much, at the time, but would come to obtain certain concessions later on.

Unlike Saudi Arabia, where the population was used to large desert areas, Oman presented itself as a Kent-like region, with more tropical plants. The roads were winding and manicured.

*The history of this sultanate was impressive. They had designed
boats with flexible, woven hulls that had been sailing since
before Christ. Having learned of the American Revolution,
they offered George Washington a pair of Arabian horses
transported on these boats. In exchange, they received a rifle,
which was displayed in their national history museum.*

Slave traders, they established a co-sultanate on the island of Zanzibar and bought the slaves their touts provided them with there. They would then transport their cargo of slaves to what is now Pakistan. The Pakistanis would pay in silver. Today, beautiful pieces of chiselled silver can still be found in Oman. It is not uncommon for an Omani to have a second wife in Pakistan. As for the wealthy Zanzibaris, Sultan Qaboos offered to participate in the governing and development of the sultanate; a proposal they accepted.

Our relations with Iran had taken a new turn since the shah had been replaced with Imam Khomeini. The new regime seemed to be closer to a police state than the previous one had been. The imprisoned populations, which had often been made up of the shameless upper bourgeoisie under the previous regime, had since varied considerably. It was the families who managed to escape that incited the West against the new government. While what the West had seen from this vital change in Iranian politics had been the rise of obscurantist clerics to power, I believed a closer analysis would reveal several positive results.

The first was a legislative chamber being established, which actively participated in political life. Outside Turkey and Israel, it was the only example of democracy in the Middle East. Admittedly, objections do exist to religious power rejecting a candidate from standing in an election. From a Western approach, this does seem undemocratic. The West does not, however, get offended when, for its own elections, parties choose one or other candidate as more presentable. In both cases, selecting a candidate in such a fashion has somewhat regal implications.

At the time of the shah, only he, the Prime Minister and the Royal Court Minister were aware of current affairs. When the new administration came in, I noted that we were now able to deal with problems executing ministerial decisions at an administrative level. It was a positive step towards the decentralisation of power.

Then, with the shah's regime being overthrown, the Iranians took their destiny into their own hands. Intellectually, the Iranian approach to reality changed completely. In the shah's time, everything that happened was blamed on the English, then the Americans. Now the Iranians took complete charge of their politics. Objectively, they now saw themselves as the subjects of international relations. This difference was of primary importance. If fact, this was probably the most important change Imam Khomeini made to Iran. Upon reflection, I think that even if there does come to be a change of regime in Iran, this achievement will not be taken back.

The Iranian Ambassador to Brussels once explained to me that Iran's persistence when it came to irritating all the other governments was voluntary. Thus, with no other way out, the Iranians were forced to make their own decisions and stand by them. The Iranians kidnapping American diplomats in Tehran was only the beginning of this new confident attitude towards securing their destiny. In doing so, the Iranians followed the brilliant three-thousand-year-old tradition kept by the Persian Empire.

In religion, Khomeini was in line with Sayyid Qutb's fundamentalism, though he added an essential element to it. He became the champion of the oppressed. Oppressed by whom? By the West, and more particularly, by the United States. This attitude made him popular with Muslims, though he was criticised by other religious people that accused him of using religion as a political factor.

Like that of the shah, this government remained dependent on oil revenue. A large part of the economy was firmly in the grasp of those in power.

Finally, Iran was waging two wars at the same time — one against the Kurds, the other against Iraq. For a people who favoured gardening over warfare, it was a tough pill to swallow. The West believed that the government would not survive these two battles. History would prove the opposite to be true.

Taking matters into their own hands, they took to developing the economy. In the midst of the wars, they connected remote villages to electricity and water grids and built countless buildings in Tehran and other cities. From 30 million inhabitants in 1970, the population rose to 60 million. Agriculture was developing, and military equipment left behind by the Americans was copied successfully. New SMEs were emerging. All this contributed to an educated, wealthy, dynamic bourgeoisie being formed. For a reputedly obscurantist religious people, they seemed to be reasonably open to what the future would bring.

This is a fundamental difference when compared to the neighbouring Arab countries that depended on the West.

Since the advent of the Iranian revolution, our trade with the country had halved due to the bleak atmosphere created by American policy. Outraged by the imprisonment of American diplomats in Tehran, they had decided to break off trading with Iran. The economic reality differed to policy, however, in that I learned that the United States was Iran's leading trading partner, though this trade was carried out via roundabout routes, in particular via Dubai.

Before a meeting in the ministry about measures to be taken against the Iranians, following them having taken the American embassy hostage, I noticed an advert in the International Herald Tribune: if you want to do business with Iran, write to a particular PO box in Zurich. The embargo therefore came down to the percentage this kind of intermediary would take. It should be noted that, while it was easy to bypass an embargo when delivering consumer products (wheat, steel, etc.), this was not the case when it came to selling products of known origin. The meeting chose to evict two Iranian diplomats who the Iranians had decided to call back a fortnight earlier.

During a routine visit from the Iranian chargé d'affaires, we discussed the possibility of boosting our trade relations. We developed a scenario that would help break down the resistance felt by the Belgian government.

As a first step, the Iranians sent an official delegation made up of officials to resume contact with Belgian businesspeople. My part in the matter involved organising a meeting at the Federation of Belgium Enterprises, where these officials would hold a conference. It drew a large crowd and was visibly successful among the Belgians. Iranian officials requested a meeting with the Secretary of State for International Trade and invited him to Iran. This visit took place a few months later, and I accompanied the Secretary of State to Tehran.

In Tehran, the authorities showed us around the cemetery filled with those who had died in the Revolution. A president, ministers, senior officials, fighters and, among them, many children. So many deaths in the name of a regime could only help make it stronger. The new generation, which had not seen the perversities committed during imperial times and had never got the chance to leave their country, knew nothing other than what they were taught.

A dozen ministerial interviews were arranged, as we already had some notable contracts. Soon, our business took shape once again, surpassing previous figures.

A meeting with one of the Iranian ministers was limited to him presenting a declaration of good intentions concerning Iran. The rest of the hour spent in his ministry gave the Belgian delegation a chance to hear a presentation on the Quran. Leaving the meeting, our Minister, who was exasperated by the monologue he had been subjected to, told me that the only difference between himself and his Iranian colleague was that while the Iranian would say *"au nom de Dieu"* (in the name of God), he was more likely to mutter *"nom de Dieu"* (Goddammit / bloody hell).

> *As tradition dictated, my Iranian colleague and I drew up a press release. When it came to signing it, I noted that the text typed up by the Iranians was precisely as we had agreed, except they had added: "In the name of God Almighty". My minister refused to sign it. I explained that nobody read these press releases, which were not printed by the newspapers. He agreed to sign it.*

Iran was at war with Iraq at the time, but our political and trade relations remained positive with both countries. The day before I left for Tehran with the ministerial delegation, the Iraqi ambassador called me, demanding an explanation. "I thought we were friends and then here you are, going off to Tehran". I informed him of our sound economic relations with both countries, but that if he forced me to choose, my choice might not be what he was expecting. We left it there. On the morning of my return, he called me with an invitation to lunch at the Cercle Gaulois as proof of the continued good relations between Belgium and Iraq.

I have also, incidentally, been on several visits to Baghdad. What is striking, the first time you visit, is the quiet confidence of a city that was once one of the most important global centres of culture. Today, it is in the hands of an ambitious group of men who seek to dominate the Middle East. In the wider picture, where the Middle East is concerned, the Shah of Iran being overthrown provided Saddam Hussein with the opening he needed to make Iraq a benchmark country in the Middle Eastern Arab world. The Saudis, who were undoubtedly richer, proved to be unable to play a military role. Thanks to their oil reserves, they were content with having a certain amount of leverage in discussions within the OPEC and financing the expansion of Islam.

Iraq was one of the most powerful states in the region thanks to its military-type state apparatus and a well-trained army. It has only existed as a state since the end of the Ottoman Empire.

Formed of Sunni Kurds in the north, Sunnis in the centre and Shiites in the south (Shiism's central holy places are located in Najav, in southeastern Iraq), Iraq, which is managed by Sunnis, maintained a cohesive population thanks to its army and its secret police.

Iraqi territory is primarily made up of desert lands. The fertile regions are arranged around Mesopotamia. The oil regions are located around Mosul, on the edge of Kurdistan, and to the south, in the Shia region of Basra.

In 1958, the royal regime established by the British was overthrown and replaced by the Ba'ath party. It has remained in power ever since, acting with severe brutality.

The Iraqis have difficult relations with all their neighbours, except Jordan: with Syria, despite the Bassists being in power on both sides; with Saudi Arabia and Kuwait because of their oil wealth and the monarchical character of their government; with Iran, despite the presence of Shiites in the south and the commercial circles of Baghdad; and with Turkey.

Despite these bad relations, there was a certain collusion between the Iraqi, Iranian, Turkish and even Syrian governments, who came together to manage the Kurdish problem.

Iraq had been waging war on Iran since 1980.

Our relations with Iraq were difficult but good. The contracts we had managed to gain were important, and we provided technology and equipment for a variety of industries. In general, Saddam Hussein's Iraq benefitted from good relations with the West, more particularly with the United States. The latter had incited and helped Iraq wage war on Iran, encouraging officials to use the former Iranian imperial army troops who had taken refuge in Iraq to do so, among other things. Saddam Hussein agreed to wage this war because he wanted to recover the entirety of the Shatt al-Arab, the left bank of which he had had to cede to Iran following the Algiers agreement (1975). However, the Shatt al-Arab was a significant delta for both the Tigris and the Euphrates. It housed oil terminals, the Iranian ports of Abadan, and Iraqi ports of Basra.

During one of my trips to Iraq (1983) with our Minister, several Iraqi Ministers announced that once the war with Iran was over, Iraq would attack Kuwait and Saudi Arabia. These ministers had clearly been issued with a watchword. The information was coordinated among the ministers to ensure that we had been made fully aware of their intentions. Upon my return to Brussels, I made a note of what had been said. It was not until a few years later that Mr Hussein would put the policy into practice. Iraq invaded Kuwait.

The allies arriving prevented them from successfully conquering Saudi Arabia. Doing so would have allowed Saddam Hussein to control not only the oil in Iraq, Kuwait and Saudi Arabia, but would also have granted him access to the Suez Canal and the holy places of Islam.

One of Iraq's neighbours, Transjordan, now Jordan, played an essential role in the fight against the Israelis in 1948, thanks to British aid provided to the Arab Legion. Since the very start of the monarchy in 1930, the sovereigns, who were backed by the Bedouins — the backbone of the army — had had difficult relations with the Palestinian population (2 million Palestinians out of a total population of 4 million). In September 1970, "Black September", the Bedouins crushed the Palestinians. This significant Palestinian presence led to relations between Jordan and Israel becoming difficult.

Jordan's economy remained fairly limited in terms of its expansion, however, because most of the country was covered by a desert. The port of Aqaba developed somewhat, serving as an access route to Iraq.

Our economic relations with Jordan were good, though of little consequence. The links between King Hussein and our Sovereign, on the other hand, were excellent, and a visit from Crown Prince Hassan, who was skilled in economics, was a success.

We had good relations with Israel, a relatively new state despite its long history. Two parties dominated domestic politics. Firstly, the Labour party, which was essentially made up of Eastern European emigrants. They founded the first *kibbutzim*. Within the movement, the Histadrut trade-union owned the industrial companies of the highest importance.

The other party, Likud, was an association of right-wing parties, its ranks formed of North African and Eastern European emigrants.

A friend of mine, the Israeli Ambassador, told me that he booked the harvest days off every year because he would go back to his kibbutz to help pick the grapes. Why? Because the Kibbutz had funded his studies — as they did for each of their members —enabling him to go on to have a good career. Indeed, most Kibbutz did not pay their members for the work they did, covering all their costs instead (education, health, etc.). This system has had very favourable echoes among the European youth who have gone to live in a kibbutz for a few months.

In regional policy, Israel began to lose its image of being a pioneering state, the inventor of the kibbutzim, becoming, instead, the oppressor of the Palestinians. Young Europeans partially share this perception of Israel. *In situ*, the situation was far less clear-cut, with the arguments put forward by each side carrying their own weight.

Israel, a relatively developed country, found it difficult to fit into the still largely underdeveloped Arab world.

The Israelis settled in Palestine thanks to an agreement entered into between the Westerners and the Jews. The Muslims played no part. This was all the more annoying to the Muslims, as they had never failed to take in Jews who had been persecuted by the Christians, though on the condition that they did not form a state within the Muslim world (the position taken by the Ottoman Empire).

Over the years, following the various violent pogroms the Jews had to endure in Europe, including the Holocaust, immigration continued, accelerating after the Second World War. The idea of creating a Jewish state where Jews from all over the world could live and, if necessary, take refuge, became popular. Though the Palestinians' opinion was not taken into consideration, the idea had the West's approval and, in particular, that of Great Britain; the country with tutelage over the region.

The Camp David Accords (1978) and the Egypt-Israel Peace Treaty (1979) put an end to the 1973 war (the Yom Kippur war) with Egypt and dealt with the position Jordan could occupy should it also join them. Egypt reconquered the Sinai. Not a word was heard from the Palestinians, except for a first possible degree of autonomy to be negotiated with Jordan, Egypt and the elected representatives of those countries.

President Sadat of Egypt realised that, to gain this agreement, the barrier of mutual distrust that had formed would need to be broken down. Aiming to do just that, he went to Jerusalem (19 November 1977) and made a speech that was very well-received in the Knesset. The other Arab countries saw this agreement as a betrayal, leading to the Arab League excluding Egypt from its ranks at the Baghdad meeting. Under Secretary of State George Ball summed up the agreement as follows: "We bought the sands of the Sinai from Israel for an exorbitant price ($3.2 billion in American aid) and then we paid Egypt dearly ($1.8 billion in aid) to take them back."

It was in this international context that I was sent to Israel to examine the possibility of developing our bilateral trade within the framework of our good relations. The Israeli Ambassadors in Brussels have always been of a very high calibre, thus demonstrating the country's interest in Belgium. Several thousand Belgians are of Jewish faith and have family ties to Israel. While the community in Brussels is more focused on the liberal professions, Antwerp, probably the most religious Jewish community outside of Israel, controls the diamond market. Thanks to this position, fairly close production links were established with Israel.

To me, this mission was a journey to the source of the Holy Book's three religions. While a palpable tension could be felt between Palestinians and Israelis, a Christian presence in the region was not free of complications. Indeed, our consul in Jerusalem explained that since Napoleon, the Franciscans had been established as guardians of Christian holy places. This meant they were watched over by rival Christian communities on a daily basis.

It was due to these circumstances that he had experienced a curious episode. A small broken window in a church was being repaired. The church was considered to be a holy place, but the Orthodox Patriarch paid for the repair. The Catholics and the Armenians intervened immediately because it was down to the owner to pay to fix the window. There was no middle ground in sight. Therefore, according to the Napoleonic rule, the "Catholic" consuls – which included the Belgian one – would serve as mediators. If this failed, a decision would have to be made by the country's civil authority, in this case, the Israelis. You could not make it up.

I made my way to Foreign Affairs, where I was to have my talks. I was hosted in a wooden barrack. Only certain ministries had been granted stone buildings then. I was also amazed at the extent to which inflation had become a part of daily life. So much so, that wages were paid taking into account the inflation predicted for the following month. We bought newspapers with cheques because paper money devalued so quickly. It was risky to keep cash, even small change. The newsagent would deposit his cheques the very same day he got them, as the banks would increase account balances on an almost daily basis to follow inflation.

In our bilateral relations, the major problem faced was the agreement entered into between the Arab states to boycott any company that did business with Israel. There was an office in Damascus where all the disputes took place. This office sourced the livelihoods of several Syrian lawyers. I had to sort out cases involving Belgian companies that had been put on Damascus' blacklist. The most frequent reason for this was Belgian companies accusing one or other of their competitors of having relations with an Israeli or Jewish firm outside Israel. At the request of these boycotted companies, I requested that our Embassies in the Arab countries take action before the competent authorities. I managed to get some of these decisions annulled thanks to pressure put on lawyers in Damascus and lobbying.

The fact remains that this boycott policy annoyed exporters, especially those who exported a branded product. Exporters of unbranded products were less likely to be boycotted, as it was more difficult to trace the origin of their products.

It should also be noted that the Israeli authorities showed little inclination to pursue a more dynamic policy in our bilateral trade relations. This visit did not, therefore, lead to any spectacular increase in our trade.

As I walked through Jerusalem, I noticed that the churches would ring their bells over loudspeakers next to mosques that were playing their call to prayer over speakers. On the Jewish side of the city? Silence: you had to go to the Wailing Wall to see the Jews pray.

One day, the Israeli Ambassador came to see me with a request that the terms of the agreement (which was still being negotiated) for Spain's acceptance into the EEC be altered. We bought a large part of our citrus fruits from Israel. Spain entering the common market, where the production of oranges had improved remarkably, would sharply reduce imports from Israel. I replied that one of the aims of the EEC was precisely the free movement of goods. He retorted that it was the Israelis who had sold the Spaniards the technology used to produce citrus fruits in semi-desert regions and that they were now falling victim to their own technology.

The UN considered Jerusalem to be a land without political authority (no embassies had been placed in Jerusalem, rather, they were all located in Tel Aviv) as was the west bank of the Jordan (which had been annexed by Jordan and then occupied by the Israelis). Such was the fundamental legal ambiguity that underpinned the region.

The first piece of evidence as such was that neither the Israelis nor the Palestinians could imagine circumstances under which this patch of the Middle East, between the Dead Sea and the Mediterranean, could live in peace. This double incapacity made life difficult for both, neither side knowing what it was like to lead a quiet life.

These two peoples are among the most gifted on the planet. This led me to question both the Palestinians and Israelis. A logical conclusion would be that they would take control of the Middle East, together. On the one hand, they would have access to superior Israeli technology and the financial expertise of the Jewish banks. On the other, the presence of the Palestinians in most of the operations conducted in the Arabian Peninsula, particularly in the oil sector. Together, they could form a concentrated pool of intellectual and financial resources that could make them a very important force. The Arabs would be relegated to the second most powerful force. This new alliance would play a significant role in the world.

Apart from the Israelis and the Palestinians, who had any interest in seeing the rise of this new force? The West? The USSR?

The Arabs were aware of this problem and reluctant to give up the free reign they enjoyed over their property, opposing both the Israelis and the Palestinians. The Arabs incited the jihad, for no other purpose than to create irreversible tension between the two peoples that would last for a generation.

To support this analysis, I will provide you with a quote from a Palestinian poet "when I was in an Israeli prison, I knew that I was Arab; when I was in an Arab prison, I knew that I was Palestinian".

The Palestinian representative in Brussels told me at length about the problems they faced with the Arabs. In 1976, for example, the Arab League recognised the PLO, which had been created in 1964, as a government in the same right as the other members of the League. The Palestinian Authority did not agree to the PLO being recognised as a government (not even under the title of government in exile). The reason? Not to please the Palestinians, but to be able to consider them foreigners rather than refugees, thus limiting their rights to property, access to public offices, etc. It was therefore a way in which to safeguard against the omnipresence of the Palestinian people.

Another example: the Arab League had never been in favour of a rapprochement between Palestinians and Israelis. On the contrary, whenever possible, it has voted on resolutions or taken initiatives which, appearing to favour the Palestinians at first sight, serve only, upon second reading, to incite hatred. Suffice to say that the Arab ambassadors in Brussels were unable to admit to this in public, though they acknowledged it in private.

Faced with these problems, which seemed insoluble at first sight, life went on. It was not unusual to see Arabs, Israelis and Palestinians doing business together.

Egypt was the centre of the Arab world, particularly when it came to politics, culture and religion, as evidenced by the prestigious El Azar University. The country's history, which is several thousand years old, has been marked more recently by important events, the repercussions of which rippled through the Arab world due to both their political and economic significance.

These events made the situation in Egypt quite unstable. Sadat had been assassinated two years previously, and Mubarak was seeking to establish his authority. To take power, he would need to overcome the substantial legacy left by recent years.

The Arabic word for Egypt is "Misr", a term which means protected land. It is in the centre of the Arab world.

From 1954 to 1970, Nasser was in power. Although he had been dead for several years, his aura continued to cast a shadow over his successor, Mr Sadat.

What did this shadow entail? At first, Nasser had had close ties to the American CIA. Not having been successful in gaining funding for the Aswan Dam, however, he turned to Moscow.

In 1956, he nationalised the Suez Canal, provoking an Anglo-Franco-Israeli armed reaction. Diplomatic intervention from the Americans and Soviets stopped the military intervention. This marked the end of Western European power.

Despite the increasingly omnipresent bureaucracy he implemented, Nasser retained a "direct bond" with the people until the very end. This bond was created thanks to him having been the first Arab leader to abandon literary language. He spoke to the people in their own language, one that was simple and that could be understood in other Arabic-speaking states. He was skilled in transforming each defeat into a victory thanks to his very moving rhetoric.

What was his political and economic philosophy? Liking neither capitalism nor communism, he chose a third path. His discourse was secular. He refused to be "the Oriental chained in a mystique of circular vision of history punctuated by divine Providence". In 1964, Nasser inaugurated the Aswan Dam, built with the help of the USSR.

His policy led to profound changes: an Arabisation of the administration was systematically pursued to counter the powerful Copt minority as an affirmation of national independence. As such, Nasser proclaimed his policy of neutrality in Bandung in 1955, which implied a break with the British.

President Sadat (1970—1981) would follow.

Having conducted his policy side by side with Nasser, Sadat succeeded where Nasser had failed. He reconciled Egypt with the West, brutally breaking from the Muslim Brotherhood. He restored Arab honour by having his troops moved east of the Suez Canal in 1973 (Yom Kippur War) and reopened the Suez Canal to international traffic in 1975.

Sadat rising to power was also the end of an era. From then on, an openly pro-Western policy was pursued. Religious fundamentalism was tolerated, having been condemned by Nasser. Speculations surrounding the new wealthy population began thanks to oil, especially in the Arabian Peninsula.

But this new policy did not prevent a very large part of the population (those that were not oil renters) from falling into poverty; a source of constant humiliation given the weakness and fragmentation faced by the Arab world. The most important factor, however, was that Sadat did not have a special bond with the people like Nasser had had, and was said to be a hostage to the powerful.

In addition, Sadat's arrival in 1970 provoked the "October Document" of 1974, which was a "de-nasserisation" policy. It was the start of an agreement with the United States, and an "Egypt first" policy instated to recover the economy through reconciling with Israel. Sadat's time in power was punctuated by his visit to Jerusalem (1977), the Camp David Accords (1978) and the Washington Peace Treaty (1979) between Egypt and Israel.

The Arab countries then excluded Egypt from the Arab League, though they did not seek to wage war on Israel alone. Egypt reduced its military forces and pursued a policy of opening up to foreign investments with the creation of free zones. The only continuity with Nasser's regime was Islam being maintained, as well as a robust, autocratic power. The problematic circumstances Sadat found himself in where the Muslim Brotherhood were concerned were what led to his assassination in 1981. By that time, the Muslim Brotherhood had already successfully committed most of the liberal professions, locking these professions exclusively to Islamists.

The coming to power of Mubarak was still full of uncertainties: would he be the man to guide Egypt? Though he did carry on Sadat's policy at first, he executed it less provocatively. Politics remained tough vis-à-vis the Islamists. Some significant works were carried out (telephone network, underground, etc.), but the government was unable to eradicate poverty.

The alliance with the United States remained firm, and Egypt managed to regain its place in the Arab world, re-joining the Arab League.

Which were the economic problems faced by Egypt?

The Egyptian economy mainly survived on four sources of income: rites of passage through the Suez Canal, tourism and exporting raw materials: oil, gas, cotton, and the salaries paid to migrant workers abroad (Saudi Arabia, Libya, etc.).

It faced a severe handicap in that the only farmland in the country was in the Nile Delta and Valley, while the rest of the country was a desert. The most logical procedure would have been to leave the Nile Delta and Valley to agriculture and place the towns on the edges of this area, in the desert. The country had a farmable surface area the size of the Netherlands to feed a population of 60 million people (more than four times that of the Netherlands).

The population of Egypt was increasing by one million people annually. The persistent poverty in which most people lived forced the government to subsidise bread and housing. It was not, however, encouraging more food to be produced or new housing to be built. Finally, while certain private sectors were developing relatively well, most of the economy suffered under the weight of their finicky, corrupt administration.

What were the political problems faced?

Following attacks by the fundamentalists, Mubarak's government -operated heavy-handedly. For a country with such a glorious past, this was difficult to live with.

In foreign policy, Egypt being excluded from the Arab League following peace being made with Israel was considered a necessity by the other members of the League, in terms of public opinion. The procedure itself, however, was dramatic, as the League was losing its binding agent. For Egypt, this exclusion of the only Arab country that had taken Palestine's side, and done so with arms, was a bitter reward.

As a result of this peace treaty between Egypt and Israel, the United States government committed to allocating a similar amount of aid to the Egyptian government as they had to Israel. This semblance of equality did not successfully deceive anyone, as Egypt's economic problems were infinitely more difficult to solve than those faced by Israel.

Peace with Israel allowed Egypt to reduce its military budget and devote itself to an economy of peace to a greater extent.

Our relations with Egypt were good, though underdeveloped. They dated back to the 19th century when, encouraged by King Leopold II, Mr Empain installed trams and built Cairo's Heliopolis district.

As a means through which to develop these relations, the Egyptians approached me to create a sort of forum where businessmen and people interested in Egypt would meet. This project duplicated the operations carried out by the chamber of commerce and never saw the light of day.

It was in this climate of uncertainty surrounding the new government that the Belgian government agreed to invest in working on the stability and development of our relations. I went to Cairo to negotiate an economic agreement that would encourage the strengthening of these relations. Shortly after, we would deliver a boat for tourists travelling to Upper Egypt. Elsewhere, we were also present in the beginnings of Egyptian nuclear research, and I negotiated a nuclear deal with Egypt.

Libya was considered a problem by the United States government. The latter had decided to sever diplomatic ties with Libya and asked the Belgian government to protect American interests in the country. As a result, and due to this being an economic problem, I was frequently in touch with the American Embassy.

The American authorities portrayed Mr Gaddafi as dangerous. They inflated his importance as an enemy by claiming he was responsible for an aborted attack against General Haig, NATO's Supreme Allied Commander. Seeking to determine the danger Mr Gaddafi actually posed for myself, I took to asking Egyptian and Tunisian Ministers questions at any meetings I found myself in with them. These were Libya's neighbours, after all. They informed me that Mr Gaddafi had sought to increase his country's landmass by trying to detach some of its neighbours' provinces and attach them to his own country. Despite the vast sums paid, however, he was unsuccessful. The degree of nuisance attributed to him was described as close to zero.

He was an intelligent man who had a deep understanding of the relations between the West, the USSR and the Third World. Cramped in his own state, he sought an international role. It was with this objective in mind that he worked on forming unions with Egypt and Syria, though these were short-lived.

One day, speaking via our Embassy, Gaddafi offered himself up as an intermediary to try to settle the latent conflict between the Israelis and Palestinians. The United States rejected this offer because it did not want a relationship with him. I intervened, telling them that if he were to succeed, it would be all the better, and if he failed, it would only be to his detriment. But the Americans continued to refuse.

It was in this state of Libyan relations with the Western world that a Belgian company approached me, informing me that, for several years, it had been playing the role of nuclear adviser to Libya. All the role essentially encompassed was assisting the country in using a Soviet research reactor.

Mr Gaddafi wanted to build a nuclear power plant, thus making Libya the first African country to have one, apart from South Africa, which was still implementing apartheid policies. His desire was unrelated to any economic necessity whatsoever. What the Soviets proposed would be very expensive. The Belgians made a counterproposal that would cost half as much. Construction was expected to take a minimum of twenty years. Before it began, however, a Belgian-Libyan agreement would be necessary within the framework of the IAEA (International Atomic Energy Agency, a UN body based in Vienna).

My interlocutor readily agreed to this last point and got the Libyans to approve it, in principle. I spoke about it with the Belgian government, specifying that if I were to be given the green light, I would easily be able to get Libya onboard.

The Belgian government agreed, and I got Libyan approval too. We negotiated two agreements in as little as three days. The first concerned developing our economic exchanges (they made promises about placing large orders in various areas). The second agreement concerned nuclear power, which, compared to the bilateral agreements that already existed in the world, were the most severe. All it covered was the construction and use of a power plant. Uranium enrichment was not mentioned.

In addition, I managed to get a verbal promise from the Libyan delegation that they would not interfere with Belgian interests in Central Africa, having beforehand managed to convince the Belgian exporting company and the Ducroire Office to divide the contract up into independent elements. In the event of Libya violating this political agreement, the Belgian government would be able to bring the construction of the plant to a halt without the Ducroire Office having to pay the Belgian exporting company the whole amount still remaining under the contract.

I then requested the Belgian government agree to allow me to initial these two documents. As a general rule, it would have been the Ministers who signed this type of document. I was informed that the government no longer wanted the agreements, even after they had been drafted according to their terms. The government asked me to explain as much to my Libyan interlocutors. The unlucky Libyan negotiator who had been tasked with getting this agreement through was persistent. He took to phoning me from his hotel room every day to find out when he could come and initial the agreements. I was consistent in my response each time, replying that my authorities had changed their minds and were now refusing to enter into the agreements. He would then give me the same reply every day: that he understood that consent to these agreements could take time and that he would call back the following day. After a fortnight, he left for Tripoli.

I then learned that many companies were bidding to build the plant, some of which were American. Since the Belgians had been ousted for political reasons, I spread the word to prevent any other company from winning the contract silently.

It was clear that the actions taken by our political leaders could only serve to irritate Mr Gaddafi.

A few weeks later, Gaddafi went on a trip to Central Africa, opening "agricultural centres with mosques" in Zaire, Rwanda and Burundi in spectacular fashion. During these inaugurations, he launched violent diatribes against Belgium. He would go on to fund these agricultural centres for many years, establishments that would soon become centres of anti-Belgian propaganda.

We had passed up an opportunity to develop our foreign trade, to broadcast our excellent nuclear know-how abroad and prevent anti-Belgian policy from being pursued in Central Africa. It would have been much less damaging for our relations to have refused to negotiate these agreements from the very start and to have limited our company's participation to merely an advisory role. After this failure, Gaddafi began a more intense anti-Western policy. Western stupidity surrounding this nuclear power plant had landed us in a considerable amount of unnecessary trouble. The plant would have been completed at the turn of the century, at the earliest. The closer we came to completion, the less Gaddafi would have hurt the West. Our general policy towards the Maghreb, however, was another story.

Our general policy towards North-western Africa was in line with what we had developed within the European Community.

If we were to examine how relations had evolved between the northern and southern shores of the western Mediterranean, the first observation that can be made is that relations have been good when there is some semblance of political unity. This has been true since as far back as the Romans, through the High Middle Ages and, for a while at least, during the French presence in the region.

It was for this reason that the European Commission proposed that the Mediterranean states meet, so that, together, they could work towards gaining the means necessary to build a new alliance: this was the Euro-Arab Dialogue.

The second element was a high birth rate in the north-western African countries compared to a meagre rate in Europe. In only a few years, the population of the Maghreb would reach 200 million people, a population equal to that of the entirety of the Economic Community in the late 1970s. This population was concentrated within a relatively narrow slice of the geographical region. It was governed by ministers who sought to industrialise the country over developing its agricultural practices.

The result was a high strain being placed on European Community countries due to the high immigration rates of young north-western Africans. When I was appointed to the desk, my ears were still ringing from Algerian President Boumediene's speech at the 1974 United Nations General Assembly. "One day", he declared, "millions of men will leave the Southern Hemisphere to go to the Northern Hemisphere. And they will not go there as friends. Because they will go there to conquer it. And they will conquer it with their sons. The wombs of our women will give us victory". The speech was made following the constitution of the third-world organs and President Boumédiène riding high on the OPEC's victory, the latter having just increased the price of oil.

Europe's reaction, and Belgium's in particular, was multifaceted. The first concerned the North African immigrant populations in Europe, including the Turks in Germany, though these came from the eastern Mediterranean. This marked the start of the implementation of rules to slow immigration. Immigration was welcomed by Europe, as it allowed for the continent's economic development, though this theory applied exclusively to workers. It would only be later that family reunification policies would also be implemented, authorising these workers' spouses and children to join them in Europe.

The second direction aimed to stimulate economic development in these three countries, particularly agricultural, so as to reduce the population's drive to emigrate. Our cooperation and export policy was being drawn up in such a way that it lined up with these policies. Turnkey industrial units were flying off the metaphorical shelves, as were agricultural development projects.

These countries' reactions have been far from excellent. They did not gear themselves towards developing their economies in any significant manner. Here are a few examples.

Algeria was very rich, both in terms of its subsoil and the farmable land in its northern coastal region. The country's landscapes were superb. The French were deeply settled into the country. They created cogs in a state that was inexistent prior to it being colonised.

Algeria, a country that gained its independence at the expense of a bloody eight-year war, was marked by the departure of French officials and the arrival of this new Algerian elite of businessmen. This new elite had inherited the intellectual rigour passed on by French universities where they had done their studies (the French National School of Administration, the École Polytechnique, Mines ParisTech, etc.).

This elite built a model administration through rigorous planning, though it did not meet the needs of the circumstances it faced. In addition, it had to deal with the victorious army and the FLN, who supported it. These different currents formed the basis of certain errors made early-on.

Algeria was a significant power within the Maghreb. Thanks to its oil exports, gas in particular, the country had a sizeable income. Despite an old gas contract between the two countries, relations with France were tense. The United States also bought Algerian gas, though to a lesser extent. The USSR's politicians were surrounded by a certain aura of greatness, especially when it came to military aspects.

While this new player admired the Soviets' industrial successes and sought to imitate them — something it was able to do thanks to its gas sales — it did not care much for agriculture. Now independent, Algeria abandoned its legacy of agricultural exports, a practice implemented by the French colonisers. As a result, farms were abandoned, and cities saw their populations increase. Algeria's birth rate allowed the country to not only make up for the large numbers of deaths caused by the war with the

French but also to substantially increase the overall population. The result has been a growing impoverishment of the population as a whole. The Ministers would explain that the government refused to build new urban housing in a bid to limit the exodus to the cities, generating, instead, an overcrowding of existing buildings.

Relations between Belgium and Algeria, especially with the FLN, the party in power, had existed since the Algerian war. Belgium had provided military assistance to help the FLN in its fight against France, as well as allowing Algerians who fled their homeland to take refuge in Belgium.

Several Algerians approached me with tales of the time they had spent in Belgium after the war. Another noteworthy point was that the first official visit any Algerian President went on outside the Arab community was to Belgium, a move that inspired a strong reaction from the French. During this visit, I showed the Algerian Minister of Foreign Affairs the acidic articles printed in Le Monde and Le Figaro. He responded by saying "so much the better".

Algeria appointed an influential figure as Ambassador to Belgium as, grandson of Abd-el-Kader and son of an Englishwoman, he spoke Arabic, French – having been a student at the National School of Administration in Paris — and English – also having studied at English universities. He was one of the chief negotiators of the gas agreement with Belgium.

When I took up my new post, I found two Belgian-Algerian agreements on my desk. The first, which was signed, related to gas deliveries to Belgium. The novel aspect of this agreement was that it contained a clause that linked the price of gas to that of oil. This agreement would serve as a model for other agreements of the same type, including the Franco-Algerian agreement, which was renegotiated at the request of the Algerians to the dissatisfaction of the French.

This Algerian gas agreement was an important component of our fossil fuel supply. We had long-standing contracts with the Netherlands and Norway relating to purchasing the gas they were yet to extract from the ground. The Belgian government saw this gas as our strategic reserve. While we were waiting to use it, the government entered into two agreements with two more distant producers: the USSR and Algeria.

Soviet gas was supplied via a pipeline through central Europe. At that time, Algerian gas arrived via the French LNG terminal. The expectation was that this gas would have to come to Zeebrugge as soon as the LNG terminal there was completed. This large terminal exceeded Belgium's needs, which meant it could be used by European consumers thanks to the connection between Zeebrugge and the European network. This contract was already a closed deal. I did not have to get involved. The completion of the Zeebrugge terminal and its utility when it came to importing Algerian gas, a few years later, would meet all these forecasts.

The second agreement, which had not yet been signed, aimed to encourage the construction of turnkey industrial plants in Algeria, by Belgian companies. As I read the text carefully, I discovered that the Belgian state intended to guarantee the successful completion of the construction works at the price agreed when the contract was signed. This clause was, of course, opening up a door to questionable practices. An unscrupulous entrepreneur who had provided us with a cheap quote so as to land the contract stopped midway through construction. They were replaced by another company whose additional production costs would be paid for by the Belgian state.

This problem was all the more acute since half of Belgium's Ducroire commitments at the time related to Algeria.

With a new government rising to power in Belgium, I managed to get a cessation of the process of signing the agreement granted. Our former Minister of Finance came to see me one day. He told me that the previous governments' Ministers had approved the signing of the agreement. He was the only one who had opposed it, thus causing the stay of proceedings.

I then let the Algerians know that we would need to renegotiate the agreement, adopting the usual terms of economic cooperation agreements. They agreed, and the new agreement was set to be signed a few months later.

During a visit to Algeria, the Ministers informed our ministerial delegation that they faced severe problems when it came to maintaining their industrial units. Back in Brussels, I shared this information with our industrialists, who immediately came together in a consortium, ready to carry out maintenance work to various Algerian factories. I forwarded the proposal to Algiers, though I received no response. Several months later, the Algerians rejected the agreement, doing so as a matter of principle. We will do it ourselves; they said. The case fell apart.

While I did not get the chance to go to Tunisia, I did maintain excellent connections with the country thanks to their Ambassador in Brussels, Nourredine Hached, the great trade unionist Farhat Hached's, son. Alongside Mr Bourguiba, Hached senior was the only Tunisian politician to have a street named after him in each village, thanks to the role the two men had played in the country securing its independence. I had two problems to solve, both of which were typical of industrialised countries in developing counties.

The first was an agricultural centre we set up in northern Tunisia. Our scientists succeeded in tripling each cow's milk production and quadrupling the yield per hectare of cereals, without importing anything. It was simply down to a rationalisation of their local resources. After several years of success, we decided to stop funding the centre. I proposed to the Tunisian government that they take it back and make it a School of Agriculture. It could educate countryfolk from across the Maghreb (north-western coast) and from certain countries of the Mashriq (north-eastern coast), where the amount of rainfall was similar to that found in northern Tunisia. Curiously, this was of no interest to them. Would they reject development entirely?

The second stumbling block was a Tunisian law providing for a tunisification of foreign investments after a certain period had elapsed. However, several leaders of Belgian SMEs, seduced by the country's climate and way of life, sold their business in Belgium and invested in a new SME they founded themselves in Tunisia. After a few years, this capital was confiscated from them. I asked the Tunisians what they would think if we were to reciprocate the measure. They promised to alter this punitive law.

In Morocco, we had not faced any significant problems in the areas in which we had made any significant investments. In terms of the Maghreb, Morocco was the only kingdom and the only country where the official state religion was Islam. King Hassan was a descendant of the Prophet and Commander of the Faithful. It was in this capacity that he chaired the Al Quds Committee (Committee for Jerusalem), which allowed him to have relations with Israel. He had an excellent network of contacts across Africa and intervened several times with Marshal Mobutu, at our request. The Soviets bought a large part of the country's phosphates. The French were still very present.

Behind this optimistic facade, however, the King faced snarling socialist opposition, which he put behind bars, sometimes harshly. Relations with the United States were good.

> *We had sold Morocco some new sets of trains for the Rabat-Casablanca line. Unlike the old trains, which operated at between 18 and 24 mph, they reached up to 87 mph. Our first task was convincing the Moroccan railway authorities that they needed to keep the doors closed. The most unexpected development, however, was on the day of the inauguration itself, when the train killed several sheep and chickens on the tracks. The animals were not used to having to clear the way so quickly.*

Mauritania set off to a difficult start, but thanks to President Ould Daddah, its northern region, a region populated by the Berbers and the Arabs, was seeing some development in the mining sector (iron and copper), and the country's southern region, with its African population, of its agriculture. In 1978, Ould Daddah was deposed and the regime destabilised, the state being subjected to coup after coup.

We had noticed that one of the most important fish stocks in the world could be found along the Mauritanian coast. Many Russian, Korean, Japanese and Spanish boats would fish there, though they did not have permission. The authorities placed a Mauritanian naval officer onboard these boats to monitor their fishing practices. However, as soon as he got on board, he would be taken by the hand and plied with drink.

We proposed that a centre that would catch, process and sell the fish be created. I even offered our helicopters to patrol Mauritanian waters removing foreign fishers *manu militari,* if necessary. The windfall this contract would have brought to Mauritania was substantial in terms of jobs and royalties received.

The contract was drawn up fairly quickly as far as the Belgians were concerned, though it got lost in the twists and turns of Mauritanian politics. This was a shame, as the contract presented was balanced.

Upon making routine contact with one of our shipping companies, I was informed of the competition they faced from Eastern European carriers, who were not regulated by the shipping conference. This conference was an agreement between shipping companies that operated between one area and another (e.g. Northern Europe and the Middle East). It regulated prices and sometimes the sharing of revenue. I wrote a note, and the service in charge of transport problems took over the case. An agreement was drawn up, according to which the Ducroire guarantee would only be acquired definitively once proof that the transport had been carried out by a Belgian company was produced. In the years that followed, I noted with pleasure that Belgium was the only country within the European Community that saw its share in maritime transport increase.

I also tried to draw up a contract template for construction practices, that would work both in the public and private sectors. I intended to safeguard both contractors — ensuring they would be paid on time — and owners — ensuring the quality of any work done. Insurance companies have told me that, unfortunately, the critical mass necessary to provide this type of insurance is non-existent.

4. Head of the Economic Service of Sub-Saharan Africa (1984—1986) in Brussels

The first analysis of Africa, which was shared among many of the continent's most intelligent personalities, highlighted the decline of the continent. A drifting economy that was unable to pay its debts, where disease was beginning to take its toll once again (notably malaria and AIDS), in short, political and economic irresponsibility combined with a general apathy.

Several events had marked Africa's most recent history.

Firstly, the tradition of slave trading, in which tribal chiefs got rich selling slaves to the Arabs and Europeans. Today, African analysts believe that this pattern has perpetuated — it is country leaders who deal with the foreigners, getting rich at the expense of the population.

The continent was then colonised by Muslims, followed by Christians, who brought with them the practice of writing as well as a new system of government. The result was a destabilisation of the existing hierarchy and the introduction of a new set of values. The rivalry between Islam and Christianity became more intense in the 1970s. Christians inherited the advantage of being settled in the South of the continent, though they were intellectually linked to the colonisers. Islam defended the poor against these colonisers. In the North, where Islam was already well-established, it was unassociated with the colonisers.

African universities would study the problems caused as a result of colonisation and assess the different methods used to colonise a country. They informed me that Belgian policy was considered the least imperial because it took into account the interests of the colonised populations.

Finally, there was the decolonisation of these countries, beginning after World War II alongside Pan-Africanism and the interplay of non-African powers in Africa.

These powers, which were only able to act in Africa due to the Cold War between the USSR and the West, sought to prevent any state rich in subsoils or agriculture from falling into the sphere of influence of their adversaries. African heads of state, who were well-aware of this rivalry, used it to their advantage.

Among the main countries involved, France took on a unique role by maintaining military bases in several African states, as well as two Franc zones in which there was monetary parity. The United Kingdom, Belgium and Portugal managed to maintain ties to their former colonies. Germany, a primary provider of funds, kept a low profile.

The USSR managed to gain privileged links with individual states, such as Ethiopia and Angola. It helped South Africa's (anti-apartheid) ANC. The country remained a potentially dangerous rival in the context of the Cold War.

The United States was pursuing an African policy to satisfy the black minority in the US.

Beijing's China was attempting to prevent Taiwan from establishing itself in Africa by building presidential palaces and, in Tanzania, even a railway.

Japan obtained important contracts but implementing them was made challenging due to anti-Japanese xenophobia.

Israel was very active, mainly in the fields of the military and security. The Scandinavian states posed serious competition, thanks to their funds. I have found these states have often crossed my path.

The EEC deployed an open-door policy on African products, a

stabilisation of the prices of certain raw materials and a policy of non-intervention when it came to any political problems faced. This policy became the subject of the Lomé Conventions. The former Caribbean and Pacific colonies were also included.

I kept in touch with either businesses or governments in most African states. They managed the formal sector of the economy, which included both public sector operations and private companies that were recognised, assisted and regulated by the state.

This sector was experiencing supply difficulties due to strict regulations, inadequate transport infrastructures slowing down the rates at which products were sold, difficulties in being granted bank loans and, possibly, their currencies depreciating, and making imports too expensive.

A remnant of colonisation, this sector often contrasted with the traditional system, with which I also managed to establish some rare contacts.

I read a study conducted by a Belgian on this traditional economy, in which the focus was Swaziland. The study demonstrated that the head of any company had neither control over the company's economic actions nor of their own cut of the profit. A company's treasury would be managed according to pressure placed upon it by the community, society and religion. Upon the death of said manager, the succession regime would frequently bring an end to the business.

Whenever I met a head of state, I was amazed by the way in which they exercised their authority. It always reflected the contempt in which the leaders held their people. Among themselves, African heads of state considered that the oldest of a group would always be the wisest.

After several years of economic euphoria in our relations with the Middle East and North Africa, I spent two years dealing with shortages in Africa. Most of the work came down to managing the loans we'd granted each country. Without going into tiresome details, I'll make a quick note of several constants I observed.

The debts these states owed to Belgium varied from country to country. They had sometimes arisen due to Belgian exporters on secret commissions inciting these counties to enter into unnecessary contracts. I prevented these contracts from being established whenever I got the chance. When it came to the quality of the equipment delivered, I explained to our businessmen that if they tried to get one over on a governmental institution, they would lose their market credibility.

African governments approached me several times, asking me to verify contracts they were in the process of signing, which had been issued by other countries or international organisations relating to replacing equipment. I would send an expert who would work out any anomalies in the equipment they already had in only a few hours.

> *An Ambassador had told me the cranes in their port had stopped working. Experts from the World Bank and Scandinavian aid funds decided that these cranes should be replaced. I asked our experts to go there to check them out. Bewildered onlookers then watched as they asked for a knife and started cleaning the rail the cranes slid along. They were completely encrusted with dirt. Once they had cleaned a few metres, they started the engines and, to everyone's surprise, the cranes slid along them easily.*
>
> *Another time, an Ambassador told me that international experts had declared his country's army's fleet of 500 trucks unusable. I sent an expert who checked several vehicles. They found that the diesel they had been using was impure and small dirt particles had blocked the engines. All they needed was a screwdriver and a little compressed air to disassemble the part that had become blocked and clean the dirt out.*

After these free demonstrations of our know-how, our businessmen, who were seen in an extremely positive light, found they were granted contracts more readily.

To these considerations, I would like to add that in Africa, the World Bank frequently played the role of "export aid" to rich countries by agreeing to fund their projects. It would have been better for it to limit its aid to African companies, even if that had meant asking for technical assistance from better-equipped companies.

As I examined French-speaking Africa, I noticed a reasonably even struggle for influence taking place between the two former colonisers,

Belgium and France. This struggle materialised by a Belgian presence in certain former French colonies and vice versa.

It was due to this dynamic that we developed fairly strong commercial relations with Cameroon, Senegal, Congo and the Central African Republic. We took a stand in the name of Abidjan, the capital of Côte d'Ivoire, in a debate over the definition of chocolate within the European Commission. We were processing uranium from Niger to Hoboken. We were building the Trans-Gabon Railway in Gabon, a vital railway line for exporting wood. In Madagascar, we participated in developing the country's agriculture. We tried to get into Guinea. The latter, which did not have a significant French presence, was suffocating under the leonine contracts it had entered into with the USSR, mortgaging the future of a country with very rich soils and subsoils.

Conversely, the French were very active in Rwanda and especially in Burundi. As for Zaire, Marshal Mobutu led a balanced policy between Belgium, which had gained large contracts in the country, and France, which served as a prop to raise the stakes. Needless to say, we were keeping a watchful eye on the situation.

Marshal Mobutu, who had been in power since 1965, was bathed in an aura that had reached across Africa because of his Zairization policy. This policy was a means with which to nationalise foreign private companies established in Zaire. Also, being one of the oldest African heads of state, he exercised a substantial amount of influence, one that could even be described as a decision-making authority, over his fellow heads of state. He deliberately chose to side with the West, a brave move in an Africa seeking to profit from the Cold War.

Marshal Mobutu had a firm hold on the levers of power and his Prime Minister, Mr Kengo, sought to strengthen ties with Belgium. When Mr Kengo came to visit, I held a meeting with Belgian businesspeople at the Federation of Belgian Enterprises. The Zairians' tone was optimistic, the Belgians' more cautious. Only a few businessmen believed in the economic future of the country, thus supporting the President of Zaire. The Belgians were not as afraid of street disturbances as they were of a new version of Zairization being implemented and affecting their businesses. Furthermore, the government's financial policy was hardly the most confidence-inspiring.

Production of copper, the primary national resource, fell sharply due to an insufficiency of investments necessary to keep the mines operational, as well as the export routes not functioning well. Besides, demand for copper was declining worldwide due to optical fibres being used in telephone networks instead. Under these conditions, General Pinochet's supply of copper from Chile seemed like a wiser choice.

During an interview with a Zairian official from Gécamine, and owner of the copper mines, he told me about the grievances he had against Mobutu; that he took action based on his military background and had no understanding of the economy. This made sense to me, as Mobutu believed that proper management was the type that increased its own assets. It would have been even better management to breathe some life back into the company.

In Rwanda, tin was the only major problem I found in our bilateral relations. Rwanda had moderately profitable tin mines. They belonged to a Belgian-Rwandan group. A fund in London stabilised the worldwide sale price of tin by buying tin when prices fell and selling it when prices rose. The degree of influence of this fund was measured by its financial capacity to act. Malaysia had the largest tin mines in the world. The country decided to sell its tin at a loss. The London fund reacted, though it soon ran out of steam. Prices fell, and Rwandan exports were marginalised. The company thus resigned itself to closing the mine. The Malays then brought the price up to normal, benefitting from one less competitor.

This Malaysian action was worrying at a time when third-world producers were coming together to protect themselves against rich countries exhausting their goods. It demonstrated the neutrality of their feelings and their absence of solidarity when faced with an opportunity to improve their financial interests.

Angola has traditionally been significant to Belgium for three reasons: the mouth of the Zaire river lies between two separate parts of Angola, Angola proper and Cabinda; Belgium's participation in Diamang's diamond mines; and the Benguela railway, used for transporting copper out of Katanga. Unfortunately, the civil war raging in the country stopped these operations.

Mozambique, a country of equal importance, housed an exit point for copper leaving Katanga, in Maputo. Unfortunately, due to insecurities, this copper had to be exported via Durban or Port Elisabeth, increasing the delays.

Finally, the Cape Verdean authorities expressed a desire for Belgium to participate more actively in the development of their archipelago.

Ethiopia is located in the very centre of the Horn of Africa. This region is made up of Ethiopia, Somalia, Eritrea and Djibouti. Close to Asia and not far from the Mediterranean, its geographical position naturally attracts several races, religions and civilisations.

That said, the region did not undergo a long colonisation. The Italians held Ethiopia for five years, Eritrea and Somalia for around sixty. Taken by force in 1947, Somalia was then returned to Italy in 1949, the latter remaining in power until the country's independence in 1960. Within the region, Ethiopia presents itself as the only organised state, comparing itself to the nomadic Somalis who were prone to tribal disputes. It should be noted that, of the five existing Somali tribes, three lived in Somalia, one in Ethiopia and one in Kenya.

Ethiopia, however, underwent significant imbalance due to both ethnic and religious problems.

Ethiopia played a crucial role in Africa. It was in Addis Ababa that the Organisation of African Unity was set up, bringing together all the independent African states. The history of this country traditionally dates back to the Queen of Sheba. More recently, Italian colonisation forced the Negus into involuntary exile. At the end of the Second World War, Ethiopia regained its independence, and the Negus returned to his throne, in a palace guarded by lions. Towards the end of his life, in 1974, a coup d'état inspired by Moscow had him overthrown.

Economically, Ethiopia presented itself as one of Africa's wealthier countries. Between 1985 and 1986, the news shared by the media showed an Ethiopia that had been bled dry. A terrible food shortage caused by drought was described. Western governmental and non-governmental organisations were moved and began transporting food by air to the most remote parts of the country; collections were organised in Western Europe to buy food.

A deputy was doing his shopping in Brussels one day when he noticed that the beef came from Ethiopia. He put a parliamentary question to our Minister, asking how Ethiopia was able to export beef if its population was facing a famine. A Belgian businessman who had just returned from Addis Ababa told me that the situation in the country was calm. One could find more at the market in Addis Ababa than in Brussels.

I will explain these differences in appreciation. Ethiopia had the largest beef herds in Africa and exported part of their stock. These exports were frequently made to Egypt or their neighbouring countries, and occasionally to Europe. However, the population of the Tigray province, which sought more autonomy, independence, even, was creating severe problems for Addis Ababa's pro-Moscow government. The same was true for the state of Eritrea. To get these provinces to obey them, the government used the old African food shortage tactic. This was also why Ethiopian authorities were curbing the sending of food by Western Europe. Planes were not granted landing rights. They parachuted food and medicines in, despite the ban imposed by the Ethiopian government. The gravity of the situation prompted the USSR's satellite countries, led by Poland, to also parachute in food and medication.

Africans I spoke to about the situation told me that they did not understand this Western compassion. In times of war or revolt, the government used all the means available to it. One must not be unnecessarily sentimental.

In English-speaking Africa, the competition faced was more in the fields of the economy and commerce, unlike in French-speaking Africa, where it was more political. Good contracts were thus entered into with Kenya, Zambia and Zimbabwe.

In addition, Rwanda, Zaire, Burundi and Tanzania still benefitted from Belgian-British agreements providing for the passage of goods through Tanzania when they were both imported and exported from Rwanda, East Zaire and Burundi. These agreements provided for the use of "Belgian docks" in the port of Dar es Salaam. Although we were no longer a party to this agreement, we often benefitted from all the facilities it provided.

When it came to diamond production, our relations extended to Botswana and Namibia, alongside South Africa.

South Africa's apartheid policy was perceived very differently from one country to another. The other African countries viewed it with a sense of awe. The governor of the Central Bank of Mozambique explained to me that his country's economy generated an income equal to that generated by a single skyscraper in Johannesburg. There was only one thing they wanted: to be able to live and work in the country. Only wealthy African businessmen were granted legal permits. They would buy a house and open business centres in South Africa. A third of the foreign workforce, i.e. a good million people, lived in the country illegally.

The countries most firmly set against South Africa — the only states that took steps to demand that we cut our economic relations with Pretoria — were its competitors in the mining and agricultural fields: Canada and Australia. Belgium played a leading role in the country's economy, importing diamonds, via London, to Antwerp; coal, fruit and vegetables to Ghent; and gold coins (Krugerrand) to Belgian banks.

With the exception of Libya, all the other African countries maintained economic relations with South Africa. Arrivals by plane all took place at night, so as not to arouse the population. Cape Verde, the only African country that seemed indifferent towards apartheid, allowed South African aviation lines to stop there en route to Europe.

South Africa was developing a dominant position throughout southern Africa, including Zaire. The country's influence manifested itself in several ways.

South African radio broadcasted a detailed programme in all the tribal languages.

The government controlled access to the sea by owning the only operational rolling stock, used to transport metals from Zaire and Zambia and agricultural produce from Zimbabwe. Exports were shipped out via Durban and Port Elisabeth. Incoming produce was imported to these countries as well as Burundi and sometimes Rwanda, when the railway line via Dar es Salaam broke down. By playing on the rates and frequency of convoys, South Africa was able to regulate, or even temporarily suffocate, one or other country.

A short trip to Swaziland, on the border between South Africa and Mozambique, shed light on the general problems faced by this region of Africa. The first problem I found related to constitutional order. When they left the country, the British granted it a constitutional monarchy and a parliamentary and justice system, like theirs, where the judges wore wigs. Three years later, the tribal leaders gathered around the King and decided to return to their tribal traditions. According to this tradition, the King would marry the daughters of tribal leaders, which meant he would have some hundred wives at his disposal.

A chain of South African hotels dominated the tourist market. A country not subject to the laws of apartheid, it became the place par excellence where the white population of South Africa would go to visit the black population of Swaziland. The highest rates of HIV-positive diagnoses could be found among white South Africans. This figure, which had been dutifully omitted by the South African government, was shared with us by the WHO.

Like Lesotho, Swaziland was both financially and economically dependent on South Africa. The three countries were united as one economic entity, a factor that allowed South Africa to add "made in Swaziland" labels to exports sent to countries where it would have faced sanctions incurred due to its apartheid policy. Though only a few tens of kilometres from the port of Maputo, Swaziland barely used the road or rail links that connected the two. The famine faced in the country due to the long civil war had made Mozambicans rapacious. Goods transported were looted as often as our ancestors' stagecoaches had been robbed.

When Zimbabwe was decolonised as a result of the Lancaster House Agreement, signed in London on 21 December 1979, my position as deputy chief of Protocol led to me helping set up their mission in Brussels. The new President, Robert Mugabe, seemed to have positive relations with his country's white minority, a factor demonstrated by him appointing whites to his government. He asked them to stay to run operations. Somewhat absurd scenarios would follow. Mugabe would make big speeches castigating the Whites, then, behind closed doors, would reassure the very people he had spoken out against, telling them that they were nothing but electoral speeches.

The white minority, which mostly worked in agriculture, brought in most of the country's foreign exchange earnings by exporting agricultural produce.

My last trip took me to Malawi, where I was sent to accompany our Minister. It was a small, forgotten country formerly known as Nyasaland. President Banda, a doctor, decided to develop his landlocked country. In order to ensure the secure export of any produce, the main problem the country faced was being forced to limit its production to goods that were easily transportable by air. The closest port was in Mozambique, where access had been rendered impossible by the latent civil war. The same applied to transit to South Africa via Zambia and Zimbabwe.

The most surprising event of the trip was our interview with the President. He welcomed us by telling us that he knew nothing about Belgium except what Caesar had said. He proceeded to quote the beginning of "Commentarii de Bello Gallico", in Latin. He explained that, like it or not, the Malawians had had to familiarise themselves with the Europeans. And how would they do so without studying their past? He therefore instituted schools where Latin and Greek were taught, geared towards the children of the bourgeoisie. He then added, sarcastically, that he had found the teachers in Britain, where the languages were no longer considered necessary.

He told us that while the country's apartheid policy was in full swing, the President of South Africa had invited him on an official trip. He accepted the invitation, inciting fury among his African colleagues. According to tradition, upon arriving in Pretoria, the two heads of state exchanged guest lists for each of the meals they would hold in honour of the other. The South African list was exclusively made up of white names. Mr Banda's list of both black and white South Africans was rejected. Malawi turned down South Africa's invitation. The South Africans swiftly changed their minds, accepting the Malawian list after all. He told us that, thanks to me, for the first time, they had sat at the same table as the black people they so despised. He added that if his colleagues did the same, politics would end up progressing in South Africa.

On my return from this trip, I packed up all my papers before leaving the Department of Foreign Affairs.

IN THE END

Ultimately, what has stayed with me from my years of service? Do I look back on them fondly? I would have to say yes, and I believe that many who have shared my line of work also share this view when it comes to their careers.

The bits and pieces I picked up along the way have each left their mark. Every location I was posted to revealed a different source of wonder and a new opportunity to learn about the energy sources powering an entirely different world, and a deeper understanding of mankind. Each has formed one of many anvils upon which my vision of the world and personality have been forged.

What can I claim to have been the constant features throughout my time?

Relations between people who live in the same country respond to a balance of power. In any society, the governing forces are divided into three groups. The leading group, which is made up of the fewest numbers, manages society, encourages the state to develop and enhances knowledge.

The second energises society. It is meticulous and follows the rule of law. It weaves the very fabric of the economy and keeps the country's morals alive. When it believes that the first group is no longer fulfilling its duty, it becomes the instigator of reform, of revolutions, even.

The last, the largest in number, carries out the orders given by the first two groups.

In relations between states, some constants are still relevant to this day.

Religious civilisation, the hidden side of politics, has come about as a result of centuries of daily routines, key phrases and a joint vision of the world. Nowadays, however, unbridled materialism has fundamentally changed the way in which mankind approaches religion. Our new standpoint is somewhere between two extremes. One is limiting religion to key times in our lives (birth, marriage and death). The other is recruiting fanatic followers. Religious civilisation remains, however, a bond of loyalty between members of the same community.

What has become of the two great protagonists of the Cold War; the USSR and the United States? Thanks to the efforts of Pope John Paul II, who was heavily supported by US President Reagan, the Russian empire has disintegrated. In return, Reagan asked the Vatican to condemn the theology of liberation in Latin America. This theology sided with the poor against big business. The end of the Russian Empire marked the end of the Cold War. Russia is now seeking the new position it will fill in the world.

The United States appears to be the only superpower to have recovered from its defeat in Vietnam. Reagan gave them confidence in themselves. But they have never been the same since. During the Cold War, like the Soviets, they maintained the power of an absolute deterrent. Each feared the other and did not dare consider taking military action. The end of the Soviet empire also brought an end to this absolute deterrence.

If I were to analyse the USA's military power, I would note that its navy's firepower was equivalent to the entirety of that of the other navies combined. It reigned over all the seas and ensured freedom of navigation. Its air force was also very powerful, and the country had numerous military satellites.

The US economy has probably been the biggest victim of globalisation. Many American companies no longer manufacture their produce within the United States. Even research has become a net importer. The only area where they retained a considerable advantage was defence.

The world of Islam had gone in search of itself. A few have tried to propose a direction it should take, but none has been able to serve as an example for the entirety of the Muslim world. Nasser was the first to try to lead the Arab world as a whole. Khomeini brought religion into politics, making foes among the ranks of the religious. Finally, Mr Mahatir, the former Prime Minister of Malaysia, wanted to prove to the devoutly religious that economic development could go hand in hand with Islam. Nowadays, Muslims are relentlessly venting their frustrations against the West, the Chinese and the Indians through their attacks. But these appalling actions do not lead to any tangible proposals being created.

Three notable countries have been able to manage their resentment against the West. The first is Japan. Following its military defeat in 1945, the country has since taken economic revenge on the United States. Next, it was China's turn. The country had been humiliated by the West's assault at the end of the 19th century. Thanks to Mao Zedong, who unified the country and made education compulsory, and Deng Xiaoping, who opened the country's floodgates, China began developing. Finally, India. Having reconciled with the United Kingdom, the country began building an economy based on the techniques of the future.

What about Europe? Sorrowful spirits minimised the influence exerted by the continent. Personally, I take issue with this pessimism. While the first Europe, of the Inner Six, came about as the result of a fundamental reconciliation between the French and the Germans, it has since become the guarantor of continued peace. The other 21 States that have since joined the European Community have only sought to profit from the extraordinary economic adventure that is the European Union. The influence exercised by the Union's policy is that of a moderator who seeks appeasement and peace. This human policy contrasts with the US's traditional war-based policy.

A final fundamental point has caught my attention. Around the world, attitudes of women and towards women are changing. They feel freer; now, they choose the number of children they have. They are taking more and more control of their own lives. They are enacting the immortal words of Simone de Beauvoir: "you are not born a woman: you become one."

Having established these few considerations, I now turn the page with determination. We have to keep looking to the future; all the past can do is satisfy those who are curious. Waking up the morning after my last day, I realised I had already forgotten the Department of Foreign Affairs' phone number.

Printed and bound by CPI Group (UK) Ltd, Croydon, CR0 4YY